KEEP MOVING FORWARD ON YOUR JOURNEY TO HAPPINESS

Nohemi Molano Lewis

Happiness and Wisdom Adviser from Hawaii.com sm

"WE ARE THE CHANGE"

Keep moving forward on your journey to happiness

Re-discover how you can find it, keep it, and make your dreams come true.

Nohemí is an Award Winning International Journalist and Speaker, Writer, Poet, TV Director, Artist, and Author of twenty-seven books,

-some also published in Spanish and French

Nohemí Molano Lewis

Happiness and Wisdom Advisor from Hawaii.com sm

"Malamapono a hui hou"

Me 'oukou ka welína ò ke aloha

Published in Hawaii, USA by
BetterwaysPublishing.com sm
E-mail: **BetterwaysPublishing@earthlink.net**

Keep moving forward on your journey to happiness

Keep moving forward on your journey to happiness

"Play the harp well; sing many a song, so that you will be remembered."
"Sing Your Song of Happiness!"

"This great book will increase the number of people with opportunities to be happy with insight, on this world of sadness."

English First Edition

Nohemí Molano Lewis, Author, Journalist, and Artist
Happiness and Wisdom Advisor from Hawaii sm

**This excellent book will guide you to find and keep happiness.
Choice is a process of creation…
1st Step - Choose to be happy, and then keep it.**

To my loving husband, partner, and friend, Michael Lewis, who has been my grounding force, as he nurtures and gardens me and my book, husbanding not only my work, but my deepest heartfelt and trusted dreams, with kindness, love and strength, and for taking care of my health and wellbeing

For his visionary thinking and capacity to understand, forgiving mistakes,

For his admiration for my dreams with humility, and for his courage, throughout our paralleled and difficult trials,

For uplifting his wife, when at times, had to use additional tools to support her truth; lighting her road, providing the best medicine to keep her healthy and out of the ditch and avoid her going down,

Thanks, Dear Husband Michael for making my dreams comes true to geminate the seeds of Happiness and Health, and nurture and keep them through maturity.

Nohemi

Keep moving forward on your journey to happiness

Copyright © 2017 by *Nohemí Molano Lewis*

Book Cover created and designed by *Nohemí Molano Lewis*

Book Edited by *Michael Lewis, Editorial Consultant, Artist, Photographer*

First Edition
By Nohemí Molano Lewis
All Rights Reserved

ISBN-10: 1975813987   ISBN-13: 978-1975813987

Library of Congress Cataloging-in-Publication Data Control Number
<u>2017913375</u>

Published and printed in the United States of America by
BETTERWAYS PUBLISHING

www.BetterwaysPublishing.com

E-mail: **BetterwaysPubishing@earthlink.net**
Honolulu, Hawaii

"Malamapono a hui hou"

Me ʻoukou ka welína o ke aloha

(Affectionate Hawaiian Greetings with Aloha)

<u>**_Some of the Other Wonderful 27 Books, by Nohemí Molano Lewis_**</u>

<u>**_(In English, Spanish, and French)_**</u>

<u>**_English and French Works_**</u>

COLOMBINA Searching for Happiness (English)
COLOMBINA À La Recherche du Bonheur (French)
Happiness Does Not Have To Be A Project It Is A Journey (English)
Keep Moving Forward On Your Journey To Happiness (English)

<u>**_Poetry in English_**</u>

A Journey Through Life with Wisdom to Share
Ashes / Reflections / Sunset

<u>**_Works in Spanish_**</u>

COLOMBINA Buscando la Felicidad
Ángeles de la oscuridad
Cómo poder aliviar la tensión y tristeza
Pruebas de cariño
Se ha quemado el 'último cartucho

<u>**_Poetry in Spanish_**</u>

Alborada
Álbum familiar
Cenizas
Gotas de agua
Las Rosas de mi Huerto, Sutilezas, for Spanish Associates, Sacramento.
Semblanzas y Recuerdos, for California State University, Sacramento.

<u>**_And Of Course Bilingual Editions for Children in Spanish/English_**</u>
Aprenda sus números – Learn Your Numbers
Buenos amigos – Good Friends
Mi hermosa tortuga – My Beautiful Turtle
Mi querida patita – My Darling Little Duck
Nuestro paseo – Our Walk
Conchas del mar –Sea Shells

To analyze and understand that life is not a project. Our years keep going, and the fingerprints left on the physical and spiritual realm are tangibles and real. –Just looking in the mirror, we understand where we are – Through the process, we make individual and specific choices, learning to thank the gift of friendship, and growing in understanding and spirituality. **Keep Moving forward on your Journey to Happiness**, analyzing that a kiss from our children, the smile of a baby, or a family celebration, produce more light in our life, that a constellation of stars.

In the meantime, to pursue A Journey to Peace and Happiness, and Understand the concept; we could follow the theories of psychologists, spiritual advisers, or gurus. –We get to the conclusion that we cannot absolutely acquire it, if we still have anguish and despair…

– "No person is transformed emotionally, or physically, to act in this world –by just reading wonderful books", all kinds of material, attending universities, receiving the information about the subject of Happiness, and implanted it in their hearts… –We eventually figure out that we need a Spiritual Path to Higher Levels of Consciousness, Creativity and Spirituality!

Had been living long years, smiling, or crying… –Even though, I consider that the great changes that the years had given me I had obtained by teachings to exteriorize the gift of love, thanking life for this reward of friendship… and, as a result received the Gift of HAPPINESS.

–Dr. Dan Baker, Ph.D. and Director of the Life Enhancement Program at Canyon Ranch have devoted his life to teach people how to be happy. He stated, *"Apparently, most of us could use a little tutoring."* –he continued, *"Research has shown that the root of unhappiness–fear–lies in the oldest, reptilian part of our brains, and negative reactions are often dictated by primal instincts. We are literally hardwired for hard times."*

In his book "What Happy People Know", Dr. Baker uses evidence from the new science of happiness to show us, "how we can overcome this genetic predisposition toward negative reactions and lead and truly reach, a happy and healthy life."

Then, he transcribes the statement of Aristotle, in The Nicomachean Ethics *"Happiness is the whole aim, an end of human existence".*

According to him, *"A poor rich man–he looked so pale and drained. He was living a life that held no happiness, and he needed help. He had everything the world could offer–money, freedom, friends, and family... (but) one thing he needs most: simple happiness".*

"This man was one of the wealthiest people in the American Southwest, rich in the resources that should bring happiness. At this moment, he could have been anywhere on earth, with anyone he wanted to be. Moreover, here he was very sad! *It will not take you long to learn what happy people know and learn how to feel happy for the rest of their days. It will take longer, however, for you to work these lessons into the heart of your life, until happiness becomes a habit and unhappiness feels foreign."*

Then, Dr. Baker stated, *"Happiness is neither a mood nor an emotion. Mood is a biochemical condition, and emotions are just transitory feeling."*

"Happiness is a way of life composed of qualities such as optimism, courage, love, and fulfillment. It is nothing less than cherishing every day. – did you get it?"

Statement from Denis Prager, on his book *"Happiness is a serious problem"* he stated –"First, I have not written this book in the belief that everyone who reads it will become happy. The very idea is preposterous. *To be happy requires knowledge about how to achieve happiness (i.e., wisdom) and hard work and self-discipline to put that knowledge into practice".*

Then, he continues, *"I could say, Feeling good all the time was our only requirement, then, the answer would be Yes." However, recent research suggests that an even-keeled mood is more psychologically healthy than a mood, in which you achieve great heights of happiness regularly–after all, what goes up must come down."*

"Furthermore, when you ask people what makes their lives worth living, being happy… they rarely mention anything about their mood! They are more likely to cite things that they find meaningful, such as their work or relationships. Recent research even suggests that if you focus too much on trying to feel good all the time, you'll actually undermine your ability to feel good at all–in other words, no amount of feeling good will be satisfying to you, since what you expect (all the time) isn't physically possible for most people". –I agree!

He found in interviewing people they arrived at similar conclusions. *"Happiness is Not Feeling Good All the Time. People have often asked whether a person who uses drugs every day, is happy. –Again if feeling good all the time is our only requirement, then the answer would be yes. Again, recall that recent research suggests that an even-keeled mood is more psychologically healthy, than a mood in which you achieve great heights of happiness regularly. Again, after all, what goes up must come down".*

"Again, they are more likely to cite things that find life meaningful, such as their work or relationships. Recent research even suggests that if you focus too much on trying to feel good all the time, you'll actually undermine your ability to feel good at all–in other words, no amount of feeling good will be satisfying to you, since what you expect (all the time) isn't physically possible for most people". Don't you agree?

Another report "*Happiness is Not Being Rich*, or to be able to *Afford Everything, while living below the poverty level*; – it certainly makes it seem to be hard to be happy, but *people, at the poverty level, can be happy, since they have already learned that money does not appear to buy happiness*, because it is *a state of mind*. Imagine you unexpectedly get extra money to buy a new car, but now have the inconvenience to learn how to drive, to pass the driving test, get insurance, and deep down you prefer to live with your family in your happy farm…You probably be exited in the short term, but it would only be a matter of time, before your expectations change to fit your new life. Before you realize it, you probably readjust to your old happy time, as you were before you got the new car! –This holds true for new houses, new gadgets, and all of the other material goods that people spend so much time pining for".

Other friends, state, "the old adage", "Are we there yet?" is often applied to discussions of happiness, as if a person works towards happiness and one day it "arrives". –"Contrary to popular belief, – unless you are one of the few who won the *genetic lottery* and are somehow wired to be naturally happy, it takes regular effort to maintain happiness".

Most established techniques for becoming happier– is like keeping a gratitude journal, for example of habits, not one-shot events, and most life events that make us happy in the short–term, like getting married, or being promoted, fade over time, as we adapt to them.

–Do we want short gratifications, or long time goals? Or the positive deep feelings that go with their accomplishments? –A reminder of our goal is to find Happiness and keep it! Right!

The result has been to bring peace where there was pain, and suffering has disappeared, to be replaced by happiness.

What is the real meaning of happiness?

Let's say that happiness is a combination of how satisfied we are with our life –for example, *finding meaning in the work we do – and how good we feel on a day-to-day basis.* –Both are relatively stable. –*That is!* –... Our life changes, and our mood fluctuates, but *our general happiness is more genetically determined than anything else.* The good news is, with consistent effort, this can be offset. *Think of it, like reflecting about weight: how much are you going to eat; if you are as active as you want to be, your body will settle at a certain weight.*

Let's analyse this assertion ... *if we eat less than we like, or we exercise more, our weight will adjust accordingly*; right? *If that new diet or exercise regimen, becomes part of our everyday life, then we will stay at this new weight...it becomes a new biological "set point". If we go back to eating and exercising the way we used to, our weight will revert to where it started at a different "set point."* So, the same thing happens with *happiness.*

We have the ability to shift feelings–and with consistent practice, we can form lifelong habits for a more enjoyable and fulfilling life... Now, we know how happily we are, having gotten the tools to make the charges to attain happiness on a daily basis.

I think it can be easy to find and keep Happiness...if you know how!

Happiness and emotional fulfillment are within us if we are persistent and wanted to keep it. We all want to feel happy, now we have to find ways to keep it! Do not waste your time, try it, you will be surprised the way you can bring happiness into your life!

Try this...
–*Be with friends that like to smile... Stick with those who are joyful and let it rub off on you. Do not be afraid to acknowledge your values, being fair, expressing your own beliefs. Accept the good.*

Look at your life and take stock of what is working, and do not push away something, just because it is not perfect. When good things happen even they are very little ones, let them in. Do not be afraid to look at what you really want, and be sure you are getting it. Imagining receiving what you want, it is a big part of achieving it.

Always, try to do what you love. Maybe you cannot play soccer every Saturday, swim every day, or enjoy concerts, occasionally, but as long as doing the things you love, you will seek and find your real happiness.

Find your real purpose. If you are contributing with groups, you will tend to feel better about your life. Most of us want to be part of something greater than they/we are, simply because it is rewarding to feel we are contributing something to making something better or the world a better place.

Listen to your heart. You are the only one who knows what fills you up and float your boat; despite your family or friends may even think you would be great at something that is not you or fit your comfort level. Again, listen to your heart. You have to because it can be challenging to ensuring your bliss…most things we do have to work at. Just be smart, but keep your day job for the time being.

Impose you… not others. It is easy to feel that someone else is responsible for your success, but the reality is that it is really your duty. Once you realize that you have the power to get where you want to go! *Stop blaming others or the whole world, eventually you will find your answer. However, it is not enough to hear your thoughts. You have to choose to move forward and act upon them!*

Be open to change. –Try very hard! –*Change*, is one thing we can count on. –Believe it! -*Change will happen, so make emergency plans and ardently glide yourself through it just for the experience.*

At times, let your boat sit in the harbor... Your boat can lay at rest unworthy of serious concerns as you plan. Go with the flow if it seems right for you. Those who love us treasure our kind memories, jokes, kindness, and peaceful nights—these are the rewards. You will know where and when you fit somewhere – then just do it!

<Happiness and fulfilment are within us to grip, but sometimes, just out of reach... Understanding what works best for you, is the first step in finding more of them. We have to endure, and trust, –the guide that never fails... Pursue solitude, observing the calm ocean, watching the birds flying across the mountains, and the colorful (Hawaiian) trees, reflecting the rays of the afternoon sun... and, all the nature's beauty, knowing that inspiration will come. Trust your intuitive side felt with no fear"–This is the calmness before the storm". Then be bold!

<Remembering also, Gratitude is the beauty of life! At the end, we experience more moments of contentment than distress. Following these simple guidelines help us to find authenticity in your daily life!" – We have the right to achieve our dreams, we only have to wake up and choose to pursue them and do it! – *Nohemí*

In Hawaii, we honor the true meaning of ALOHA...

Akahai   Hawaiian... *Kindness*, expressed with *tenderness*.

Lōkahi   Hawaiian... *Unity*, expressed with *harmony*.

'Olu'olu   Hawaiian... *Contentment*, expressed with *agreeable thoughts*, *words*, and *actions*.

Ha'aha'a   Hawaiian... H*umility*, expressed with *modesty* and *humbleness*.

Ahonui   Hawaiian... *Patience*, expressed with *persistence* and *perseverance*.

Thank Life for the time delay. . .
Not all of our dreams come instantly.
We would be in distress if they did.
The element of time delay serves us.
It allows allow us to reassess.
We should think about what we want
to be able to make new choices.
Life is at the other side of the window.
We only have to move the curtain - and
Keep Moving Forward To Peace and Happiness-
Making Our Dreams Come True.

— Nohemi

Keep moving forward on your journey to Happiness

I was a woman in need of going forward… have to forgive myself and forgive others… This is a necessary correction for the mistakes we had made… *Forgiving others is the only way to live a happy life; it reflects the law of Joy and happiness, analysing that giving and receiving are the same.*

Forgive others and forgive ourselves; through forgiveness the thinking and actions of the world reverses. Holding nobody as prisoner of guilt, we all become free… I know many children hold prisoners their parents for errors of misconceptions, or inexperience, or lack of awareness… —but holding no one prisoner of guilt, we become free. Misperceptions and allowing nothing from the past to hold us back, we are set free, can start fresh, returning to Spirituality.

"*Perception is a mission of the body,* and therefore if inaccurate can represent a blockage to our knowledge. Perception sees through the body's eyes and hears through the body's ears, and induces the limited responses which the body makes. The body appears to be largely self-motivated and independent, yet it actually responds only to the intentions of the mind. If the mind wants to use it for attack in any form, it becomes prey to sickness, age and decay. (A Course in Miracles)

Keep moving forward on your journey to Happiness

Is a process in life that many people loathe, because *moving forward is a time that requires us to make changes.* Being creative, and able to make our dreams come across in life, is a true test of a person's maturity level, and a spot-on test of the confidence that we have within ourselves, to succeed in the completion of the dreams and goals that we have in our hearts. —We must be able to look forward, having the capacity to move ahead, with gratitude, harmony, beauty and joy as well.

 "We must" *resist, looking back, trying to overlook and judge our past, because the past can only be lived but once, and the mistakes we made, we cannot make again, but we can learn from them. We can choose to make wiser decisions, and learn from our experiences in order to become the best person possible, moving forward in our lives."*

Even if life is filled with ups and downs, *—we do not have to go up and down, just go forward*! Don't ignore everything or everybody in your life, —some are blessed. — Especially family, friends and people, who truly need help that you can provide.

Remind yourself to remain quiet and send loving energy. Remember the *Power Of Intention. —What matters, is in our hearts! And, remember, there is always hope in the face of uncertainty*!

Gratitude is the beauty of life! At the end, we experience a simpler way to apply the techniques that helps us to find authenticity in your daily life."   *— Nohemi*

Feeling *gratitude* and not expressing it, is like wrapping a present and not giving it."

— William Arthur Ward

I would maintain that thanks are the highest form of thought; and that *gratitude* is happiness doubled by wonder."

— G.K. Chesterton

Advance

Before this book could be written, I had to reflect of what was not working in my life. Perhaps for the first time, I had to be heartlessly honest both inwardly and outwardly. During this period of profound introspection spiritual principles such as harmony, gratitude, love, forgiveness, self-consciousness and being creative, became the catalyst that helped me define a life of my own.

One morning, observing the ocean from the window of my home in Hawaii, I awoke the realization—almost imperceptibly, I'd become a happy woman, experiencing more moments of serenity that distress. Feeling confident again, I decided to write a downshifting lifestyle book for everyone who wants as I do, to live by their own luminosities.

I started carving this book A Journey to Peace and Happiness and realized I have to publish it right now... Why waiting for what is coming next?

"The truth is, unless I let go, unless I forgave myself, unless I forgive situations, and others - unless I realize the negative conditions are over, I cannot get Peace and Happiness." "LET'S START TODAY".

Sometimes the people we want most in our life are sometimes the people we are without, until we learn to let go...– We do not understand that there is no point in holding on, until we learn to let go. Until then we will never realize that we deserve better.

Too often, we make a mistake trying to create a lifetime relationship with a seasonal person... Not everybody who comes is mean to stay. Let go learn the lesson... and choose to move forward...

Stop trying to hope that mistakes will correct by themselves. We just have to learn to let go, and realize that not everything is mean forever.

Starting today, we need to forget what has gone... Appreciating what still remains and starts the Journey To Peace and Happiness to what is coming next.

Iif everyone is moving forward, success takes care of itself, opening new doors learning and doing new things and since we're interested in leading ourselves to new paths; we don't even loose curiosity.

Testing to the maximum, we could explore, until we satiate our doubts... we can make progress without giving up; just keep learning the importance of reaching old age, rationalizing that we have lived plenty and have being contributing efficiently to society...

Hope reading this book, through its gentle
Phases of enjoyment, helps you to find
Authentic life you were born to live.
If you do not believe in your own capabilities,
Who will?

— *Nohemí*

"There are painters who transform
The sun to a yellow spot, but there
Are others who with the help of
Their art and their intelligence
Transform a yellow spot into the sun"

— *Pablo Picasso*

I decided to help me and to help others.

Decided to write this book **Keep moving forward on your journey to Happiness,** despite so many years of writing and lecturing about other subjects, until recently struggling with the issues of *Next Time, Tomorrow, Past Experiences, Pain, Sorrow,* and *Hope…*thought, *"Why waiting until tomorrow?" –Then thought it should help me, and help others.* That was why, decided to assemble these thoughts right away!

Create productive energies! After all, the innovative artist is an inner child to infantile thinking. Remembered when Mom expressed doubt or disapproval of her daughter's creative dreams… *Carl Jung* answered the question of beliefs, *"I don't believe. —I know. —Realize the creative energy is an artist in the inner adolescent, to a childish thinking; and using it, is our gift to people".*

Remembered our Great Winston Churchill's words, "You have the power to change anything, because you are the one who chooses your thoughts and you are the one who feel your feelings. You create your own universe as you go along." — Understand that we have to follow the subject, to complete the CYICLE OF A GOOD, GREAT AND HAPPY LIFE.

These subjects are very important about *how I could deal with Grief…* Sure, I did not, either… and later, did not wanted to be in misery, *therefore I found the way to live in peace*; and my readers could learn to deal with their sad past also. Assuming, that everyone else did the same, and was cured. That mean, *they found the steps* and followed them, —somehow someway they acquired joy! Yes, my desire is, to remind everybody that *with determination everybody could find contentment using personal experiences to guide my readers.* Remember, that *Perseverance* is also very important!

Analyzing these phenomena, I say follow A Journey to Peace and Happiness! These steps are our alternatives to get happiness, peace, success and grow. —We have to perfect the subject! We have to complete the *CYCLE OF A GOOD AND HAPPY LIFE! CHOOSE!*

Everybody, without exception, want to be in high spirits! I know. I did *a*nd I am! The family wanted… YES, we finally accomplished our goal! Therefore, now it is the right time to follow A Journey to Peace and Happiness. Move over; supervise your own thoughts, even if this will take us a lot of work. This is where the journey to joy begins! — *By Your Choice to follow the suggestions in* **Keep moving forward on your journey to Happiness** you will make it to happen. All you have to do is "Choose It" and "Do IT"!

Kept Happiness, provided Lectures, found regularly inspired, showed interest, and motivated others, which is the purpose of this handiwork. You can be part of the solution too! "Slow down and enjoy life. It's not only the scenery you miss by going too fast; you also, miss the sense of where you are going and why".

Explore with this book and "learn how to improve your awareness, on how we can experience the Delightful Presence, within us and in all life, not just as a passing inspiration, but as a constant inner Self-Realization.

Further in our personal Quests of Constantly Moving Forward, we Adapt, Adjust, Readjust, Survive, Reinvent, and Fine-tune, go Past Superficiality, Keeping Our well-earned Balanced State of Mind. From there, continue Finding and Keeping Happiness by Being Creative. – This has been the main reason to write this book, believing that everyone who read it will become motivated to Keep Moving Forward, Making the Dreams Come True! -Create Your System gathering the skills to overcome stressful situations, to create our own goals working toward Peace and Happiness.

***Nohemí Molano Lewis -** is an Award Winning Writer of Novels, Political History; Newspaper Journalist, Poet, Radio and Television Celebrity, Journalist, Anchor and Talk Show Host in California, and Costa Rica. Also, a Prizewinning Poet at the International Society of Poets and. —Born in Colombia, South America, and citizen of The Unites States; performed at the "Alberto Castilla Conservatory of Music", in Colombia, and with the Vienna with Boys Choir.*

College Professor and Dean in the USA and Costa Rica; honored by Sacramento State University for her book of poetry in Spanish "Semblanzas y Recuerdos"; successful columnist in USA at "El Hispano Newspaper; "Para Todos" Spanish Magazine; and English publication "Culturs" in the USA. Nohemí interviews famous personalities, writes stories for newspapers and magazines regardiong the Pacific Aviation Museum in Pearl Harbor, Honolulu, Hawaii. Nohemí is also a recent Guest Speaker of CUNARD's "Interstate Corner" on the Queen May 2, World Cruise.

Here I am on ***"Cunard's Queen Mary 2 on a Cruise Around The World"***, on January 16, 2016; left Hawaii at night, arrived in New York nine hours later, boarding the number one cruise liner in the world at the age of 86, as a Guest Speaker for *"The Cunard Interest Corner."*

Program 1. Discover here How You Can find Happiness

Program 2. Having Alternatives, Making Choices —the Basis of Human's Emotional Health

Program 3. If we want to Make Our Dreams Come True. Be Happy, and Move Forward

Program 4.   Be creative…We possess the Inner Wisdom to Make our Dreams Come True

Program 5.   With Belief and Creativity We Live, and Keep Happiness

Bearing in mind, a year ago, my Dearest *Sisters Chila, Leo, and, Grandson Giovanni,* passed away, leaving our family in pieces. Let us think, "There was a time I was afraid of dying, but now that you all are there, I am no longer scared, and look forward to when we will be together again". At that time, was slowly recuperating from the enormous personal losses, looking every morning at my Sisters' and Grandson's darling pictures, which I have at home on the wall in the hall, wrote poems of love and remembrances, which was read at her service by my Dear Niece Betty. Nephew Jim's family honored his mother, aunt (me), and grandmother, by reading poems to her soul. Then, members of the family attended the *Service* organized by her dear friend Reyna and roommate for more than thirty years. —Very *Sad from these sorrowful facts, I wrote…*

Went gloomy, tried hard to sleep
Waiting for the birth of the sun
To clear the days to sing
-Love is patient and is full of bliss…

BLESSING HER NEW FRESH DAY
By *Nohemi*

There was a young moon
With a bright stream of light
Falling down at the hillside
     Holding out her guns
With hope at the moon's light
Coming down at the highland
     Cuddling out her arms
With hope at the moon's light
Bowing her head among her guns
     Sobbed at her gloomy home
With no signs of anything
But the soft gleam's strips
     Leaving home with broke bare walls
She found herself at the riverbank.
There was no other sound
     Than the rain on the ruined roof
And the basic snowing of birds
On the limbs of dried aged trees
     The absence of human beings
had become a nuisance!
     But then, in the new morning
The sun dried new great hair

     Smiling at the new bright day
She suddenly found herself
     Very happy at the hillside,
     blessed the new fresh day!

Have a mind that is open to everything
and attached to nothing. – Dr. Wayne Dyer

–Disbelieved when *a police officer in Colombia assassinated Dad,* at the time he was ready to vote on a Presidential Race, leaving his children, in limbo... I was very young, and my mom sent me to live with Aunts and Uncles. Was very happy, then, then, dear uncle was murdered, when he was riding a burro coming happily home.

–Then, *Brother Vita, already blind,* due to a car accident where he lost his eyes; burned and died from a Kerosene stove from his kitchen, stroking a match and the gas was on; he actually died alone, since his wife passed away a few months before, and his kids were sadly orphans.

–Dear *Beautiful Sister Helen, –just twenty-five years old,* with three little beautiful children, took her life in desperation of knowing the infidelity of her husband. Father, being guilty, placed the three lovely children, on the bed, next to her, wearing her gorgeous wedding dress.

–Little *Brother Fabian only nine years old* was playing with a dear friend, during Christmas Time; falls down from the rooftop and crashed his head, dying a few days later... -Cleaning his blood, decided to be near him, until he closed his eyes at death.

–As soon as young *Brother Gabby barely thirty-five years old,* finishing the first section of the football game with his two sons, he dropped down with a mortal heart attack, living his three children orphan.

–We had to face the death of a sixty-five years old' *Mother,* from a heart attack, after suffering many tragedies of her family, living two young daughters –*Leo* and *Chila,* orphans, who I continue taking care of them.

–The heart attacks of *Brother Charlie,* after agonize the absence of his dear kids. Then the death of *Brother Gustav, Sisters Leo, Martha* and *Grandson Giovanni...Being very sad, Life crashed and burned.*

We try to comprehend the sadness at death of loved ones, as events that all of us experience during lifetimes. Sadly, we have to open our minds to all realities.

All these calamities, made think about life! We may have episodes of sadness, even long after they died. Our minds may be confused pondering about it. –Even though death is a natural event, we may find it difficult to concentrate on just about anything... We may be able to focus our attention, but all we can focus on, is on the one we loved who died, or how he/she departed this world, or thinking about life together before they died.

Circumstances alone do not make us Happy or Unhappy. It is the way we react to circumstances, that determines our feelings. – Best is to focus on happy events.

Enjoyed and tried to understand the story of *"The bird on the branch"*. *"A tired bird was resting on a branch for support; it enjoyed the view and safety it offered from dangerous animals. Just as it had become used to that branch and the support and safety that it offered; a strong wind started blowing and the branch started swaying back and forth, with such great intensity, that it seemed that it was going to break."*

But the bird was not in the nest worried for it knew two important truths. One was that even without the branch it was able to fly and thus remain safe through the power of its own two wings. The second is that there were many other branches upon which it can temporarily rest. –But we do not have wings!

This small example represents the ideal relationship between us and our interactions, possessions, social and professional positions. *We have the right to enjoy all these, but cannot as long as we are depending on them, or are afraid of losing them. They are all in a state of change and can disappear at any time.*

Our real strength does not lie in those external ephemeral things, but rather on our two internal wings of love and wisdom. – These must become our security base, our source of enjoyment and happiness. Enjoy material things, but do not be attached to them.

Understand that Self Confidence is a special mixture that the Life force has prepared to help us to overcome the challenges of life. Michael Bernard Beckwith reminded, "We live in a universe in which there are laws, just as there is a law of gravity. If you fall off a building it doesn't matter, even if you are a good person, you are going to hit the grown, unless you have a parachute." –As a teenager had a deplorable issue suffering painful ordeal–. As a result, my own voice became suppressed. **–And now, can sing with love and happiness. "From now own, nobody can make me feel inferior or unhappy, without permission!"**

87th birthday July 11, 2017, received a cruel message from my dear second son - felt as *an accident victim* walking away from a crash - felt 1000 years old, like a catastrophe target without purpose after walking from a smash; *felt my life had been hurtled and burned! Felt as without a body - without life...It Sent me to the hospital! I Choose To Move Forward - Reconnected with my inner strength and rose above it. –Now, at 87 years young, again, have to repeat, "Nobody can make me feel unhappy, without permission"!*

First impact was losing his Love; then, pain on Body and Brain.... After, I had to relearn how to open new ways of coping, and how to live a new type of life. How much abuse can I take - thinking he got away with it? Moving Forward I survived and Kept My Happiness!

It is easy to focus on negative events... so, expressing gratitude, being thankful for our life, showing appreciation for people in it, or simply saying thanks to a person who holds the door open for us, makes us very happy...-Husband always holds the door open, making wife, very happy, getting in!

Grateful people are likely to be happier, hopeful, and more energetic. Express positive emotions more often. -Be sure not to become a victim for commitments made long time ago... time and laws change. Gratitude helps us to cope more efficiently with trauma and stress, enabling us to overcome bad situations more quickly. –Happiness depends on us; if we want it, or not...Choose!

–Happiness is about what we think, what we say, what we dream, and what we do with love and compassion. –The fastest way to avoid painful episodes, we have to add passion to our labor, - like writing poetry, or publishing books to help ourselves and other people...IT WORKS WONDERS!

CHAPTER 1

Creating Different Alternatives

"I had an inheritance from my father…It was the ocean, the moon, the stars and the sun."   – *Nohemi*

Remember, that the misfortunes do not come from Divinity at all…There may be a sense of loss at coming to this conclusion. In a way, it was comforting to believe in an all-wise, all-powerful Spirit who guaranteed fair treatment and a successful conclusion, who reassured us that everything happened for a reason… Even as life was easier for us when we could believe, our parents were wise enough to know what to do and strong enough to make everything turn out right.

Husband, who provided us no financial help, abandoned the children and me. It took many years in Colombia to save thousands of "pesos" to buy a few "dollars", with no help, and at the same time took good care of the kids, feeding and educating them, and fulfilling the dream to raise and educate them in USA. –I did it!, with "a Resident Visa". –With faith, determination, and working very hard, I succeeded because I had determination to Moving Forward!

Already in USA, besides my regular job, learned to make *wigs* and *toupees*, for a Beauty Shop in Los Angeles; and while my kids were playing at *McArthur Park*, was inserting hair by hair on a wooden head covered with silk; with this additional job, was able to make extra money to buy better food for my kids. At one point, they were attending a Private Catholic School. —By the way, the famous actor and singer *Frank Sinatra* ordered one of these hairpieces; and he was very satisfied with the job, for that reason, got a wonderful check from the owner of the store! *—Always, believed we get rewards from special places, and for a job well done!* Likewise, I taught college at night. Recognize, you probably had your own challenges, but with courage and determination, I am sure you succeeded too!

Sons and daughter are now professionals, already married and divorced, graduated from College, obtained good positions in industry, managing successful businesses. Oldest son came back from Vietnam with many Medals and graduated from UCLA in psychology, got married and had one handsome son, and a beautiful daughter. Grandma had the chance to hold both beautiful grandchildren in her arms. – Through the years tried to be with them, in sicknesses and healthiness. They remember grandmother, and she remembered them… *As you know, love for family is forever and ever, until we all move to another home, or we are unable to do it due to old age, dealing with lack or energy!*

WROTE THIS POEM FOR MY GRANDSON
© *Nohemi*

"Here at home, after years of inspiration
Sit poised over the computer
Waiting to move the mouse with numb fingers
Trying to strike remembrances
From those years of the past

"The future mom was pushing and sweating
With painful happiness and expectations
"This is a serious stuff, mom, you know!"
–She murmured…

At that instant all I was able to do, was to pray,
Sent little angels to ease the pain, comforting her
After long labor, my precious grandson's head
Suddenly appeared…Welcomed him to life…

Flames burned senses, brightened, for the first time…
Then, softly winds touched grandmother's face
Run my fingers on his soft face
While the lights still shining!

"Since that day, I think of you, dear grandson"…
when the little birds chirp in the trees…
when the butterflies frolic, on the flowers…
Think of you, when the sky drops tears…
From the silvered clouds, I think of you.

Think of you, when glance at the ocean in the mornings
With its waves caressing the kind, beach…
I think of you, when the softly breeze
Plays happily on the wrinkle face…

Think of you, when the seagulls fly low,
-almost touching the white sand…
Think of you, noting the moon on peaceful knights…
dancing through the windows into the eyes…

Think of you, when the seagulls fly low,
Almost touching the white sand
Think of you, when twinkling stars adorn dark nights,
Sometimes falling from the distant sky

Felt your heart, as you slept on my tummy
For many years and times in the past
Smiling, you held grandmother, very, very tight
Miss your soft words, when you started talking

In other words, miss you all the time…
Even now, at old age, when I go to sleep glancing
At your bright-brown eyes, viewing your pictures
Since this is a reality of this far away life!

Now, still miss your soft gentle words…
Your tall figure, your brown bright eyes,
 Your forever, lovely smile, and kindness,
 All days and all nights…
–The love, which is lovable in you–.
–This is the blessing of being a Grand Mom. – Nohemi

"It was a pleasure for Grandmamma *Nohemi*, for years and years to keep grandchildren's company, on summer vacations, Christmas, birthdays, very often when parents needed a babysitter; as their *friend, in sickness and in health, always with love.* One thing briefly became obvious. *Practically all of the Happy Grandchildren were on the cusp of life.* ---

Time changed… want to tell you a story about the time when later celebrating happy days, had been very miserable! Sadly, I remember my personal story… "My younger son finished high school, went to the country where he was born, with the desire to meet his father… One week later, came back very angry, and wanted to talk to his mom about a serious issue. "I want you to tell me the truth!" – He said to mom. "Didn't father want to come back to see us, his children?" -Father said, "*I did not leave your mother… Traveled to the capital of the country to get a job, and ten years later, when I wanted to come back home to live with my kids, you mother said NO!"* Very desolated said to son, *"This is one of the most dreadful pains I have had in life! You should know that it was not true!"* –I said, with great pain! "He abandoned the family! – *Your father wanted to come-back after ten years of being a drunk, never chose to remember he had responsibility to support his family and raise his kids! You know, it was very hard for mother, being very young, without any help from him, in any deed, or money to support our kids. Remember, as a mother, I never thought to abandon my darling kids!"* –Then... *"I was working day and night... to keep the kids alive! - Not only that! Merely slept two or three hours each night, since managing many jobs at a time, to fulfil the dream to raise and educate the orphaned kids. "With so many ups and downs, tried to cope with life, always filled with lack of means to more easily deal and coped with them!"* ...–*Thanks to great efforts, we survived, and yet alone, facing all challenges, I was able to legally stablish them in this great country, USA! Then, Thanks God, they had everything they needed or wanted! –Good education... speaking two languages to get a great future!"* –Then, *drying tears, of happiness, continued...*

Now at old age almost nighty in sight, still receive sad letters from these darling orphans...Is this fair?" (–At old age, they are still so unkind!) Just recently, husband had to take wife to the emergency hospital three times, dealing with more heart attacks! – And before this time, was dealing for years with tachycardia and high blood pressure, for abuse from them kids.) ***If we cannot remove the Fear, we cannot remove the Problem!*** *With time, faith, determination, positivism, and believe... –I tried to live in peace!*

Last time, friends came to celebrate a birthday... After we finished our lunch, and placed the beautiful flowers in the living room, they brought a little card as a present... we smiled!–Time went by... -I was enjoying the time!

"After raising darling kids, helping also with grand-kids, painting special lovely cards, and making charming presents during kindergarten, junior, and high school graduations, in addition, and many week-end celebrations for so many years... Playing with them, including with participation of my new husband, making very large kites for them; cooking together aromatic cookies; and near December, we were preparing special colorful gowns for darling kids; and rehearsed The Nativity"... "Afterward making the previous presentation of the Birth of Jesus, with kids, and grand-kids, at daughter's home, we had a darling show at Christmas Season, making everybody very happy, admiring the "special performance". Then, unkindly, heard daughter from behind, "Move, Nohemi, I want to take some pictures" –¡No kindness... no thanks...no appreciation! – Always keep lovely prints of remembrances, of precious days, giving me faith for better days...! - Life continued always with confidence...

-VERY SAD MEMORIES- Unfortunately, remember another personal sad issue... "Gus, one of my dear brothers was devastated, not wanted to take care of himself! Between my oldest brother Charlie and me, bought a gorgeous piece of land on oceanfront on the Atlantic Coast, for him to spend the rest of his days in that paradise." Sadly, he couldn't enjoy it, since he was assassinated." Younger son Joe *bought half of the big lot from oldest brother that we bought in partnership. Son came to me, his mother, to request the other half as a gift!" "As a mother, I have been always very happy helping... I agreed to give to younger son Joe, the other half of the lot, **free of charge**!* Then, informed him, *"We have to make a legal transfer of the property, immediately at the Colombian Consulate, here in USA!"* (This "so call agreement" happened more than 20 years ago).

I, his mother begged him to make the transfer of my gift to him, as soon as possible, because I was already very ill and old, reaching retirement and I didn't want him to miss the precious lot...However, through more than twenty years, due to his procrastinations of not bringing documents with him, or sending me erroneous formalities, never cooperated in transferring my beautiful ocean side lot to him. (The one he asked me to give him and the last undeveloped one, in the area, that worth lots of money!) We had to transfer the title to his name, at either Colombian Consulates in Los Angeles or Atlanta, or San Francisco, California.

Now, after all that time and losing almost all his investments, he again went to visit his country of birth… "Mom, the half of the lot is still in your name!" I was retired after so many years of work and helping raising grandkids, very ill, with high blood pressure, heart problems, and high levels of cholesterol, living now with my husband in Honolulu, Hawaii… –Son called mother with panic! He suddenly remembered THE GIFT FROM HIS Mom" -the beautiful lot at the gorgeous beach on the Colombian Atlantic Coast, his mother gave him free of charge, more than twenty years ago… Now, after all that time, losing all his investments in the USA, he remembers the beautiful lot…

At this point, son requested to his old mother, now partially blind, with four heart attacks, tachycardia, also, caused by stress from family; and barely walking… to travel from Hawaii to San Francisco! -To please dear son again-, to present to the Consulate the transfer of said lot to her son's name! *Son sent by fax the documents, to San Francisco, after we had to fly from Hawaii, find a hotel, and a restaurant to feed mother, due to her with special diet, to please, him again.* The General Consul read the first paragraph, in which I, his mother, was transferring the ownership of the lot on the Atlantic Coast, to son. –After carefully reading the request, The General Consul and the Lawyer, sadly informed: *"The Law had changed in these twenty plus years!"* **"Mothers can no longer give TO SONS ANY GIFT OF REAL ESTATE IN OUR COUNTRY**

ANY MORE!" *(To avoid family lawsuits, contesting family gifts from mothers to sons, due to litigated jealousy by those not receiving the same treatment, this is the reason why that country passed the new law!) Now, sons must only buy property from their mothers at market value, paying all the taxes, to prevent more litigated jealousy!"*

"Son, you lost the lot… Procrastination is not a friend!"

Then, what was very sad, son *wanted his mother to use illegal documents to force the transaction without the legal document through the Colombian Consulate! In other words, son wanted his mother to commit an illegal act, giving her son the lot free of charge, after the new law was in act. –Even though, his mother might have to go to prison, if that dishonest transaction went through! – He even told family members some lies saying mother had swapped him the lot for some other property in Texas, which was or is, not true! That was finally it…I told him to correct the lies or I would not help him in any way and give the lot to someone else…like to "a poor person". Years went by with nasty correspondence from son… In addition, these years, still insisting, being so nasty with his mother, through nasty correspondence and electronic messages, which hurt his mother with a heart attack!*

A few years later, Brother Luis (definitely a poor person) was asking Nohemi, his sister, to help him to save his old truck, since he did not have funds to fix it. And, since I, always help people in need like I helped his daughter Margot with the big down payment to buy her own home in Bogotá, and she lost it!.) At his request, I contacted a dear friend Myriam, who lives in New York, to kindly convert my check for one thousand dollars and sent the cash thought an International Bank, since I Nohemi has been very ill, making very difficult to make the transaction, living in Hawaii. Dear friend Myriam, who always kindly, helps, in cases like this; sent one thousand dollars that converted in pesos, -considered a great gift-; and Brother Luis received it in time to fix his truck.

Later on, Brother Luis wanted to help with the solution of the said lot... since I always trusted him; I sent him a power of attorney to give him authority over the lot. He traveled to Tolú, where the records of Real Estate Transactions, takes place. They informed Brother Luis, "Before any transaction can be done; you have to present the receipt of paid-up real state property taxes that probably will be huge, after so many years; then with the authorization from the Colombian Consulate in US, you can process the transaction." ...

Then Brother Luis called his sister, (Nohemi) with the sad news, that he could not do any transaction, because he needed the authorization from the Colombian Consulate, to sell the lot... I sent throughout the same process, another thousand dollars to cover his expenses to go to Coveñas, to get the Registration Office which paperwork did not work; explaining to me to go back to The Colombian Consulate in mainland...TO REDUE THE PAPERWORK.

I told my Brother Luis, "Please dear Brother Luis, send me back the documents*...since now the transaction could not take place. I repeat, "Luis, when I recuperate, after so many health issues, due to the issuess with my adult sons; I will go with my husband to the Colombian Consulate in San Francisco, since in Hawaii we do not have a Colombian Consulate". (-Since you are my brother, -not my son, we will do the transaction.) I told Luis, "Please, return the paperwork back to me! Then, Dear Brother Luis, said, "Let me keep these forms; I want to preserve them in my personal files as a Dream that this transaction couldn't go through, and therefore I cannot become a rich guy for even a few minutes!"*

-Since always trusted him, (my dear Brother Luis), I was feeling sentimental about the words from him, and I agreed.-

In the meantime, son went to Colombia, to see HIS LOST LOT! Talked with the person he installed in the lot as a caretaker for these many years, without paying any rent, and he said, "Congratulations, the lot has being sold!"

Immediately, dear son sent several e-mails, including a heartless one, causing her mother a heart attack, with some emergency trips to the hospital! –This was the brutal E-Mail from son Joe… "You are a crook! **You gave the lot to Uncle Luis**, *three months ago! Now, he owns it! You, are also a horrible mother, you cannot give the lot to two people…You are a crook! -Do you know something? "Now you had lost all your three sons!" -I was petrified!*

Was this, a merciless treason? -It looks like My Dear Brother Luis had found an illegal way to transfer the lot to himself, without informing his dear sister Nohemi about the transaction, which was not supposed to happen!

After these incredible issues, Dear Michael took his almost dead wife, helped by the nurses at the Ambulance, to the Hospital with another heart attack! Since then, been very ill; counted the days to be alive! -Through positivism, and faith in the future, survived, giving me a chance to be happy again. I know, my dear readers fully understand the behavior of beloved family, that imparted so many disappointments in life, but I never hate them… I only want to live in peace, forgiving people that need to grow. (Families could have similar issues, but survive). When I was a little recuperated, decided to send an e-mail to Brother **Luis' son**, because he lives in the same city, and he usually helps his father with computer communications. ANALYSE THIS… you probably doubt I had more sadness…

According to him, "his father was helping me, Nohemi"… "*You, Aunt Nohemi, are an UNKIND person; you gave authorization to my father to sell the lot! Now, he has too many debts! That is your fault!" –I could not believe this atrocity! (HE DID NOT MENTION THE OTHER $1,000.00 DOLLARS I SENT TO HIS FATHER FOR THE EXPENSES GOING TO SEE THE LOT! To get rid of nightmares, and forgive family's abuse… I decided to put all this issues behind me, choosing to live in peace! Since Brother Luis, was a very poor father with dozens of kids, and grandkids, I forgave him also, as I have always forgave the abuses of so many other people! Yes, all of these issues, made me VERY SAD, BUT I LEARNED! Knowledge or not, it is their responsibility!* **I SIMPLY JUST FORGAVE, SINCE WE WANT ON OUR JOURNEY TO LIVE IN PEACE AND FIND HAPPINESS!**

I want to recall for My Dear Readers, how incredible episodes happen in life… When I was a little recuperated, decided to send an e-mail to Dear Brother Luis's son, since he lives in the same city of his father, and he usually helps him with computer communications… Please analyze this issue… To get rid of nightmares, and forgive family's abuses… I decided to put all these issues behind me, choosing to live in peace! –After receiving the following message last night, in my dreams… (later on, I read it in a Sacred Book!)

"King Solomon Makes a Difficult Decision, also…

One day two women came to **King Solomon**, *and one of them said: 'Your Majesty, this woman and I, live in the same house. Not long ago my baby was born at home, and three days later her baby was born. Nobody else was there with us.*

One night while we were all asleep, she rolled over on her baby, and he died. Then while I was still asleep, she got up and took my son out of my bed. She put him in her bed, and then she put her dead baby next to me.

In the morning when I got up to feed my son, I saw that he was dead. But when I looked at him in the light, I knew he wasn't my son.'

'No!' the other woman shouted. 'He was your son. My baby is alive!'

They argued back and forth in front of Solomon, until finally he said, 'Both of you say this live baby is yours. Someone bring me a sword.'

A sword was brought, and Solomon ordered, 'Cut the baby in half! That way each of you can have part of him.'

'Please don't kill my son,' the baby's mother screamed. 'Your Majesty, I love him very much, but give him to her. Just don't kill him.'

The other woman shouted, 'Go ahead and cut him in half. Then neither of us will have the baby.'

Solomon said, 'Don't kill the baby.' Then he pointed to the first woman, 'She is his real mother. Give the baby to her.'

Everyone in Israel was amazed when they heard how Solomon had made his decision. They realized that God had given him wisdom to judge fairly.

You My Dear Son Joe, according to the Law of God, or the Law of Life, had lost "The dear Baby"; The Lot in Colombia free of charge your mother gave you, more than twenty years ago, with your responsibility to change the title to your name at the Consulate. (We did know that the law had change) even though, we have the responsibility to be honest.) –If we do not comply with the laws of life, we have to pay the consequences!

And now, dear son you are twisting the guilt to your mother, for you not owning the great land, since you never made the effort to travel to the Consulate, during more than twenty years, to change the title to your name, before the change of the law, which prohibited mothers, to transfer to their sons any real estate property. The Consul stated "Dear friend, Acting Consul Nohemí, you may tell your son, "Sorry Son, in life we cannot twist laws without consequences." -Son I helped a needy member of the family, I gave it to Brother Luis, who is probably happy indeed!

"Beloved son Joe, you are very energetic; consider the following concept of your inner reality... which determines responding to situations in your daily life. Those responses are the energy you have inside to give away, as love for mother, sons and grand-daughters...

-If you get angry, is because you have anger in your body, like anything in the universe, your thoughts are a form of energy; everything you feel and experience is a result of energies...You get back what you put into the world to give away to others.

-Don't hold back just to maintain the equilibrium... Don't sacrifice your honesty and peace of mind, just to keep from rocking the boat. Refusing to face reality, just to keep up easy facade, isn't doing any good. Be totally honest with yourself!

-Just recall, low energy attracts low energy, like Anger, Hate, Shame, Guilt and Fear; not only they weaken you, but they attract more of the same. By changing your inner thoughts to the higher frequencies of love, harmony, kindness, peace end Joy, you will attract more of the same, and you will have those higher energies to give away to others. Just place honesty to work, forgiving people's mistakes; since we are still not perfect, we can reach understanding and translated into action!

*–**Remember beloved son... These words are a gift from your dear Mom, before she dies.**"*

Dear readers, as you can see, all I am offering in this book is the awareness that we can return to a full-time compassionate state of mind and inspiration, which is the true completion and ending of Our lives! Want also to ask, "Are some of you, dealing with similar issues? Sometimes in life, we try to guide family members to the high road, but for "some reason(s) it does not work! –If I have been able to forgive the sadness produced by my own kids and be happy after all; you all can do the same, living happily and at peace, as it is going for me!

Our mind is the means by which we determine our own condition, because mind is the mechanism of decision; it is the power, by which we separate or join, and experience pain or joy accordingly. All is possible through our own joint decision, but mind alone cannot help us. -Your will is as free as mine...The forgiven world becomes the Gate of Heaven, because by its mercy we can at least forgive ourselves. We came to this world to be creative with or without mistakes; with inspiration and faith, we can learn to be compassionate, being in harmony with each other faith.

WE HAVE TO LEAVE THE PAST BEHIND

To take care of frustrations, we enjoy visiting Ko Olina, in Hawaii where appreciate on our daily walk along the beach... always in the near-by grassing path, admire our dear friends the red headed cardinals...

Stopped for a while... These amazing creatures, who always adorn the path, with their mysterious waking on the green grass... turn around to us, and then, fly away... I understand these cute creatures, avoiding human contacts, but when I am around, walking with dear husband, these little birds want to cheer my life for a few minutes, and they know this precious moments are enough for me to thank God for his love and kindness. I feel grateful for these magic moments near Makaha, on the Northwest Shore. How this cute little red head birds inspire my life!

Remember then, "When the student is ready, the teacher will appear". When I became sad for injustices of the world, the Happy Redheaded cardinals manifested to me, returning myself to Peace and Happiness.

CHAPTER 2

"Being interested in others is one of the Secrets of Happiness"

"The world is so empty if one thinks only of mountains, rivers & cities; but to know someone who thinks & feels with us, & who, though distant, is close to us in spirit, this makes the earth for us an inhabited garden."

— Johann Wolfgang von Goethe

Iwas also paying It Forward, helping others and the community. It is never too late to help people in need. If I could not see the world very clear, due to being single-sighted, not having depth perception; with tachycardia for a long time, diabetes, and high blood pressure, *I still did the (my) best*!

Spent time traveling, to attend birthdays, graduations, anniversaries, funerals… hugging and helping parents and kids. Had the pleasure to visit, and contact with them, and in cases of need, helped them too. Know for sure you had done similar things! *Felt the sad tours of the past, but now arrived at the land of happiness!*

Had been reaching out, helping family or dear friends, with their *wants and needs,* also assisting people in need...–Helping grandchildren have memories like walking and skipping on the road to elementary school, when they were innocent kids; not just contaminated with negativity which deceases singing, "*Today is a beautiful Day... Today is a beautiful Day... Today is a beautiful day... and nobody can deny.*" –Tears of happiness rolled down their cheeks, remembering all those delightful days! *– And you, dear friends keep those wonderful experiences deep down in your hearts, too and share them!*

Before retirement, decided to marry a great man, *Michael,* – who met a year before, around meditation classes, at the *Rosicrucian Lodge.* –At that time, just came back from my childhood country, attending the funeral of a Dear *Brother.* –Affected by the loss, I was very sad, and *Michael* helped with kindness and thoughtful gestures to lessen the great pain. A few months later, he proposed we get married.

–Sadly, my children did not approve this great man, who is a few years younger! –They prognosticated our marriage would not last, even a few months! Moreover, we had been happily marriage for twenty-five years! -Of course, with difficulties, since they always insisted mother to divorce this great man. –We wanted a happy life together and we have been blissful ever since! *All of these challenges made us stronger, blessing our own lives. –You, dear friends, could have also some gloomy experiences that sadden your lives, but with faith, you can overcome them!*

After few years in California; we moved to *Padre Island, Texas*; and then during vacation time, took care of daughter's children... enrolled them, at the Aquarium Summer Camp, to learn about life at the ocean… Grandma was driving a big van, husband bought just to be able to take them to their "entertainments at the Aquarium and at the Yacht Club to learn how to sail".

Then, we registered the darling grandkids at an art academy, with a Professor of Art, to learn drawing. Grandson, seven years old, completed a very artistic book of caricatures, or comic strips; Granddaughter, had severe allergies, and with special love and care, I cured the disease, happily very creative finished also her art book. Years later got their College Degrees, and Grandson got married, being happy and prosperous as a Car Designer at *Tesla*.

Almost at the same time, oldest son's children were very successful, and later, got their College Degrees; Erik has a Web Design Studio founded his business in Washington State.

Other grandchildren are attending College, specializing Psychology, Art Design, Mathematics and Music.

At our retirement, we established our residence in *Hawaii*, "Our Paradise", trying to manage our new happy life; celebrating holydays, with wonderful Hawaiian' friends … –Still writing for magazines, as well as publishing books, taking care of each other, doing our best to be happy, always moving forward, in love and living in peace! *–For sure, dear readers, always try to enjoy places and people that bring you peace and happiness!*

–Whatever the subject is or was, determined to improve the quality of life, on this trip of life, and stages a muting over a sterile life…

That is why, at this time we enjoy all days, months and years –whenever husband takes his wife. –Even, "around the world", with a big smile… –I am always fulfilling life, leaving behind the ancient days, after losing Mom and Dad, brothers and sisters, aunts, and one grandson… *–Trying to thank nice friends, and forgive, harsh* *people... –Blessing every minute, day, and night." – Those are challenges that make us grow! –There is enough in life to be happy!*

We took advance courses of Meditation at Ananda and at The Rosicrucian Fellowship, organized groups helped people to deal with stress or sadness to teach them to *Move Forward* and regain *Happiness*, enlarging our list of "Dear friends". –Bet, you do or will do the same to share keep living happy and at peace!

There are still trials, One day, out of the blue, received a big manila envelope containing *the cruelest written message from a dear daughter! After read it, placed it in the garbage can. Remember, to live happily, we have to leave the problems behind!*

Later, husband, and I planned to go on a world trip for four months... This time, The Neurologist said, I know this vacation time, will be great for your well-being.*"*

–Meditated for a while, and then thought, "*I know this cruise will be god for me, –physically, emotionally and spiritually!"* *Michael* believed in my words! I left the message at the clinic to rescind the surgery! Immediately after, we booked the cruise!

Once confirmed the reservation for "Our Great Adventure around the World." I did not want to think about the sad issues anymore! Started packing having hope!

Then, the telephone rang, – it was my first grandson...– He invited us to his wedding... "Dear God!" I, *yelled* – "Husband just confirmed the reservation for a cruise around the world." "Sorry Grandma I didn't have time to invite you way in advance! However, do not worry! I do not want you to cancel that great event to celebrate your 86 years birthday and your wedding anniversary. Please, grandma, go! I will be happier to receive the blessing on my marriage, from the Great Queen Mary".

–"And, by the way, dear Grandma" –grandson continued– "You already gave us your blessing with that gorgeous Wedding Present at the resort in Palm Spring, when I came to meet you to introduce my dear fiancée Sarah! –Remember?" "Yes I Do."

–At that moment, recalled the beautiful moments spent with dear Grandson since the day he was born.

–Because I have the gift to be sociable, with the ability to arrange all kind of events, and interesting discussions, I was involved in new discoveries, especially in this wonderful land of Hawaii; noticed this was a day full of surprises, to be prepared for just about anything.

Organized the lunch for our dear friend *Okalani Tally*, native Hawaiian, and Cultural and Spiritual Practitioner, a Kahuna, –who lives in Honolulu. *We talked almost about everything, as to have balance, understanding, patience and, of course, to live happily from deep within the mind and heart.*

Now, *we were celebrating the slight* recuperation, after many health issues… We invited our friend *Okalani* to have a good time with us; went to one of our favorite restaurants in *Kailua*, and had a worthy lunch… After lunch, observed our usual friend and server at the restaurant, limping, then, detected a big scratch on her knee… Immediately, without hesitation, our friend *Okalani*, bended down, grabbed her leg and started examining the swollen part, then tenderly, Lomi Lomi massaged her knee, giving some treatment, and *Anne*, our dear friend and server, very grateful for the unexpected treatment, hugged him and us.

–This is the way he is, very kind! We had met Okalani at a restaurant in downtown Oahu a few years ago; was having a lot of pain on the shoulder, and had an appointment to get surgery the next week! *Okalani*, came, and asked, "I guess you are having a lot of pain… wait for me, after work is over, I will give you a treatment!"

–We look at each other observing his kindness, *husband* said, "Thanks, we will wait." –That was his place of work! He was the General Manager at that fancy restaurant!

After most of the customers left, he came back… "Tell me where, do you have the worse pain, please". Placed his strong kind hand on my rotator cuff and closed his eyes… Then, started feeling like the wings of a kind bird, blowing some air… Next, after just a few minutes, he said, "The pain is gone! –isn't it?" Just very relaxed answered, "Yes, I feel no pain." That night, and for many days I felt good, it there was no more pain"!

Now, – many years later, we were celebrating his birthday at home; *Michael* prepared the food… Decorated the dining table with colorful napkins, and helped to set up the salad; then, in the center of the table, we place the wonderful cake, decorated with orchids and with his name, a phrase, *"Happy Birthday, Dear Okalani"*.

On my birthday, – one month later, after we met – We invited him as special guest to have lunch with us… — Looking at the window, observed our dear friend *Okalani,* with a huge flower arrangement, as tall as a very high bush. Coming in, he had to bend his body to allow the base with orchids, ferns, and lace, to get inside the door. I just noticed, he is about seven feet tall!

"Oh God! Who arranged this gorgeous center-piece of colorful Hawaiian flowers?" –"I did! -said dear friend Okalani. "This is part of my hobbies, but it didn't take me time to prepare this humble present for my dear friend". By-the-way-, "Have a Wonderful Birthday, Dear Friend *Nohemi"*.

–Since then, many years ago, we celebrate our birthdays; *Michael's, Okalani,* and *Nohemi,* at our "humble home" filled with love!   Alternatively, to change the routine, we choose different restaurants with good Hawaiian food.

Two years later, we were having lunch at home to celebrate again his birthday ... and he noticed at both occasions our art pieces were still on the floor... "–I will be back in July when we will celebrate *Nohemi*'s birthday. To hang your beautiful art at the wall... –It was very nice of him, of course! Look at husband's eyes, "he had been so very busy, with no time to decorate the big wall, besides we were waiting for 'an expert'!!"

"I know the structure of this building is so strong, with iron, rocks, cement and blocks, covered with more cement and other strong materials to sustain the building against tsunamis, earthquakes, and other inconveniences of the Islands of Hawaii... – Okalani commented to us.

"If you allow me, I will hang your pictures, had seen on the floor since we met."   –And he did what he promised, always smiling! The next week he came in with gorgeous lei of white-scented jasmines to celebrate his friend's birthday, and the necessary instruments, hammer, special nails, and do not remember what else!

He did not need a ladder, since he is so tall, and handsome! Had lunch, sung a *"Happy Birthday"*, and almost immediately after, he started to take measurements of the pictures, and the wall; inquired our opinion to the right place to hang the art that we had on the floor for years, since the time we moved to Hawaii.

After he finished the great job, the place looked so gorgeous! "It was magnificent!" I said. –This has been the best gift we ever received in Hawaii from our dear friend *Kahuna Okalani Tallet*!

Guess what happened! Drinking his magic Hawaiian leaves named *Mamaki Tea*, my blood pressure and diabetes, have been greatly improved. I was blessed finding this wonderful Hawaiian friend.

-When we invest our time, we make good decisions about something that we want to accomplish, whether it's to have good grades in school, be a good athlete, be a good person, or make a good trip, go down and do some community service... Helped somebody in need, whatever it was we made a choose to do... We were investing our time in being very cheerful and happy paying it forward, since 'what goes around comes around'. Keep Moving Forward on our Journey To Peace and Happiness, Making our Dreams Come True-. (From time to time, we felt isolated after many family incidents; (sons probably believe that mother forever keeps solving all their economic needs, but I realized eventually, they should have responsibility for their own families. −As a result we decided to move far away.

-Sadly, remember when oldest son falsely accused husband Michael of "Elder Abuse." via the District Attorney of San Diego. "Recalled, *Michael* signed a *Quick Claim*, before we got married; -son thought the real state property, was still in jeopardy-. *He thought mother was leaving this property in a Will to husband Michael.* – Since the investigator did not find any glitch; son was obliged to pay mom overdue profit of more than twenty years. (He did not pay mother anything! Neither mother pursued the case.) After mother's retirement, he finally reimbursed some funds! In the meantime, -like many families,- mother was always helping adult sons, daughter, grandchildren, and great grandchildren, but they never appreciated it. ***We Grandparents sent Grandson Erik a graduation present for graduating from college, for him to come to Hawaii, and we had a wonderful time with him in Oahu and Kauai. He went back to accept a position at Microsoft.***
-Remember, Good friends and children, are like stars... you do not always see them, but you know they are always there−!

CHAPTER 3

Giving our best in everything that we do reaps rewards that last a lifetime.

**Do not judge each day by the harvest you reap,
but by the seeds that you plant.**

—Robert Louis Stevenson

E Como May

Now, I would give you a flavor about my last "*Paradise on Earth*"... but, remember, to talk about Hawaii, it would take me years and years... since "*this Wonderland*" has at least a hundred thousand years of all kind of multicolored stories". —According to writer *Yunte Huang, College Professor in Hawaii, his* concoction was-"*how shall we say it– and intriguing people*". —He also called Hawaii "*The Sandwich Islands*", and "*The Archipelago*".

The Hawaiian Islands are unique in their geology, geography, biology, and culture. These islands are the most isolated landmasses on Earth. Located 2,400 miles from the nearest continent, North America, the archipelago stretches nearly 1,600 miles from the volcanically active "Big Island" in the southeast to Kure Atoll in the northwest. There are 132 islands, reefs and shoals altogether. *This chain of islands* sitting on the Pacific Lithospheric Tectonic Plate is moving West Northwest at approximately 3.4 inches per year. Due to this geographic isolation, there are no native land reptiles or amphibians and only two native mammals, the Hawaiian *Hoary Bat* and the *Hawaiian Monk Seal*".

With the tranquility of the ocean, we discover our own piece of paradise! With warmest aloha, we welcome you now to the Islands of Hawaii...

Kauai, with magnificent sea cliffs, canyons, and foliage distinguished as the Garden Island.

Oahu, *Known by Waikiki* beaches, world-class shopping, Pearl Harbor and the North Shore. The third-largest island in the Hawaiian chain has 112 miles of coastline with 30 miles at its widest point and 60 miles long. It is by far the most populous of the Hawaiian Islands, and home to its capital city, Honolulu.

Molokai, *is* where you find Old Hawai'i char, mule rides, and famous Molokai bread.

Lanai, *Hulopo'e'* is a Bay, –with pine-studded uplands.

Maui, the Valley Island; with top-Notch-whale-watching, art Mt. Haleakala, and the winding Hana Highway.

Hawaii, The ever expanding island that has an active volcano Mt. Kilauea's Volcano National Park, where we get information on volcano activity and wonderfully diverse scenery with gigantic powerful observatories, Except unpredictable weather, the climate from rainy and chilly near the *Kilauea Summit* to warm and dry at the end of *Chain of Carters Road.* *–Volcano National Park is a 2 1/2 to 3 hours' drive from the Kailua Kona area.*

Hawai'i Native Wildlife offer nature lovers all the beaches, mountains and tropical greenery one could want… Animal lovers appreciate the islands are also rich in native fauna, most of which are endangered species. It is a true treasure to come across these creatures, so please treat them as such! In addition, we have federal laws that prohibit close contact.

Let us talk about *Sea Turtles. Green Sea Turtles are* affectionately call *Honu* in the islands. *Green Sea Turtles (as well as the Hawksbill Sea Turtle)* we find swimming at snorkel spots and sometimes basking on the beach. The largest hard–shelled sea turtle is an aquatic herbivore that crops a variety of seaweed off the reefs using a finely serrated beak. They have a natal homing instinct, and the majority returns to the sands of their birth the French *Frigate Shoals* in the North islands to lay eggs. However, an increasing number are nesting on beaches of the main Hawaiian Islands. Listed as endangered species in 1973, it is illegal to harass, capture, or kill green sea turtles and beachgoers should watch them from a distance. Summer is sea turtle nesting season, so we admire them for afar.

Hawaiian Monk Seals we find only in Hawai'i, this endemic pinniped has a round head covered with short hairs, giving a "monk-like" appearance. The Hawaiian word for the silvery-gray seal is *Ilio-holo-i-ka-uaua* meaning *"dog running in the rough seas"*. While seals mostly live among the uninhabited Northwestern Hawaiian Islands, they sometimes travel to the main islands, and are seen napping on beaches. –This is an endangered species with a declining population of 1,200. *Monk Seals* should be left alone;

while seals may appear ready to play with swimmers, be advised they can be rough, and can cause serious harm in their playfulness.

Let us learn about *Nênê, the Hawaiian Goose-proclaimed the state bird in 1959; the Nênê* resembles the Canada's Goose in appearance. We find them during spring-summer on golf courses, where the birds hatch their young; or in Hawai'i's national parks. These beautiful geese favor the native foods of the uplands, when not rearing goslings and can maneuver hash terrain, including rocky lava flows. These endangered species with about 900 living on Hawai'i Island and as many as 1,100 more combined across *Maui, Kauai,* and *Molokai.*

Now, let us talk about *Waikiki,* in *Honolulu,* this city is more than a visitor destination–every grain of sand on the beach has a story to tell, and you can learn some of them. The morning hours are perfect for a quiet walk along Waikiki Beach from the Natatorium War Memorial to the Hilton Hawaiian Village. –Close your eyes, and pay attention to the calming sound of waves lapping on the shoreline and feel the cool sand between your toes. Grab any spot on the beach and take in the splash of sunrise colors, watching *Waikiki* awaken.

The Waikiki *Natatorium* opened in 1927 as a tribute to more than 10,000 service members from Hawai'i who served in World War II. It is design as a living memorial.

One great idea because a crowd gathers on *Kuhio Beach* every Tuesday, Thursday, and Saturday at the Hula mound across from the Hyatt Regency Waikiki Beach Resort and Spa; here you can enjoy Hawai'i's *hula halau* (hula groups) performing in the rays of the setting sun.

There are some wonderful places to visit, *The Arizona Memorial at Pearl Harbor…*The *Diamond Head State Monument…*

The *Hanauma Bay Nature Preserve...The Polynesian Cultural Center...The Honolulu Zoo...The Atlantis Adventure, and Waimea Valley,* which offers cultural activities, archaeological sites, botanical gardens, a waterfall, shops, and restaurants.

Did you have enough? Get a canoe ride and you will enjoy our tropical paradise and learn more about the people of Hawaii.

It is amazing to know, Hawaiian Islands have the most *endangered plants*–as the palms–, among many others; over 90% of the native Hawaiian plants found in undeveloped and mountainous zones of our islands do not exist anywhere else in the world.

These paradisiac *Hawaiian Islands* are among the last places on Earth discovered and occupied by humans. Before A.D. 100, there is little evidence of human contact of any kind. The first significant colonies of ocean voyaging Polynesians were established around 800 A.D. Modern contact was made in January of 1778, when English explorer Captain James Cook first encountered the Hawaiian Islands.

Since we have been living in the Islands of Hawaii, we always have admired each one of them, for their unique beauty... For example *Oahu* features myriad sights and attractions, such as the crashing waves with the mirroring kaleidoscopic colors of their waters –Every day according to the weather, the shade of the waters are paradisiacal different, and thus making the ever changing crashing waves of the island incredible to see!

North Shore is the quintessential place where visitors and locals alike come to enjoy three treats: *sun, sand,* and *surf!* Moreover, it takes about an hour to get there from *Waikiki...* In addition, you can enjoy the Bohemian *Haleiwa Towne's* shops!

We enjoy *Hanauma Bay*; it is not too far away from where we live in *Hawaii-Kai...* "He magic of *Hawaii* comes from the stillness, of the sea, the stars… and the things we like to do best here, and cannot be found in a brochure or any other place!. I want to be frank with you, my readers, even at my age of 87 going on 88, I still enjoy things like feeling the peerless winds and looking into the colorful world of corals and tropical fish, snorkeling in gentle bays and inlets which creating calm special places in the romantic inner waters, ideal for snorkeling and swimming.

Other times, husband drives us near the Diamond Head… The story said, over 300.000 years ago, a volcanic explosion occurred along Oahu southwest shore, creating a saucer-shaped crater that sprawled across more than 475 acres. Thousands of years later when a British sailor came across the remains of calcite crystals, thought of at that time to be diamonds, he named it "Diamond Head" to describe the beautiful mountainous extinct volcano.

On the other hand, drive around Oahu… in direction of the Ko'olau Summi… As we came to view a mountain on a small offshore island in the ocean, I said to Michael, "It looks like a hat because it has the shape of a hat." "I didn't know My Dear Wife; you knew the name for that little mountain!" "No, I did not! I was just kidding!" I said to my wife. I guess people call it that way, because it looks like a Chinese hat." "Yes, of course" I said", people named it 'China Hat' because it does look like a gigantic Chinese hat."

I learned that other writers such as *Robert Louis Stevenson, Jack London, Mark Twain* (before he became *Mark Twain)*, explored the "Sandwich Islands" as these islands were then called in the early 1800's. Then, they people also called "The Archipelago".

Remember, the favorite sport of Hawaiians, is surfing! They do not call it "hart work!" … They call it, "having an affair with the ocean!" Now I share with you Hawaii's most unique surf contests.

One day, we were sitting with five surfers who are on the forefront of the progressive surfing movement to understand how they define "progression," ... how their home-breaks (local favorite surfing spots) molded their surfing styles and what new "aerials" and "rotations" (their new developing stunts) we can expect to see in the future... They gave us a history ...

The Haleiwa International Open continues as a contest tradition for 47 years; we had the opportunity to admire at the 47th annual *Haleiwa International Open,* held at *Haleiwa Ali'i Beach Park,* on December 26th to 28th. This event is as legendary as its contest heritage, thanks to two factors: Monumental Swell and the areas "Eclectic Group of Local Surfers".

The Monumental Christmas Days December 26-28th played on, as the event held on, even with heavy offshore winds. One of the highlights of the event for decades has been the Masters division, and this year was no different. *Style maestros Ross Williams, Jack Johnson, Matty Liu, and Lifeguard Adam Lerner gave Haleiwa a good run down.*

With the best conditions of day two, we observed, very excited, some of the Champions... *A 20 years old Seth Moniz* proved that not only he is growing in stature and maturity, his wicked backhand is improving as well, which helped him finish fourth overall.

Koa Rothman won the 2017 Da Hui Backdoor Shootout. The conditions were the best the contest has ever seen! In addition, we were fascinated to assist for the first time in life one of the best free Surfing event in the world!

Let us go back to the wonderful information about the architectural styles in *Honolulu*, the capital, which is in European style, if we analyze the "*Iolani Palace*... Same as the Alexander and Baldwin buildings, that covers the entire city block on Bishop Street. –If we analyze the *Hawai'i State Capitol*, it reflects Hawaii's bold and progressive appearance into the modern age.

The best way to describe the magnificence of a rainbow and kaleidoscopic colors of *Leeward Oahu*, you have to visit the coastline to agree with me that its coastline boast some of the best surf spots e.g. *Makaha Beach*. A visit to these beaches will reward you with pods of dolphins that frolic in the open ocean. The sheds of the sky are like gold and flame.

From Kawaihoa to Makapu's, the Ka Iwi Cost on Oahu, we appreciate traveling through the coast-line to observe, among many beautiful views *The deep End* on the *Crest Hill*; from there we are in a different world! No more houses, no more malls... Before *Ka Iwi*, the rugged and wild stretch of coastline, between *East Honolulu* and *Windward Oahu,* we always feel like we might be in heaven.

Ka Iwi is the first glimpse of the *Hawai'i* drama of volcanic creation and destruction is visible... a raw land of lava outcroppings, stream-carved gulches, windswept beaches, crushing surf and plunging sea cliffs wreathed in a salt haze. The ocean is a rich indigo, and on a clear day *Molokai, Lanai* and *Maui seem to float on the horizon!*

Oahu has hundreds of beautiful places... breathtaking kilometers of sand beaches with topaz water; considered as some of the best beaches in the world!

–When listening to Hawaiian Music, feel transported to the heavens! We had a chance to spend the first half of the show of Grammy Award-winning guitarist John Hammond, bringing his

signature blues style to Hawaii... Since then, wanted to rest and get inspired... (Always listen to all kind of Hawaiian music; you can do it too, even if you do not live in Hawaii).

–Remember some cute statements, from the Associated Press, about asking four candidates running for President, to name where you came from, *"Rosary beads" -said Joe Biden; "Olive burgers" from the "Pickwick in Chicago," –replied Hilary Clinton. In addition, our Ex-President Barak Obama, said, "The photograph in my office of "The Cliffs of Oahu, South Shore" where my mother's ashes are scattered". –He was referring to the area bellow "Lana'i Look out", one of the pullouts along Ka Iwi's coastal drive, between Hanauma Bay and Sandy Beach, near Honolulu.*

All Hawaiian Islands preserves agriculture everywhere! One of the most precious are the The Koa trees, which are used in many gorgeous artefacts locally, and around the world; and do not forget cocoa and coffee.

Hope you had enough information and had the desire to visit these gorgeous islands...

–Since writing articles for magazines and newspapers, had interviewed famous people around the world; so I conferenced with individuals and got their opinion. "If you visit *Oahu, Hawaii*, don't forget the sentimental *Pearl Harbor Museum of Art*... all of you should observe and respect it! –Studying this iconic spot of history, like *Kumu Lopaka Kapaui, you have to stop at Pali Lookout*, which, according to the story, *Kamehameha's* fate was sealed as the one who would unite the islands"... Let us come to visit it and enjoy one of the Great Places on Earth!

Now, want to inform the readers about a sentimental event that takes care every year in Honolulu, Hawaii...

A CHANCE FOR GRIEVING AND HEALING *–Positive energy and support from thousands fill the annual Lantern Floating event in **Hawaii**.* This celebration *"Many Rivers, One Ocean"* was the home for one of the celebrations of *"Lantern Floating Hawaii"* ceremony with more than 50.000 people to *Ala Moana Beach Park* with about 6,000 lanterns, were set afloat in the traditional *Memorial Day event.*

"Kawehi Adkins-Kupukaa was just 14 years old when she died in a horrific car crash in Ewa Beach, just days before Thanksgiving 2012. Her death devastated her family in ways they could not adequately express. Two years of shared grieving have hailed the family to regain a semblance of orientation, of daily balance, but the desire to keep Kawehi Adkins-Kupukaa alive in memory remains stronger than ever. "She was just awesome, so vibrant," –said aunt *Sharlene Kupukaa"… –she was the life of a party, and she was also helping others*–taking care of her grandmother, who is blind, and watching her six nephews,,. –She was a beautiful, loving girl." *Kupukaa* was one of the thousands of people who gathered at Ala Moana Beach Park on Monday to participate in Lantern Floating Hawaii, the annual ceremony of remembrance sponsored by *Shinnyo-en Hawaii* and *Na Lei Aloha Foundation.*

Kupukaa and about 20 families and friends spent the late afternoon beneath a massive tent decorated with a large banner emblazoned with her niece's name and image. "A lot of people have stopped by. –*Kupukaa* said. "So we got to tell them about *Kawehi,* and we also got to hear their stories. That's what makes this event so awesome; there is a kind of healing that happens when we are all here together supporting each other."

First staged, as a fusion of the Japanese born tradition and the *American Memorial Day,* the lantern-floating event has grown into a massive spectacle that includes live broadcasts on TV and the

Internet.   This year organizers increased the number of lanterns available for participants to float in memory of loved ones to from 5,000 to 6,000.

Among all the beautiful events in Hawaii, admire this breathtaking ceremony, when the waters illuminate the ocean with incredible lanterns decorated in all colors, designed by real artists. *Shinso Ito*, leader of *Shinnyo-en*, sponsor of the event, dressed in red kimono, kindled the *Light of Harmony* with *artist Sooriya Kumar... Even the Mayor Kirk Caldwell, Lt. Gov. Shan Tsutsui, and Sgt. Rob Lee, attended this memorable ceremony.* —"Organizers calculated that more than 60,000 participants and spectators were on hand for the extraordinary event!

Now, I want to take my readers to the *Hawai'i Island*, often called the *"Big Island"*, is the largest and tallest of the 8 main Hawaiian Islands. It is 95 miles long (N-S) and 79 miles across (E-W), with a total area of 4,028 square miles. This land area is larger than all the other islands combined. Its highest elevation is 13,796 feet *at Pu'u Wekiu* on the summit of *Mauna Kea.*

Lake *Wai'au* on *Mauna Kea* is the third highest lake in the United States, at an elevation of 13,020 feet. (Every time we visit the *Big Island*, we are amazed to see 90% of the visible stars from Mauna Kea, home to 13 excellent observatories' telescopes from 9 different countries). *Kilauea* ranks as one of the world's most active volcanoes… Approximately 11% of Hawai'i is above sea level, with the remaining 89% reaching depths of 18,000 feet below sea level. This island is located in the middle of the Pacific Ocean, receiving many powerful storm-generated ocean swells, created by the winds blowing over the ocean surface in a "straight line".

It is worthy to visit the *Hawai'i Volcanoes National Park*! Established on August 1,1916; the park has a total area of 449086 acres, and it was recognized as an *International Biosphere Reserve, for its unique scenic and scientific value and became a World Heritage Site in 1987.* Another fascinated area is *"The Hawaiian Tropical Botanical Garden. A non-profit Scientific and Educational Institution, Preserves the Onomea Bay, with the Legend of Twin Rocks.*

Mauna Kea Summit & Observatory... Visiting the *Mauna Kea Summit and Observatories* gives you the feeling of being on top of the world for good reason: You're actually pretty close. Standing at 13,796 feet (4,138 meters), the mountain is Hawaii's tallest and the highlight of many visitors' trips to the Big Island of Hawaii. *The Mauna Kea Observatories* (MKO) features some of the world's largest telescopes, including equipment from Canada, France, and the University of Hawaii, due to its designation as an unparalleled destination for stargazing.

What makes *Mauna Kea* Ideal for Astronomical Sightseeing. These collections of huge telescopes are the most fantastic observatory you can imagine! The *Subaru Telescope*, the *W.M. Keck Observatory*, and the *NASA Infrared Telescope Facility* take advantage of *Mauna Kea's* ideal location near the *equator* and above most of the atmosphere's water vapor, which means a clear view of stars in both of the earth's hemispheres.

However, if you do not have a chance to visit these masterpieces of science, just go outside your hotel or resort about midnight... Look at the sky! It seems that you can raise your hand and touch the huge stars! -Then we visited the precious Maui' island. ***"Believe it, or not! –Admiring all of these wonderful treasures Got mentally away from the disturbances of our environment, escaping from this world! –Like, in meditation– "This is what I do sometimes... when I put my mind on a particular thought, my attention does not become restless hopping from one idea to another, not like living on the surface of life".***

Maui is another beautiful and prosperous Island

They grow Koa wood, meaning "warrior", strong hardwood, incredibly valuable as a building material for canoes, furniture, and the traditional material to make "ukuleles" adopted to make guitars, and other instruments. By the way, the Hawaiian music is an inspiration in all the Hawaiian Islands and with great voices interprets in a very romantic way local songs, besides mainland music.

Maui has over 200 different species of fish that inhabit *Molokini Crater*, and you will have the chance to search for them all aboard *Maui* snorkeling tours. Inside an ancient volcanic caldera that rises up out of the sea, you might also find *manta rays, sea urchins, eels*, or even harmless *sharks*. The tour stop at a spot called *Turtle Town* along the *Maui* coastline, where visitor have the chance to swim alongside enormous Hawaiian Green *sea turtles*. Cruises also go up the coast in search of *dolphins* or *humpback whales*.

The snorkeling tours begin at the *Maalaea* harbor, where you will board your boat for the excursion to *Molokini* Crater and *Turtle Town*. An snorkeling trip,with a comfortable ride, ease of entry, in and out of the water, some with ham and egg breakfast, some a barbecue lunch, a professional captain and crew, and the chance to learn about this slice of Hawaii, are just a few of the reasons this tour makes for an ideal day out on the waters of Maui. The snorkeling tour begins at the *Maalaea* harbor, where you will board your boat for the excursion to *Moloki*ni Crater and *Turtle Town*. Located off the south shore *of Kihei* and rising 300 feet above the water, the extinct volcanic cone of *Molokini* provides the opportunity to see native Hawaiian marine life like *manta rays, fish, urchins*, and *sharks*, which swim around the coral through the clear water year round. *Molokini* Sanctuary is a *Marine Preserve and Bird Sanctuary*, has been protected, so expect pristine conditions.

Snorkel to explore the underwater world, and take advantage of the water slide for more fun, especially for kids. You can also peek at the reef without getting in the water via the boats glass bottom windows.

After leaving *Molokini*, your second snorkeling spot of the day is Turtle Town, where you have the chance to swim with *Hawaiian green sea turtles* amid the calm water and coral. Then return to the boat for a barbecue lunch buffet of pulled pork and chicken sandwiches, pasta salad, and chocolate chip cookies. Next, cruise down the south shore of Maui where your captain gives informative and historical narration about celebrity homes, island history, and volcanic eruptions T-shirt. Usually the tours provide Buffet and music, all to entertain you during your day in paradise. For centuries, Hawaiians were self-sufficient, able to live off the bounty of the ocean and the fertile land, harvesting the plants and livestock they had brought with them across the Pacific, such as taro and chickens. When Captain James Cook first landed on Hawaii in 1778, he found a place rich in culture and not lacking in natural resources. –*"The Hawaiian Islands has been a paradise!"*

–*Magic after dark– A lime-green sparkle on the horizon at sunset heralds each magical night in Hawaii. Have you seen it yet?'*

Feed your ears with music everywhere on Hawaii... When friends arrive, we head to a luau for the best Polynesian Music and dance.

Spend your evening with someone whose passion is to see perform a genuine Hawaiian musician... You will feel like you are in heaven!

CHAPTER 4

A fake rose can never be a real rose; and a real rose will shed it fragrance, no matter how much it is crushed.

–Paramahansa Yogananda

Most of us know that traveling can improve our perspectives in life. It is safe to say that it is our ticket to our better selves. Now, if we are traveling with someone else, like your husband, chances are – you would grow together, making your bond stronger than ever.

On February 16, 2016 at 5 pm, we were ready to left **Honolulu, Hawaii** to fly to *New York*, to take a cruise the next day at 6 pm, to travel around the world…

Early in the morning, before taking a taxi to the airport in *Honolulu,* we observed the near-by beach… The day was gorgeous, the waves at the near ocean, were undulating with grace. –They were as it is here on any day… The early birds, including some cardinals with gorgeous red plumage, were eating some seeds beneath the canopy of the scented early day, we observed a local elderly man seating on a big rock, near a palm tree, fringed with coconuts, plucking soft tunes on his ukulele, perhaps entertaining himself before going to work. Imagine the moonlight hiding on the other side of the ocean; isn't it so great!

We arrived at the airport, very early this morning; did the hurry-up routine, after the helpers sent the luggage inside the huge airplane, to fly to New York. –Smiling, the happy steward asked, "What are you going to do in New York? Do you know tomorrow all that area will be covered with heavy snow?" –"Yes we are aware of that! Nevertheless, we always hope for the best."

Long time on the plane gave the opportunity to rest on the arms of husband; walked from time to time in the plane, trying not to disturb the passengers that were sleeping and snoring… Got some almonds that my husband had packed for me inside his jacket, to entertain my diabetic hunger; and from time to time, paid attention to the flight attendant announcing the turbulence from the bad weather…

About ten hours later, we arrived at La Guardia International Airport! Left the luggage at the special guest-room at the airport; hired a taxi to Manhattan, got a great breakfast, and there we were walking and observing the thousands of people walking in a hurry to go to work.

It was February 17th, in *New York*! We admired the skyscrapers, and visited the *Museum of Modern Art*. We went to the *Empire State Building,* to take some photos from the 103rd floor… Remembered, this was the tallest building in New York. Visited some rooms, attend to a symposium about art, bought at *Times Square street,* a *Times Magazine.*

Since we had some time, we ate at one of the most famous hamburgers, stuffed with onions, at *The Iconic Burger* in Manhattan 21st W and 52nd. *The taste was great, but the price was sower,* they charged $40.00 dollars per hamburger, explaining they used "aged beef from *Master Purveyors,* served on a *Challah Bun".* Later, we ordered a soft drink. Listen to this, Michael paid more than a hundred fifty dollars. We thought, were should be eating in Heaven.

As we all probably know, the City of *New York* is *the most populous city in the United States,* and *the most densely populated major city in North America.* The *center for international finance, fashion,* entertainment and culture; and is widely considered to be one of *the world's major global cities with an extraordinary collection of museums, galleries, performance venues, media outlets, global corporations and financial markets...* –Also *the home to the Headquarters of the United Nations.*

Luckily, our dear friend *Myriam,* who lives in New York for many, many years, –the same friend who encouraged me to present my book *Colombina* a few years ago at the *International Book Fair,* in New York. –At that time, she introduced us to this metropolis's exciting new world of extravaganza. At that time, she invited us to *Radio City Music Hall, The New York Metropolitan Area* –according to her, with population of about 22 million, which makes it one of the largest urban areas in the world! Nicknamed *"The Big Apple",* which attracts large numbers of immigrants, with over a third of its population foreign born. I was just evoking that time.

Went to the most iconic 360-degree open-air Observation Deck in all of NYC, at *The Empire State Building's* 86th floor in the heart of midtown *Manhattan.* We really felt the heart of NYC and our free self-guided multimedia tour. – Looked out on *New York*

City from 1,050 feet above the bustling streets below. – Experienced the panoramic views of up to five states from the surrounding open-air promenade or from our climate controlled viewing, and got galleries, the details about what we are viewing from every vantage point with the free self-guided multimedia tour. It is so much more than just a view. We embarked on a journey through one of the most famous landmarks in the world, where we experienced the newly restored *Art Deco* lobby and murals, the historical *Dare to Dream* exhibit, and Sustainability Exhibit.

To admire the *Statue of Liberty* and *Ellis Island Immigration Museum,* we took a short ferry ride from Battery Park. And since we did not want to miss the historic halls and galleries at *Ellis Island,* –where more than 12 million immigrants first entered America, took an audio tour to both *Liberty Island* and *Ellis Island.* (We found out that there were other tours available in different languages including Arabic, English, French, German, Italian, Japanese, Mandarin, Russian, and Spanish.)

This New York Pass granted us a free Ferry ride that took us to the *Statue of Liberty* and *Ellis Island,* that included access inside the Statue of Liberty; pedestal access was *first come,* first *served.* From there, we observed the *Masterpiece of the Oceans!*

In a few hours, we were inside the Cruise Ship after finishing the tours. Later in the afternoon, we were walking inside "The "Largest and Best Cruise Ship in the World." Guided by uniformed young men, to one of the best-decorated rooms, accommodated our belongings. Then, after lunch, we walked a little bit around the vessel to stretch our legs... and then it was time to transfer to our beautiful room.

After taking a quick shower, dressed in our special attire, to attend the first wonderful dinner aboard; and immediately after, we joined *Capitan Christopher Wells,* and his Officers for champagne (with me only a sip) to listen to the Captain's welcome' words to the thousands of "guests" in the *Queens Mary's Grand Ballroom..*

On January 17, we were excited to be living four months in the World's most Wonderful *Ocean Liner on the Queen Mary 2 Cruise around the World...*Next day, *January 18* started feeling fantastic! I sat for a while, in a red chair with a golden frame for Michael to take my blood pressure test and when I observed the results, jumped for real joy and happiness! *–That means my health had improved!* At that moment, I was feeling on top of the world!

Very relaxed, we sailed away from *New York...* Then, my husband made an appointment with the Cruise doctor. – "Your blood pressure is normal; only as a precaution, I am going to prescribe some medicine, just in case... In the mean-time you may order at the dining room a special diet." –Looked at my husband Michael feeling very happy about the results of the test, and the positive words from the Doctor... – Then, with satisfaction, seating on red chairs, of our remarkable room, husband opened the bottle of Champaign, which was on our desk, as a welcome present from the Crouse ship' Captain. I only took a smell!

–From that inordinate moment, we started the incredible cruise around the world without any worries! In route, we enjoyed the wonderful programs in the incredible Queen Mary's theater, with thousands of red chairs... *"The first night, we got surprised with the interpretation of The Overtures of the Sixties."* The band was amazing! *–We read at the program, that this group* is the best band of their kind on the world." The *Overtures* presented a faithful and dynamic tribute to pops greatest decade – the sixties. –Then, it was time to go to sleep...

Next night we appreciated the "*Appassionata,* exiting style of dance from around the world; from Glenn Miller's Swing to the tantalizing *Argentinian Tango show*, featuring some of the most incredible dances ever seen at sea. Had a wonderful dinner and again went to snooze. I was sleeping very well… getting up early in the mornings to walk 1, 2, or 3 miles a day around the ship…Always ordered diet food (no salt), just in case. After two weeks, went back to the doctor, sent to the laboratory to get a blood tests…–The results were great! –Then, appointments scheduled only once a month! – All Blood tests were normal! Michael enthusiastically exclaimed: "That's all you needed, "Peace and Tranquility!" –Remember Dear, "Our capacity for Happiness is a true measure of our greatness."

The Captain, who welcomed all of us on board for our World *mentioned,* "Our Cunard cruise ship have traversed the globe since Laconia set sail on the first world voyage in 1922. Those seeking style, sophistication, and adventure can travel only by sea. Along our epic itinerary this year, guests will have the chance to ride the famous Star Ferry in front of Hong Kong's dazzling illuminated skyline; embrace the breathtaking vistas of *Australia* and see the statue of *"Cristo Redentor,"* in *Rio de Janeiro.* –Your home for the duration of you stays with us this wonderful cruise-ship, has taken the reigns as one of the world's most famous vessels, and her scale and elegance makes her an attraction in her own right. We wish you a pleasant journey and relaxing voyage as Queen Mary 2 departs for our next port of call, Fort Lauderdale. (By the way we can sail as fast as 35 knots…if you want to water ski!)."

The champagne had been everywhere! *Sailing away from New York in style,* with the Entertainment Staff from the iconic New York skyline and celebrated with the *International Band Vibz* providing music for the occasion. *–All were impressed with the fast results! I was also amazed per the Captain chat that "the Abyssal Plain under our ship is an underwater plain on the deep ocean floor, usually found at depths between 30000m and 60000m; and, that in fact "Abyssal plains cover more than 50% of the Earth's surface".*

In our route, we were happy to be entertained again periodically by The World's Best 60's Tribute Act *The Overtures*, one of the finest and "To quote *Sir Elton John*, speaking to GQ magazine after they performed at the celebration of his civil partnership with *David Furnish*. –"I learned, this band is *just the best of their kind in the world*. –The Overture presented a faithful and dynamic tribute to pops greatest decade – the sixties. –We really, enjoyed them.

–Since I was eating a "special diet" the *Maître d'*- assigned exclusive table for two, always decorated with colorful flowers, and tonight they chose at dinner a bouquet of flamboyant orchids…The service was fantastic; the head waiter was coming to our table very often to ask, "Is the diet food satisfactory to you? Other-wise with the doctor's permission, we will change the fish for chicken, and once in a while you can have one of these wonderful sugarless desserts!" –By the way, at the second visit, the doctor allowed changing the diet, and was delighted eating every day and night something very special, like oysters, lobsters, duck and red meat (in moderation).

I commented to my husband Michael *"See darling we never give-up! Not giving up is the first step to winning"*.

On Jan 19 we were in route to *Fort Lauderdale*, had the time to better organize my gala dresses, and husband's suits versus tuxedo for husband; chose a better place for the *"Love Ducks"* these were the towels the Housekeeping Maid fashioned into cute creatures and left them on out bed each night and the fresh colorful orchids we moved to the center-table. After taking a warm shower, we got ready for another gala-dinner and show at the *Master of the Seas*. Then, we were ready to observe the wonderful cruise around the world.

(Want to comment, that we had taken many, many cruses in Europe, Central and South America, but this was the best of all! – Wish all of our friends were there with us!) At this time, we arrived Jan. 20 at 5.30 pm… at **Fort Laurendale** once, the ship left the big *Tugboat Tender* to approach the city, and the lines of tourists were then waiting for the big buses to go on tours. –Finally, they arrived with signs blue, green, red, and white. *"Please, read the signs,"* – announced the driver–, *"to avoid taking the wrong buss; and, please take the right seat"*. Everything was professional organized, with one complication; a *"disabled lady"* protesting *she wanted the front seat! To please the absent-minded' lady, the other passengers were moving back, and everybody was happy..."* When the buss attendant, was trying to seat the lady, that waited about three hundred pound, it was a challenge!"

Fort Lauderdale is as the *Venice of America* due to its expansive and intricate canal system. Learned that the population is describe as metropolitan in coastal and downtown areas and I observed diverse cultures are commonplace; with great pleasure, they welcomed all of us. Learned the estimate population is about 164,000. – Very surprise, to hear, that the city was *"The western corner of the Bermuda Triangle –.*

The beaches offer 23 miles of golden sand, lively with the spirited antics of happy vacationers. Sail the blue-green waters on a chartered catamaran, and dive beneath the surface to meet-and-greet the local sea life. Shopping and dining al fresco on *Las Olas Boulevard* is one of Fort Lauderdale's greatest pleasures, thanks to adorable shops and prime people watching.

–According to comments, *Fort Lauderdale* has become one of the top destinations for family travel on the east coast of the United States. Its beaches and wildlife reserves provide a diverse breadth of outdoor fun, while its waterfront hotels and facilities sponsor youth-friendly recreation and parent-approved activities.

Located just an hour north of the glitz and glamour of *Miami's South Beach*, Fort Lauderdale is a little more subdued and a lot more diverse. This ocean-front community is filled with artists, beautiful homes, and waterways, great restaurants and miles of beautiful beaches framed by a picturesque serpentine wall. Fort *Lauderdale* is a wonderful place for a vacation and a terrific place to call home!

You likely already know about the area's tropical climate— sunshine, warm weather and frequent quick bursts of rain. Likewise, if you are probably familiar with the sandy beaches and crowds of smiling people on vacation, you may even have chosen the perfect spot to laze away the days fishing, or a well-loved place to kayak or snorkel. While these are all fabulous draws to the region, there is much more to this thriving little metropolis of 167,000 people.

This is a city that embraces its ocean and river heritage. In fact, nearly 40,000 residents live aboard their yachts and the 162 bridges and nearly 500 miles of waterways have rightfully earned Ft. *Lauderdale* its nickname, *"Venice of America."*

We learned *Ft. Lauderdale* is a trendy smaller city; at once a mega yacht capital, beach town, and hip urban area. It merges all people seamlessly like no other place. The city earned its spring-break reputation due to the 1960's film, *"Where the Boys Are,"* but local government wisely added a business with friendly environment, that have created significant business growth.

Artists flock to *Ft. Lauderdale* to join communities like the Flagler Arts and Technology (FAT) Village and the city's art scene is rapidly expanding. FAT Village offers regular Art Walk events in the community located downtown. This tropical area, that we already had visited in the past, when we went to *The Miami Book*

Fair to promote some of my books, and afterward enjoyed *The Keys*, the small picturesque islands considered a *Tropical Paradise*.

–Remembered at the time we were visiting this colourful place, the flowers on top of the bushes were so closed, that I felt exchanging pleasantries… other time they swept by so rapidly, that I found myself running up in the park as a schoolgirl, just to keep pace; *but now I am 87 years old, I couldn't keep it up with it. So, even if I had the thought, I couldn't rush up the steep hill at the far end of the villa; then, reminded myself that I was not the energetic schoolgirl, as I once was.*

Yet the excitement pursed me on another rose garden, who have dashed out into their flowers to enjoy the sight; I tried to go up there, on top of the hill, where I catch my breath, took one last longer look, and then, again my husband reluctantly said, *"You Dear Wife, better say farewell to those adventurers, and let's share instead, a delicious ice-cream together (me 98% you just a taste)."*

After analysing the charming morning, with the bright beauty at noon, we enjoyed dinner, the blessing beauty of the stars, made a wish together, wrote lovely notes to our friends read the itinerary for next day, moved the night-stand, happily tired, turned out the lights, and after, both comfy-cosy, went gleefully to sleep.

–Next morning, after breakfast, remembering the wedding of Grandson Carlos and girlfriend Sarah, went to the chapel of the Great Ship to pray, sending a spiritual blessing to my dearest tressures in life, "my two grandchildren".

CHAPTER 5

On January 21st, in route to Amber Cove, feeling great... expecting good health, wanted, and felt it...

*After present wonderful experiences, stated...
"What we think matters... we dictate how we should feel,
in and out of our lives! – Now confirm, really trying
positively, we reach the higher and better life!*

On January morning Queen Mary headed east through the North East Providence channel and altered course to starboard, passing north of San *Salvador Island*. Throughout the day will be skirting to the northeast of the *Bahama Banks*. At evening, we passed through the Caicos passage, between *Mayaguana Island* and *The Caicos Islands*, to continue overnight on our southeasterly course.

At night, we had the chance to attend a wonderful harp concert by Shirley *Dominguez*, born and raised in Montevideo, Uruguay, presenting *"When the Harp Goes Latin"*. Her repertoire ranges from soft familiar melodies to lively ethnic rhythms covering the cultural spectrum from Greek, Italian, New Flamenco, and pop to her own Latin roots. She had shared her passion with the instrument, with audiences all over the world, and has performed for President George W. Bush, former Vic-President Al Gore, and many others. This, our first concert with her, was fantastic!

–I really started feeling well, forgetting the past, and welcoming my new "era" of health and happiness".

On January 22nd, we arrived in *Amber Cove, Dominican Republic on the Bay of Maimon near Puerto Plata* in the country's North Coast. The new facility represents one of the largest cruise industry investments ever made in the *Dominican Republic*. The project is design to re-establish it North Coast as a popular cruise destination. The last cruise ship to call at *Puerto Plata* was nearly thirty years ago.

Amber Cove is a purpose built complex, built by *Carnival Corporation*; it is situated approximately a 15 minute drive from *Puerto Plata*. The ship will berth here at *Ambar Cove*, since this resort has duty free shops, gift shops, cafes, restaurants, "Aqua zone" swimming pool, water sports, and cabanas for hire, -as a new resort, facilities are still being added.

This city of *Puerto Plata, as some know,* was discovered by *Christopher Columbus-,* in one of the famous explorer's trips to the Americans in the 1490's. This place, -better known for its Atlantic Coastline-, with more than 60 miles (100km) of beaches, coastal villages, and hotels. The beach towns of *Sosua* and *Cabarete* are, famous for windsurfing and kiteboarding, and only a half an hour away. –We had the chance to admire *the popular Ocean World Adventure Park* located on the outskirts of the city, about 20 minutes north of *Ambar Cove*; and the amazing *Damajagua Falls* are just a 30 minutes ride south.

Puerto Plata lies on the country's shimmering north coast, washed by the waves of the *Atlantic Ocean* and backed by the protective peak of *Mount Isabel de Torres, Christopher Columbus* is credited as having named it the "silver port"; although *Nicolas de Ovando* is thought to have founded the settlement here in 1502.

Its strategic location served the fleets sailing between Spain and Mexico, before suspended by *Cuba's Havana* in the 1860s. The island is a tobacco producer and exporter; and many mansions built by German merchants and investors who migrated to the city are still standing today.

The total land area of this gorgeous place is 48,730 square kilometers, with an undulating landscape rising to 3,175 meter at the *Cordillera Central* range's highest mountains, the *Pico Duarte*, and dropping to 46 meters of the *Enriquillo Lake*.

The *Island of Hispaniola* is the second largest of the *Caribbean Sea's Great Antilles archipelago*. Divided into the countries of *Haiti* – a former French colony that takes up the western third of the island- and the former -Spanish-owned- *Dominican Republic* with covers the remaining eastern two-thirds.

We had the chance to visit the popular Ocean World Park on the outskirts of the city, about 20 minutes north of Amber Cove. Damajagua Falls is just 30 minutes ride south. —By all means, the cabanas are so picturesque right on the water, and at their back yard, with fascinating palm trees, to shade the wooden slatted seats that do not need air-conditioning. -That day, a little tired, went to have dinner, and after, enjoyed the show of *Brett Sherwood, a Master Magician*.

Next day we pass through the *Mona Passage* and into de *Venezuelan Basin*, which forms part of the *Caribbean Sea*, between The *Dominican Republic* and *Isla De Mona, west of Puerto Rico.* The passage is 35 nautical miles wide and has seabed depths of over 7,500 feet. –Throughout the day, we followed a southeaster course, through the *Caribbean Sea* toward *Barbados…*

– During this journey, we were very happy helping disabled people with thoughtfulness, like holding their hands to get out of the bus, bringing them some water in hot weather, talking with old single travelers, so they could enjoy their special vacation.

–Other times, husband and I carved out our precious moments, sitting down with friends from different nationalities, in the mornings, having a cup of coffee with Tom and Sheila Sheppard, talking about their families, living so far away, or being still listening to music, and observing the ocean's tranquility waves, to find our minds and souls absorbing the gentle peace.

At one particular moment, was analyzing that, "It is not what we had gotten, or seeing, that counts… it is what we do with kindness to people, that counts". At night, featured Entertainment was incredible *Aerial Acrobats,* transporting us through a marvelous love story full of lights and color…

On January 23, At sea, in route to *Bridgetown, Barbados*, spent our precious time enjoying the sailing, near one of the huge windows near the waves of the ocean, drinking a cocktail, and enjoying the piano concert, executed by one of the invited musicians.

January 24 in Port of *Bridgetown, Barbados* … This is a medium sized island that is 21 miles wide, located in the far south eastern corner of the Caribbean It is the most easterly of the Caribbean islands, situated about 100 miles east of the Windward Islands chain. The climate is semi-tropical with an average temperature of 80 degrees with only minimal seasonal variations. *Barbados* is getting cool, by the constant trade winds blowing from across the Atlantic toward the Caribbean. The direction of these winds is remarkably constant, which have made Barbados easily reached by sailboats from Europe (downwind) but very difficult to reach from the other Caribbean islands (always lying upwind). This helps to explain why Barbados alone was not subject to repeat conflict between the Caribbean colonial powers and, once colonized by England, remained English until her recent independence.

Barbados is the easterly island in the West Indies, out of the chain of *Leeward* and *Windward Islands*. The island stands in splendid isolation with the powerful *Atlantic Ocean* on its east coast and the clear, calm waters of the *Caribbean Sea* on the out and west coasts. – It is twenty-one miles long and 14 miles at its widest point, with overall area of only 166 square miles. *Mount Hillaby* in the northern center is the highest point of 1,115 feet. The climate is a holidaymaker's dream – tropical, but tempered by the sea breeze from the northeast. The temperature hardly varies from 24 – 27 C or 75 – 80 F. and humidity is pleasantly low.

Founded in 1627 and got independence in 1966, The Island was a British colony, unlike the rest of its Caribbean neighbors, but nobody took it by force. It has an endearing blend of British and West Indian culture, which allied to the Bajan's reputation as the friendliest people in the Caribbean, waves a potent spell.

Barbados is – throughout the *Caribbean* a *"Little England"*. The market town atmosphere, Georgian houses, Parliament Square, neo-Gothic public buildings, and a cricket ground, to say nothing of the signposts to Hasting and Northing, all contribute to the impression. The total population is nearly 300.000 people, more than a third of them live in the capitol, Bridgeton.

Enjoyed *Bay Mansion* on Bay Street, which has on it one of the great houses of the past, with parts dating back to 1750; The Heroes Square is the civic heart of the town, and its focal point in the statue of Nelson, erected in 1813 on the site of "The Green" where hansom cabs wait for fares. The Admiral spent some time here during his command of the naval station at English Harbor, *Antigua*. In the square stands, the Renaissance-style Public Buildings of coral rock and the island's chief administrative offices (opened in 1874). According to information, The Barbados Parliament meets and conducts its work. The open arcades have Gothic instead of the usual rounded arches, and the windows are stained glass portraits of all the monarchs of Great Britain since *James the First*... In the neighboring streets, there are a number of elegant Georgian houses, now used mainly as shops of offices, though some are until privately occupied.

Noticed *Barbados* does not have the striking heights and lush tropical forests of some other West Indian islands... Observed the highest point of *Mt Hillaby* with 1115 feet, steeply descending east coast on the Atlantic, is not unlike Cornwall, with its long stretches superb and surprisingly under crowded surf beaches interrupted by dramatic rocks. In addition, The Atlantic rollers come crashing in, accompanied by the constant breeze of the northeast trade winds that make the climate of *Barbados* so pleasant!

Can you imagine? At age 87, after having, health difficulties with high blood pressure above average, high levels of cholesterol and diabetes... almost prepared to the worst! Now was my feeling healthy and having a good time, forgetting the sadness, being happy with life! "–There was no time to feel unhappy, or unhealthy, because I was only thinking about being positive and living!"

–We can fix most everything in life, if we want to! –But now is the time to be happy.

CHAPTER 6

Enjoyed Salvador, the real Capitol of the Brazilian State; — the third largest city in the country, after Sao Paulo and Rio de Janeiro; and one of the oldest colonial cities in the Americas.

"I have found out that there ain't no surer way to find out whether you like people or hate them than to travel with them."

— Mark Twain

We spent Five days, in route… *On January 30,* we arrived at Port of *Salvador, Brazil,* also known as *Sao Salvador, Salvador de Bahia.* Found out that its population was 2.9 million people, founded by the Portuguese in 1543, the first capital of Brazil.

A steep hill divides its Lower Town, *Ciudade Braxa.* The first elevator *Lacerdahas* connected the two since 1873. UNESCO named the *Pelourinho* district of the upper town, still home too many examples of Portuguese colonial architecture and historical monuments, a World Heritage Site in 1985. We estimate the city for the carnival celebration, and for being the largest city in the world. We admired this place, for its cuisine, music, architecture; and *Porto da Barra Beach,* which had been named one of the best beaches in the world.

Then, we took a shuttle service to approach the *Modelo Market,* and the *Elevator Lacerda* to the Upper City, from the *Salvador Cruise Terminal.* Remember, the two parts of the city, center and upper (*Ciudade Alta*) and a lower city (*Ciudade Baixa*), with very large art deco clanking electric lifts (*Elevador Lacerda*) taking 50,000 guests daily between the lower part and the upper commercial area of the city. The High City (*Ciudad Alta*) *Pelourincho,* is the historic city and the attraction for tourists and partygoers.

–January 31st in route to Rio de Janeiro. After day and a half, at 5:30 p.m. in the afternoon, passing the iconic *Copacabana Beach* and *Sugar Loaf Mountain,* and into the *Bay of Guanabara.* (*The Bosom of the Sea*), *on February 1st, we arrived at Rio de Janeiro, Brazil.*

This marvelous city is the second largest in the country, being, the sixth-largest city in the Americas, and the world's thirty-ninth largest city by population…. The metropolis anchoring to the *Rio de Janeiro* metropolitan areas is the second most populous metropolitan zone in Brazil. Part of the city has been designated as a *World Heritage Site,* named "*Rio de Janeiro …Carioca Landscapes*…a Cultural Landscape Founded in 1565 "*between the Mountain and the Sea*" by UNESCO on July 1st. 2012.

The Church of *Nossa Senhora do Rosario dos Pretos*. (Our Lady of Rosary) is at the north of the area, dates back to 1704. Following the road south, we went to *Lago (Lake) do Pelourinho*, that contains the world's largest collection of *Baroque architecture* and the stroll south does not disappoint, culminating with the wonderful baroque church, Saint Francis (*Igreja Sao Francisco*).

We admired also a wonderful museums that have been housed in the old buildings, as the *"Casa de Jorge Amado"*, dedicated to the novelist *Amado* who lived in the area. We also had the chance to visit the nearest unpolluted beaches located at *Porto da Barra*. –I learned, from the cruise-ship. The city was initially the seat of the captaincy of *Rio de Janeiro*, a domain to the Portuguese Empire; and in 1763, it became the capital of the State of Brazil.

The state of the Portuguese Empire *Rio de Janeiro*, is one of the most visited cities in the Southern Hemisphere and is known for its natural settings, *Carnival, Samba, Boss Nova*, and *beaches* such a *Barra da Timucua*, Copacabana, Ipanema, and *Albeon*. The most famous landmarks include the giant statue of *Christ the Redeemer*, atop *Corcovado* Mountain, named one of the New Seven Wonders of the World. The *Sugarloaf Mountain* with its cable car; the *Sambodromo* (Sambadrome) a permanent grandstand–lined parade avenue which is used during Carnival; and *Maracanã Stadium*, one of the world's largest football Fields. Here *Rio de Janeiro* hosted the 2016 Summer Olympics and the 2016 Summer Paralympics the first time a South American and Portuguese-speaking nation hosted both these events.

Husband asked, which one of these marvelous milestones, impressed you, dear wife? "By all means, the huge marvelous statue of Christ the Redeemer at the top of Corcovado Mountain, it is phenomenal!" Even though, we have been here before, we are happy to visit again, to see all of these gorgeous landmarks in South

America, which we love very much! Remember, every time, we arrive in these wonderful lands, we take dozens of pictures at the *Copacabana Beach*, at the *Maracanã Stadium, at the phenomenal Statue of Christ, and at the beach...* since this is such a delightful place!" –By the way, I want to remind my readers, that *Sugarloaf Mountain* is at the mouth of *Guanabara Bay*, on a peninsula that sticks out into the Atlantic Ocean, rising 396 meters (1,299 ft.) above the harbor. Its name refers to its resemblance to the traditional shape of concentrated refined loaf of sugar. The world recognized this famous place, by consecutive cableways...the shorter *Morro da Urca*, 220 meters (722 ft.) high, this second cable car ascends to *Páo de Acucar*. The Italian-made bubble shaped cars offer passengers 360-degree views of the surrounding city; the climb takes three minutes from start to finish. –Sadly, after walking so many miles, tired but happy, we decided to return to the cruise ship, since we will leaving at 5:30 p.m. today.

Note, Of course, reading the information on this book, about this magnificent country, will not be quite the same as putting on your boots and heading up into their hills...

"How do we feel, being so far away, about this particular cruise around the world?" asked my husband. *–Without analyzing all the facts, I talked relaying exactly my feelings...*

"Traveling is good for a lots of reasons... a) To increase our mental well-being;- not just for the short-term... Whether we are traveling for business, or pleasure, or to celebrate one of our wedding anniversaries, (because we have married to each other in 11 different cultures)... b) On the other hand... selling everything, to pursue a new life, or we are on the road, or had the urgency to move to sophisticated places, or for whatever reason... IT'S GREAT!"

On February 4th in route to Monte Video, invited many passengers to be with us at my next seminar, expecting well-being, amity, and happiness.

Traveling can make us a happier person by building self-confidence, providing new experiences and memories, breaking routine and allowing us to meet people from all over the world."

Tonight, on *February 4th* while the cruise ship was navigating, following the narrow channel up the *River Plate* toward the port of *Montevideo, Uruguay* we attended the comedian, singer and impressionist *Hilary O'Neal* who has had a career spanning 36 years in show business from television show in the UK, tours, personal appearances worldwide, and in cabarets. After enjoying some wonderful new friends at dinner and listening to a piano concert in one of the lobbies, we went happily to sleep; as the cruise continued the World Voyage… in route to *Montevideo*… We had the opportunity to exercise, rest, and enjoy wonderful programs, lecturers, and shows, onboard the lavish theatres…

"Never had to seek for significance of purpose before, and suddenly, I found out the visibly expression of King Solomon's. "However if the reader is not prudent, it might seem that Solomon was certain that his life was deprived of purpose. "All is vanity!" "Worthless!" –Let's analyze!

"Look carefully at what we find to be meaningless: accumulation of wealth, materialism, achievement, prosperity, power, or even wisdom! "Why did Solomon thought about these things which we pursue, –so firmly to be meaningless? –Maybe, because we cannot take any of them with us once we die. And we must (eventually) die! "All come from dust, and go to dust all go back." –This is not to say that life is not worth living for its own sake! –Over and over, Solomon urges us to live life with delight –to eat with gladness, –to enjoy life with husband or wife, whom you love and to enjoy the family.

I remember also reading, acknowledging, that we are part of a purposeful creation…that is the first and most vital step in making sense of life…We did not just happen by chance – struggling to make it through, having just, challenges! – I believe, we are here for a reason –to have good relationships, and to help people, to create and develop these beautiful places on earth. –And this has been, the right reason from day one… helping each other until we die! Being happy, of course!

Right in our gorgeous stateroom, before going to sleep, husband commented, "I want to ask you something, Dear Wife

Nohemí, Did you enjoy visiting, these wonderful countries?" –"It probably will take me a lot of time to express my opinion about so many delightful corners of the world, but right now; all I can say is, *"This has been one of the wonderful rewards of Life, like raising a family!* –Bearing in mind, since we got married, we have been in paradises, visiting other gorgeous historical areas around the world." –Now, it is too late at night; let us leave this discussion until tomorrow and now, just go to sleep!"

On February 5, our cruise ship arrived at 5.30 pm. at Montevideo, the capital of Uruguay. "According to the 2011 census, the city has about one-third of the country's total population in an area of 194.0 square kilometers. According to the 2011 census, the city has about one-third of the country's total population in an area of 194 square kilometers. The most southern capital city in the Americas, *Montevideo,* and the largest city is located on the southern coast of the county on the northeastern bank of the *Rio de la Plata.*

Spanish soldier *Bruno Mauricio de Zabala,* a strategic move amidst the Spanish-Portuguese dispute over the Platine region, established the city in 1724. It was also under brief British rule in 1807.

The area of *Ciudad Vieja* (Old City) in *Montevideo* is for tourism only, which includes the city's oldest buildings, several museums, art galleries, and nightclubs, with *Sarandi Street* and *Public Market,* which is the most frequented venue of the old city. On the edges found the *Independence Plaza, (Plaza Independencia)* including the *Solis Theatre* and the Salvo Palace (*Palacio Salvo).* We noticed the avenue basically, for its *Art Deco,* three important public squares, the *Gaucho Museum,* and the *Municipal Palace (Palacio Municipal).*

Uruguay, like much neighboring *Argentina,* is a country of grassy prairies interrupted only by scattered patches of scrubby woodland.   The grasslands extend into the northern third of Argentina and together these areas comprise one of the world's great grasslands – The Pampas! This rich soil required for high yields of grasses, cereal grain, and large herds of livestock.

Today, *Montevideo* is a city of about 1,800,000 residents, almost entirely of European extraction, chiefly Spanish and Italian stock. It is the largest city in the country and home to half of the country's population.

The only prominent natural feature seen from the sea is the Cerro, a 450-foot null with an old fort on the top (now the Military Museum).   *Uruguay* 'is called *"The Switzerland of South America"*… It is about the size of England and Wales, with a high standard of living and extraordinary democratic institutions.

It was the first state with great welfare programs in the Western Hemisphere. Like all Latin American republics, much of its early history was stormy and bloody, but the efforts of Statesman, Jose Battle y Ordonez, resulted in a 1918 constitution.

This laid the foundation for social programs that are unparalleled anywhere on the continent today and, when promulgated, were more advanced than reforms anywhere in the hemisphere, including those in the United States.

It has an eight-hour working day, paid holidays, social security for the aged, free medical treatment, legal divorce, nationalization of almost all essential industries and services, abolishment of capital punishment, separation of church and state and so on, and so forth.

We visited the *Gaucho Museum*, which is the one that you should not miss. It deals with the history of these famous men and has excellent display of their leatherwork, silverwork, weapons, and tools. At the same time, North American cowboys were creating the myth of their own.

"The vast grasslands that make up Uruguay were the birthplace and symbol of the Pampas – the gaucho. This South American cowboys arose in the 18th century and made a rough living capturing the wild horses that escaped from the developing ranches and then, using them to capture the escaped cattle. They lived a nomadic life on the plains, eating livestock as necessary, and selling hides when they needed money for tobacco, rum, and tea.

They were described as *"wild as the Indians, and just interesting, as well as obliging, hospitable, and very polite"*. The word "gaucho" some believe, to have stemmed from the Indian word for "orphan"; and the term is accurate, for they were solitary figures, as first ruled by no one. Gauchos had few possessions apart from a horse, saddle, poncho and knife, and they also have distinctive garb, –which is still worn on country ranches, or during the *Uruguayan* equivalent of rodeos and other ceremonial occasions.

They wear *"bombachas"* (they are pleated pants, worn inside calf-high boots.) A sash and leather belt was worn around the waist, into the back of which was always tucked a knife used for eating, skinning, castrating and fighting, A gaucho wore a kerchief around his neck, and over his shoulder a thick poncho, which was used as a blanket at night or a shield during a knife-fight.

Gauchos did develop a sort of crude philosophy of life that exalted simplicity. –as one early British traveler put said: *"The use of a fork is avoided, because a knife and fork require a plate, which needs to be place on a table. This requirement creates another – a table involves the necessity of a chair, and thus the consequences of a fork involve a complete revolution in the household."*

Independence Park, (*Plaza de la Independencia*) mark the end of the colonial era from the republican one. The sprawling Government House (Palacio Estevez) which is now a historical landmark flanks it.

Moreover, to the northeast, the *Palace Salvo (Palacio Salvo)*, *Solis Theater (Teatro Solis)* which is *Montevideo's majestic Opera House, featuring some of the best acoustics in all Latin America.*

We enjoyed the architecture of *The Constitution Park, (Plaza Constitucion.)* which is a colonial square on which is the *Cathedral*, which is the seat of the Catholic hierarchy, and the *Cabildo,* which now contains an outstanding museum of the city's history.

Finally, want to announce the Climate of *Uruguay*, –which has an exceptional weather– with mild summers and winters; summers are from December to March, and this is the most pleasant time during the year.

(I usually observe the human seasons, this way)…
The <u>Human Spring</u> –The happy people,
The <u>Human Summer</u> –The all kind of active individuals,
The <u>Human Autumn</u> –Their longer years, and
The <u>Human Winter</u> – is the cool season, with snow and wrinkles.

Choose to want to keep healthy, –since we do not have much snow in Hawaii (with the exception of at very high altitude), Choose to admiring the rain from the window, observing the beauty of the palm trees, and enjoying the healthy grass covenant everywhere.

Choose walking long distances and drink water during summer, observing the falling of the leaves during autumn, smelling flowers in spring, keeping life in perpetual Easter.

Choose to feel very happy, especially when gaining new experiences and insights, challenging boundaries. Traveling is perfect catalyst for happiness, as it has allowed experiencing the natural, cultural, and fabricated wonders of the world.

On *February 6,* we arrived at the Port of *Punta de Este, Uruguay…* We enjoyed this gorgeous city and resort on the Atlantic Coast in the Maldonado Department of *South Easter Uruguay*! Although the city has a year round population of about 9,280, the summer tourist boom adds to this a very large number of non-residents. This is a marvelous colonial place with architecture contrasting with buildings that are more modern. Nowadays it has a scenic shore, typical resort houses, modern buildings, a port with mooring capacity, gorgeous department stores, restaurants and pubs; and it is also home to the only Conrad Hilton Hotel in South America, also famous for its casino. We were fascinated with the *Casapueblo,* which is the icon of *Punta Del Este, –*it is by all means, as a piece of Artwork by the *Uruguayan Painter* and *Sculptor Carlos Páez Vilaró.*

Want to share with the readers, part of the special history of *Punta Del Este, Uruguay… The Republic is the second smallest sovereign state in South America –* with a total area of 176,215 sq. Km. Almost triangular in shape, it takes up a verdant nook of the continent's southeast, between *Argentina* and *Brazil,* while its southern border runs alongside the *South Atlantic Ocean,* where it cuts into the east coast, to meet the *Rio de La Plata.*

The first European to explore the land that now comprises Uruguay, was a Spaniard named *Juan Diaz de Solis,* in 1516, who name the Punta Del Este Peninsula, Cabo de Santa Maria (Cape St Mary), before his men were killed by warriors from the resident Indian tribes. Later navigators from the Old World dismissed the Uruguayan coastline for settlement as it lacked the mineral wealth that had been found elsewhere, so the Christian missionaries, were not established there until a 1620.

In 1726, The Spanish built the fortified settlement of San Felipe de Montevideo to suppress the nearby Portuguese colony of

Sacramento, which was located to its east–facing *Buenos Aires* across the *Rio de la Plata*. After successfully conquered the *Colonia* the Spanish established *Montevideo's Natural Harbor* as their principal port along the South Atlantic, and began to exploit the fertile hinterland for cattle farming.

In 1825, *Uruguay* became a separate state, getting freedom from Brazilian annexation, and its constitution approved in July 1830... However, its own Great War, which broke out between the *Colorados* and the *Blancos* (the party for its second president – Uribe) marred the new nation's independence. The war ended in 1851 but enduring political loyalties continued to polarize the country, until the mid –1860s. To the end of the decade, *Uruguay* had to join forces with *Argentina* and *Brazil* against nearby *Paraguay* in the "War of the Triple Alliance".

Despite the political unrest throughout much of the later part of the 19th century, the countries' economy grew from sheep and cattle ranches established by incoming migrants – and wool quickly became Uruguay's leading export. Wide-scale reforms were made by the Colorado government of the early 20th century, and the successful exportation of wool and meat continued into the mid-1950. After more than a decade under a military government, civilian rule in *Uruguay* was restored in 1985.

Today the country enjoys a reputation as one of the most liberal in South America. –Everybody is fascinated with the golden fringe of beaches bathed by calm waters, looking out to Isla Gorriti — a marina bobbing with super yachts, and a city center jostling with high-end boutiques... admired all of these wonderful treasures. One of the visitors commented, "Punta Del Este has garnered a reputation of the "Pearl of Uruguay".

CHAPTER 8

Ushuaia subsist tailing the beagle, to breed with a white, tan, and black coat, and long sagging ears, often used for hunting. The atmosphere is rough and eccentric; its islands are sheltered with birds and all kind breezes... Its waters have carried all type of ships, sometimes with wrecks. –This odd place is really an inspiration!

Being in foreign lands, with continuous forces to step out of comfort zone – is a great confidence–builder. Travel is the best school since I have learned so much about the world and, most important, sharing love, appreciation, and happiness".

February 7th, 8th, and 9th in route to Ushuaia... On February 10th arrived at Ushuaia, Argentina.

During the two previous days of navigating, we joined the Art Director on a virtual trip around the world as we delve into our portfolio to discuss the inspiration and techniques of some of our cityscape artists. Brazilian born Henderson Cisz is the 2007 artist of the year in the UK and has been ascribed the moniker of the "master" of the modern cityscape". *Peter Rodgers* holds critical acclaim for his vibrant watercolors whist Hungarian *Csilla Orban* paints the cities of the world with emotion, rather than with an architects mind.

Already in the tender, we were anxious to visit the capital of *Tierra del Fuego, Argentina, Ushuaia,* located in the wide bay on the southern coast of Isla Grande of *Tierra del Fuego*, bonded on the north by the Martial mountain range, and on the south by the Beagle Channel.

Ushuaia is describing as the southernmost city in the world. While there are settlements farther south, the only one of notable size is Puerto Williams, (a Chilean settlement of some 2,000 residents).

As a center of population, commerce, and culture, and as a town of significant size and importance, Ushuaia clearly qualifies as a city. Tourist attractions include the *Tierra del Fuego National Park* and *Lapataia Bay.* We can observe the park from the highway, in route to the *highway,* or, via the *End of the World Train (Tren Del Fin Del Mundo*) from *Ushuaia.* It is the terminus of the Pan American Highway.

The city has a museum of *Yamane,* was an English, and Argentine settlement, including its years as a prison colony.

Wildlife attractions include local birds, penguins, seals, and orcas; many of these species are live on the colonized islands in the *Beagle Channel.*

Ushuaia, is located at the foot of the *Big Island, (Isla Grande de Tierra Del Fuego, Antarctica),* and, the islands of the South Atlantic. Its population is about 45,000, located on the north side of the *Eagle Channel,* facing the Chilean Islands of *Navarino and Hosta.* The most southerly city in the Argentine is almost 2,000 miles from the capital Buenos Aires, and even the northern tip of *Tierra del Fuego* is 515 miles from *Ushuaia.*

The Yámana or Yaganes, one of the Indian tribes in *Tierra del Fuego,* we believed to be the earliest inhabitants of the area around the *Beagle Channel.* It was their beach fires that prompted *Ferdinand Magellan* in 1520 to call the island *"Tierra del Fuego"* or *"Land of Fire"* –The *Yámanas* were primarily hunters and fishermen, used to travel everywhere by canoe, complete with a form of fireplace in the center and the woman of the family in charge of it.

They rarely stayed in one place for more than a few days. – Today, *the Yámanas* and the other Indian tribes who used to live in *Tierra del Fuego* are extinct, killed off by famine, diseases, and European settlers. European interest and settlement, at least in the south of *Tierra del Fuego,* began with the arrival of an Anglican mission led by *Reverend Sterling* in 1869. *Thomas Bridges,* his assistant, returned two years later to convert the *Yámanas* to Christianity. He liked this remote region so much, that he stayed and carved out a farm 60 miles to the southeast of *Ushuaia.* He named it *Harberton,* after his wife' birth place In England and this estancia is open to the public today.

Towards the end of the 19th century, Argentina decided to create a penal colony in its most remote region: Tierra del Fuego and specifically at *Ushuaia.* The convicts and their guards had a profound influence on Ushuaia, as they not only constructed the actual prison buildings, but also roads, houses and a railway. The notorious prison finally closed in 1947 on the orders of President

Juan Domingo Perón. –Now, they have industries, such as television assembly plants and electronic factories. After they started in 1970, the city grew rapidly.

Can you imagine? At the age of 87, after having health difficulties with high blood pressure above average, high levels of cholesterol, heart problems, and diabetes; – almost ready for the worst. Realized how healthy and happy I had been, forgetting the sadness of life! "–There was no time to be unhappy, or unhealthy, since I have been thinking about living!" –We can fix most everything in life, if we want to! Resist at every turn! –The time to Choose to be happy is now!

We were fortunate to meet wonderful people from all around the world, so at the end of this particular tour, to Tierra del Fuego, sitting all around the table, we raised our cameras to snap a few shots from across the table. Offered a slight knowing smile; my husband's Michael's stylishly decked out in his blue blazer jacket, a tie, and his movie star sunglasses, his face partly obscured by some flowers from the centerpiece - his smile stole the show!.

Feb.7th, 8th and 9th, in route to Ushuaia. This was the moment; Michael had been waiting to have friends from around the world, sharing moments of real happiness. "It is never too late to assert oneself"…said Michael, "Choose To Be Happy", watching our thoughts, feelings and actions, he guided them right.

At the end of each day, we analyzed, "How have we chosen to live this day? To be really living is to strive constantly to improve ourselves physically, mentally, morally, and spiritually". "I understand", I said…"if a person has not become stationary, but continues to change for the better, day after day, year after year, for sure as the Yogi's say, develops a personal magnetism and we draw to us what we need. Don't you agree?"… Finally, we were ready for our close-up, and immediately after, went to our cabin to sleep.

Walking in the hills in Brazil provides the framework for a friendship.

"I believe we may use every occasion that comes to our path as an opportunity to meet real friends".

After our discussion with the Program's Director, I started to prepare the "my course of miracles", with a variety of Platforms, about HAPPINESS.   Then, decided to call the first segment, "Discover How You Can Find Happiness".

*For a few weeks, observed the announcement on the "Daily Activity Program"... –The day came February 11th.   I was so delighted so many people were interested in the **Queen Mary INTEREST CORNER, Seminar about "Happiness"**, since the "Daily Activities Program", had also various and wonderful courses* *starting at 6am, and ending at 11 a.m. We scheduled The Program and scheduled as follow,*

First Seminar, on February 11th, 2016**, *"Discover how we can find Happiness".***   Second Seminar, on March 9th, 2016**, *"Having Alternatives, Making Choices, are the Basics of Human Emotional Health"*.   Third Seminar, on March 14th, *"If we want to be Happy, we have to Move forward. "*   Fourth Seminar, on April 15th, *"We possess the Inner Wisdom to Make Our Dreams Come True".*   *This was the Fifth, and final Seminar, on **April 23rd,"With Belief and Creativity We Live, and Keep Happiness".***

Today, February 11, Greeting a young couple, who came to the Seminar a little curious... –Welcomed, then after finding them seats to be comfortable, one of them commented, "Someone looks after us and we look at each other... remember that the power of happiness is always with all of us! Mentally affirm to yourself, "I am calm and I feel happy". –Suddenly, through another door, dozens and dozens more people were coming in, and in a few minutes, there were not any seats left at all! –As expected, and now confirmed, there were people from all around the world! *To formalize, the theme about Happiness, I started the session with this line! –"May there always be warmth in your home, fish in your net, and aloha in your heart. "* Observed all people were interested in the Seminar about Happiness.

Husband Michael formally introduced his wife, "This is your friend Nohemi, who was born in a country with so many misfortunes, and sadness, she raised her kids after significant challenges from childhood and young adult hood; she chose to be happy, to be like a rose, which even crushed, exudes its sweet fragrance!"

–"She learned to survive the hard way... – You can choose to be happy the best way! –You can be a human rose, spreading the essences of peace and happiness wherever you go. " – For a five

weekly seminars she will be with you." Then, I reminded everyone, **"Look at the sun... Look at the Sunrise, It is eternally there to brighten our life; enjoy it every day of your life! We can always find Happiness at any time, since Happiness is everywhere."** *Many, many people from all around the world attended the Seminar... –Observed the place at over capacity with standing room only and attendees sitting right on the floor.*

After analyzing the meaning of ***A Journey to Peace and Happiness,*** I mentioned statements from some psychologists. *"We can create health and happiness by choice; those choices are in how we think, how we act, and how we react to the things we cannot control. —by making decisions and choices we can learn to lead happier and healthy lives, — no matter what comes our way".*

Then, I reminded the crowd, "We should develop our talents and ambitions as full as we can, to achieve greater success. Just remember, "Being successful makes you proud! These are good feelings from a job well done!" –Then, you find-out that this accomplishment did not alone make you happy, since you may start getting oppression from your boss, or you are working in a wrong field! –Analyzing will make you very proud! And the key is in doing the work you get satisfaction from your analysis of what you accomplished...you get it internally peacefully from within yourself about your job well done...it's nice, but you do not need it externally!" –If you have peace and satisfaction, you get happiness.

"*Peace* is something like happiness; you cannot say "I will be happy when..." –Your happiness shouldn't depend on the situation you're, in the circumstances that surround you. At the same time, you cannot wait for everything around you to become peaceful, for you to say, "I am peaceful." –In both happiness and peace, there is heart, strength, determination. –Heart has the power to make things happen. You have to be at peace. You have to be happy, now."

Let us learn about Meditation, the Spiritual Dynamic about happiness… "Sometimes we must undergo hardships, breakups, and narcissistic wounds, which shatter the flattering image that we had of ourselves, in order to discover two truths: that *we are not who we thought we were; and that the loss of a cherished pleasure, is not necessarily the loss of true happiness and well-being.*"

What else do we need to be happy? All too often, we list the things we want: a bigger house, a striking car, and a trip around the world, a lot of money for retirement, a new friend or lover… –The list never ends… *Pushing for more is one of the things that make us great; but, it's never wise to make your happiness depend on it.*

Letting go is not easy, but you can do it. Moreover, once you let go of even just one toxic thing in your life, you will instantly get a boost toward greater happiness! However, this is not all! Let us wait and see in our next seminar, and learn more incentives to get happiness.

–Participants were very grateful for this seminar, also to Cunard for being very perceptive in recognizing their customer's needs, for providing this valuable service to all of them. All were very thankful for this innovative and successful program. I received a standing ovation after each seminar.

I was amazed to observe big smiles and it was challenging and enjoyable to receive and answer so many questions! –After shaking hands, with almost everyone they all smiled, with their promise to be back, for the next seminar chapter about Happiness. – Husband said, "I know for sure, at the end of your great seminars, people will remember to smile everyday like you, enjoying life."

–"No too bad, for an eighty-seven year old Great-Grand-Mother!"– said Michael… who has been very proud of his wife!

CHAPTER 10

The next port, is the Jewel of the Pacific, Punta Arenas, Chile

In life, it is not where you go; it is with whom you travel.

–Charles Schulz

On February 12*th* we enter Cape Horn –in a clockwise direction–, to the Netherlands; before setting a westerly course toward the Cockburn Channel to take us into the Magellan Straits in route to Punta Arenas, Chile... –Were informed that the city was often used as a base for Antarctica expeditions.–This is the capital city of *Chile*'s southernmost region, Magallanes and *Antarctica Chilean,* are located on the *Brunswick Peninsula north of the Strait of Magellan.*

Puta Arenas (Sandy Point) is the southernmost city on of the South American mainland, deeply imbued with history and located in *one of the oldest, most remote regions of what one chronicler called the "Uttermost Realm. " Its first golden age ended abruptly in 1914 when the Panama Canal opened and ships no longer needed to round Cape Horn. The situation grew worse as wool from New Zealand and Australia began to compete with its major products.*

The largest sheep company controlling 10,000 square kilometers in *Chile* and *Argentina* is based in *Punta Arenas*, where the owners lived. Punta Arenas, more or less languished until oil discovered nearby in 1940 and with the subsequent improvement in roads. It has recovered its previous status as an important commercial center as well as a popular destination for tourist interested in exploring the *"Uttermost Realm"*.

The city is the capital of Magellan's Province, named after Ferdinand Magellan, whose ship literally was blown through the strait that also bears his name by a series of gales in 1520. The first European to see these windswept shores, he was so relieved to reach the calmer water to the west of the strait that he gave it a name we still use –"The Pacific Ocean".

Climate adds to the region's rather baleful aspect; during the austral summer, the wind blows incessantly, occasionally reaching gale force (110mph). There are many summer days, but at some point during each, low grey clouds invariably travel in from the sea to bring on a chill. During the winter, snow covers most of the region and roads become virtually impassable.

This city has approximately 120,000 habitants. The Plaza, lined with trees and spring blooming gardens, is dominated by a bronze statue of Magellan perched precariously on a galleon canon; at his feet are a mermaid and a pair of reclining Indians. Rub the big toe of one of the Indians, for local legend holds that those who do so will on day return; it's conveniently located on the Plaza de Arms in the Town Hall. -We had the chance to visit the Salesian

Museum, with exhibits devoted principally to Indian life on the natural history of the region and Tierra del Fuego.

Next two days we passed Chiloe Archipelago off the coast of Chile; located in the Los Lagos Region; THIS IS THE FIFTH LARGEST ISLAND IN South America, the largest island being Tierra del Fuego, which we have already passed on our journey to Ushuaia, from Punta Del Este, separated from mainland South America by the Magellan Straits.

Then, we listened to the some navigation information from the bridge. "We are taking the northerly course, continuing to skirt the Chilean coastline, the ship and crew were affected by The Humboldt Current; this current, named after Prussian Naturalist Alexander von Humboldt, is a cold ocean current that flows north along the west coast of South America – extending from the southern tip of *Chile* to northern *Peru*. (Believe it, or not! People continued…) *"The Humboldt Current is one of the major upwelling systems of the world, supporting an extraordinary abundance of marine life, and also "the most productive marine ecosystem in the world!"*

February 13th, 14th at sea cruising by *Amalia Glacier*; which is a phenomenal place; we enjoyed observing, and taking wonderful pictures. *February 14th* at sea, cursing a very interesting *Pio XI Glacier*.

Then, on February 15th, we were at the sea in route to Valparaiso, Chile. Early in the evening at around 6.30 p.m., on February 17th we were at The Port of Valparaiso, Chile "The Jewel of the Pacific". This beautiful city declared a world heritage site based upon its improvised urban design and unique architecture. In 1996, the World Monuments Fund declared Valparaiso's unusual system of funicular lifts (steeply inclined elevators, one of the world's 100 most endangered historical treasures). In 1998, grassroots activists convinced the Chilean government and local authorities to apply for UNESCO world heritage status for Valparaiso; then declared a World Heritage Site in 2003. Built upon dozens of steep hillsides overlooking the Pacific Ocean, Valparaiso boasts a labyrinth of streets and cobblestone alleyway, embodying rich architectural and cultural legacy. Visited Santiago Highlights, next day *visited Valparaiso, Viña del Mar, and Villa Victoria & Heritage*, The city is very sophisticate, and its architecture very attractive.

–We found pretty much anything we wanted to see, on the streets of life, promising to live happily appreciating the beauty. Husband Michael commented, *"You, my Dear Wife Nohemi, grinned at every darling place... looking youthful, smiling from your heart, even to strangers; your courageous smile is contagious, since I notice other people keep smiling at you do."* – *"Yes, I have been feeling youthful, also, letting others pursue their way; once I found pleasure to be happy, I found peace of mind."*

Next day,–crossed *Chiloe Island,* –the largest island of the *Chiloe Archipelago–,* located in the *Los Lagos Region of Chile,* people commented that this enormous ship was following a northerly course, skirting the coast of *Chile* at a range of about 20 nautical miles. *"Just remember... this is the fifth largest island in South America,* and *the largest island on Tierra del Fuego,* which we passed its other side on the journey to *Ushuaia* from *Punta Del Este,* separated from mainland *South America* by the *Magellan Straits.*

Then, the master of the seas will follow a westerly great circle track away from the South American Coast, passing north of *Robinson Crusoe* Island in the afternoon. A Great Circle is a circle on the surface of the Earth, which lies in a plane passing through the Earth's center... It is the shortest distance between any two points on the surface of the Earth. It will appear as a curved line on a chart using the traditional Mercator projection that you will be familiar with; then, at sea, for three days, in route to *Easter Island.*

February 18th, 19th, 20th, 21th crossed by **Easter Island** *for* pictures. *From the 22nd to the 25^{th,} went in route to Papeete. –At sea, enjoyed a wonderful show production "Viva Italia", –with Comedian Delsarte' characters. Leonardo da Vinci's Mona Lisa, Living Sculptures, Shakespeare's famous lovers, Galileo, and a tribute to Paganini, culminating in a stunning masked ball finale – Viva Italia! It was a phenomenal show.*

Friends at the sea, informed us of the phenomenal shows, *Bruce* made his theater debut in the world premiere professional production of *"Joseph and the Amazing Technicolor Dream-coat"*. He brought the trilling music, characters, and magic of *Andrew Lloyd Webber to brilliant life, singing favorites from Phantom, Evita, Sunset Boulevard, Cats, Joseph, Whistle down the Wind* and *Aspects of Love.* –This was one of the best nights! *After this performance, happily, we went to sleep! In addition,* guitarist *Simon Davies* performs pieces from the Spanish Baroque to the edgy underbelly of Buenos Aires with some Bach and Gershwin along the way; happy to know Simon studied at the Royal College of Music and the Royal Academy of Music, before receiving his Honors Degree at the Royal Northern College of Music, Manchester. Performing with the Royal Shakespeare Company "Band", Simon has most recently appeared in the West End fun of "Romeo and Juliet" and the critically acclaimed "Venus & Adonis". –It was a very enjoyable evening!

February 26, we arrived to *Papeete, French Polynesia.* – learned that *Papeete,* –meaning "Water from a basket", is the capital of *French Polynesia,* an overseas country of *France in the Pacific Ocean.* The municipality is located on the Island of *Tahiti,* in the administrative subdivision of the *Windward Islands.*

At the vibrant capital of *Tahiti, Papeete* is the perfect gateway to a paradise of lush tropical valleys, idyllic sparking waterfalls, golden sandy beaches, and azure waters.

"At the outbreak of World War I *Papeete* was shelled by German vessels, causing loss of life and major damage. The growth of the city was boosted by the decision to move the nuclear weapon test range from *Algeria* to the atolls of *Murrow* and *Fangataufa*, some 1,500 km to the east of *Tahiti.* "

We took a complete tour to *Tahiti Nui*, -the larger of the two islands, by car. Red and white kilometer stones, called PK give the distance in each direction from *Papeete* Cathedral to *Taravao*. Then, took a ferry to the Island to *Moorea*, which leaves from the harbor, informing the conductor, that we had to leave a certain time, otherwise we could miss the sailing. Moreover, hurrying up we observed the *Botanical Gardens* and *Gaugin Museum*.

On February 27th, we anchor in the Port of *Mo'orea*, French Polynesia, one of the *Windward Islands*, 17 kilometers Northwest of *Tahiti*. Its real name is *Mo'ore'a* meaning "*yellow lizard*" in *Tahitian*. This island had a volcano 1.5 to 2.5 million years ago. "This a romantic wedding place." There are two small, symmetrical bays on the north shore. Due to its great scenery, *Pape'ete and Morea*, had visitors from western tourists, who travel to *French Polynesia*; is also a especially popular as a honeymoon' destination.

From there, we were excited to visit the "mysterious wonders of *China* and *Beijing!* Wait, and read!

When we come together lovingly and joyfully, we naturally feel an increase of energetic love.

CHAPTER 11

Let us admire The Supreme Sights of China: Shanghai Terracotta Warriors, Grand Wall of China, and the City of Beijing.

Isn't it marvellous to follow Marco Polo's steps, during his 24 years journey? He was one of the first and most famous Europeans to travel to Asia during the middle Ages…. He journeyed farther than any of his predecessors along the Silk Road, reaching China and Mongolia, where he became a confidant of Kublai Khan. Isn't this amazing?" Marco Polo's adventures influenced mapmakers, and inspired Christopher Columbus… Can't you imagine? He inspired me, also, as a writer, to follow his steps.

I want to share with my readers, some curious comments I read in a little book, when traveling to China… "How being independent can keep you from breaking up. Members of your family sometimes do not leave you in peace! You will not have a private life if they do not like your partner, they may even try to break up your marriage! –

Gee whiz! If I had read this article many, many years ago, I could have had a peaceful marriage life! However, because I continued communicating with the naysayers it gave them the right to interfere with my happy life; almost making our marriage a miserable broken toy!

When I came back home, I realized If we could use this "advice" at least from now on, we could save a lot of pain and sorrow, and could have avoided also a lot of sadness.

It is natural to want to share as much with members of the family; however if you share everything, what do we learn? Private life is private life! Part of being independent is to keep your marriage life for yourself! It is time to take a long hard healthy look at your relationship to keep it a happy marriage.

If you feel free not to explain everything important or inform family members every move you did in your private marriage, it is consider, not to be independent.

What did we learn? Marriage should be an ongoing process, and it is simply not possible to do that, if all members of your family interfere with your private life; you do not keep the loyalty of both parties…

"Always remember…You are the marriage, and marriage is an ongoing process. It is important for both of you to have your private life! It is time to take a long hard look at your relationship, and think why you are in it. You should feel free not to explain everything to other members of your family or friends. Cataloging every move each couple makes, and regurgitating it borders on stalking and certainly, is not conducive to a sense of independence from your family…"

Now, it is not too late! "Better late, than never." THANKS DEAR WRITER! From that moment, on, "keep in your back pocket that Independence can keep you from braking up"!

March 1st, 2nd, in route to **Auckland, New Zealand**, arrived on March 3rd. This afternoon Michael and I sat in the deck chairs on the rear balcony of this great ship, holding hands, observing the waves leaving a path on the ocean… remembering the far away days, when I was raising my kids, without a father… tired, exhausted! – Realizing that it is worthy to have faith and enjoy these wonderful moments, resting and caring for each other during all these twenty-five years, with kindness! –Thank life also for this great gift of being a mother, remembering all family with deep love, even when they are interested in other kind of responsibilities…Thought about this poem from Paul M. Kramer, read a few days ago…

SETBACKS
Temporary disappointments, non-intended hold-ups
Goal inhibitors, snags, obstructions
Unexpected barriers, obstacles
Missed attempts at success

Setbacks are temporary obstacles,
Bumps in the road that slow down progress
They are the curves in life.
They are also stepping-stones to learning.

Failed attempts begets wisdom
Setbacks enhance the appreciation of success
Overcoming adversity is priceless
Don't be less than you are capable of being".

This way you take* A Journey to Peace and Happiness!**

–Let's first, again analyze what peace mean. Pacific means "peaceful", coming from the Latin word peace. We know the Pacific Ocean got its name from the Portuguese explorer Ferdinand Magellan in 1521 who called its waters "*Mar Pacífico*", which means "peaceful sea–. He said that profound statement after his very rough sail coming around the Cape! In fact, he was very happy to make it!

That day, we got up early in the morning to walk outside on the Promenade Deck, which is a boardwalk … The breeze was caressing our faces; by increasing the speed, we felt enchanted and more at easy to stroll… From time to time, we observed pictures of fantasy presented by the rhythm of the weaves, undulating as listening to music of the rain. After this was almost a daily exercise, and felling energetic we took a nice shower. Got dressed, and immediately, went to the fancy restaurant… Once in the middle of a creative drought, we sat in a gorgeous dining room, confessing each other a softly romantic conversation, as we admired the great personal feeling of rediscovery our eternal love.

–In the past, I never had the ability to dream... –Since raising my kids, I did not have time to fantasize, visualize, or even make a wish. Was therefore probably absent of dreams, and that was an emotional equivalent of chemical imbalance of the soul.

–Our table, decorated with tropical colorful flowers, with white linen and dishes started our dinner, with a great smile to continue recreating our authentic life. Had a great smile, to appreciate the diligence of the chefs presenting us every day with a variety of fruits, some fish, or chicken, or beef for husband, and, chicken or fish for me; prepared in so many skilled ways…, then a sugar free dessert, and decaf cappuccino or decaf tea.

On our way to a concert at the great theater, before the show started, began bringing a thought drought, then, I thought again, whenever there is a dry period, there is plenty of Light. –We are just blinded by dark, dust, and storms. –Sometimes In the past had many dry and dark periods, derailment of too many glimpses of dreams; then, I thought... "Arid despair often result from nurturance deprivation; not eating well, not sleeping enough, working too hard and too long without anything to look forward to." –I have to keep take breaks and smelling the roses!"

–Was thinking, after years of almost being killed off with so many responsibilities, I stopped trying so hard! –The creative manifestation of Determination occurred! The hardest things to learn were to stop, calling it an occasional halt. –Now, when I visualize the feelings coming back, I am prepared for a quantum leap into authenticity. –Into the natural world, droughts depart as suddenly and as mysteriously, as they had arrived. –Hope.

For three days, we decided to visit, *Sihanoukville*, to discover the incredible sights of *Cambodia* with a visit to the *UNESCO World Heritage site of Angkor Wat*. –This incredible Villa-Jewels of Indochina Overland visited for three days and two nights; venturing up to the Buddhist Temple of *Wat Leu*, perched high into a hill. This intricately decorated temple offers wonderful views over the city below. Next day after breakfast, headed for the enchanting *Banteay Srei Temple*, known as the *Citadel of Women*. –This petite temple possesses wonderful, intricate carvings. We had the chance to visit also *Prah Dak* to witness the lives of Cambodian country people; visited the *Bayon Temple*, the *Terrace of the Leper King, Terrace of the 12 elephants*, and the *Baphuon* at the *Royal Palace*.

We flew to **Shanghai**, took a guided walking tour exploring the narrow alleys and cobblestone lanes of the Old Town, over the famous zigzag bridge by the pavilion teahouse. We also, visited *Yu*

Garden, a classic *Ming Dynasty garden* and home with old pavilions. Among the many skyscrapers in *Pudding,* we viewed the *World Financial Center.* –Stepped aboard the magnetic *Maglev Train*, to reach *Pudding Airport*, and took a flight to *Xian.* –After a buffet breakfast in the hotel, our tour began with a leisurely walk on part of the *Xian City Wall.* –The highlight of the day, was to visit the world famous *Terracotta Warrior Museum with*

The supreme Sights of China, Seven Thousand Life-Size, Terracotta *Warriors,* and horses, acclaimed as the *"Eighth Wonder of the World".* *–The detail and scale of these incredible sculptures is sight to behold. After, we took a flight to Beijing,* where we had dinner, and went to sleep. *After breakfast we ventured to one of humankind's mightiest creation, the Great Wall of China, built in third century BC to protect China's northern border from marauding nomads and barbarians.* Visited *The Badaling section of the Wall, The Temple of Heaven, the largest worshipping architecture in the world!* –Observed the intricate joinery and dovetailing used to create the architectural details without the use of steel, cement or a single nail. *Had the chance to admire the largest square in the world, "Tiananmen Square"* which covers 34 acres. –This historic site, surrounded by The *Great Hall of the People, is the Mao Zedong Memorial Hall, also the National Museum.* Visited *the Forbidden City,* -once the Imperial Palace from the Qing Dynasty.

–Then, overexcited, to visit this greatest sights, went back to our own transportation, The Cruise Ship around the world.

CHAPTER 12

Having Alternatives and Making Choices are Basics of Human Emotional Health

"In this world one is seldom reduced to make a selection between two alternatives. There are as many varieties of conduct and opinion as there are turns of feature between an aquiline nose and a flat one."

— Johann Wolfgang von Goethe,

*On March 10th in routes to Sydney, Australia... at 11 AM. I, Nohemí had my second INTEREST CORNER, Seminar Program about Happiness, "**Having Alternatives, Making Choices**", -The Basics of Human Emotional Health."*

–This time, when we reached the door's office, – fifteen minutes in advance–, we were surprised and observed a very long line of people waiting at the entry doors, to get their seats! In a few minutes, the place was full, and when we started the program, many people were sitting on the floor! When we started the program, everyone applauded. Very interested, each brought paper to make notes.

Got the list of attendees, calling each one by their first name and Socratic I started asking questions… "Please, Sarah, why are you attending this seminar? The answer was, "Because, since I remember, I had been very sad and unhappy with the circumstances of my life". –Then, requested her to be more specific. She started her story of her life with tears rolling down her chicks, she explained about her childhood, and the time growing up.

Remembered the similar circumstances of growing up, and asked her, "Do you think anybody under the same circumstances had similar sadness?" –Lets inform you a little bit about life… Starting with the assassination of my Dear Father, as a little girl… with some very sad issues! Later, had to raise three children without a father… -"Of course, I was very sad! Even though, I had to start directing our lives. –Yes… made some mistakes… It wasn't easy!"

Starting with the analysis about Alternatives and *Making Choices* or *Decision-Making* comes with multiple options …

The process of making ethical decisions requires:

Commitment: The desire to do the right thing regardless of the cost,

Consciousness: The awareness to act consistently and apply moral convictions to daily behavior,

Competency: The ability to collect and evaluate information, develops alternatives, and foresees potential consequences and risks,

Good decisions are both ethical and effective:

–Ethical decisions generate and sustain trust; demonstrate respect, responsibility, fairness, and caring; and are consistent with good citizenship. These behaviors provide a foundation for making better decisions by setting the ground rules for our behavior.

–Effective decisions are *effective* if they accomplish what we want to accomplish and if they advance our purposes. A choice that produces unintended and undesirable results is ineffective.

Relayed, that the key to make effective decisions, is to think about *choices* in terms of *ability to accomplish our most important goals. This means we have to understand the difference between immediate and short-term goals and longer-range goals.*

After a few comments, I realized everybody understood the meaning of the subject, and many attendees volunteered to give their personal views; then, each sincerely confessed to the big group of attendees, about some episodes of a personal life…

How we make decisions in the worse circumstances, like being abandoned by father of the kids? –Make a choice, to be assertive, believing in yourself!

Yes, recognize the mistakes! Due to inexperience, being a mother at a young age in unusual circumstances! With faith, and persistence found a job; got a baby-sitter; then needed to find funds to pay her salary. *Happily Aunt Angie,* living near-by provided with a small loan… Had to work many hours a day, nights, and week-ends, not having enough time to take care of the darling kids... Sadly had to leave the very small children long hours with the baby-sitter, or with dear Aunt, instead of being with them twenty-four hours a day, as other privileged mothers do!

I started not fearing failure. *Powerful Lessons I Learned, from mistakes… –We have all heard, "To err is human, you live, and you learn. We make mistakes every day, large and small, failures. However, failure and mistakes still do not feel like an awesome learning opportunity. Know there were the limitations that make us unique and that we should embrace the stumbles and screw ups.*

We live and act in ways to prevent mistakes –not taking risks, enlarging our comfort zones or jumping outside the boxes we hide in. –Just remember… –Our mistakes and failures are gifts, jewels, guideposts in our learning and growth as people. So accept failures, mistakes, screw-ups and shortcomings, because they not only make us uniquely who we are, but also teach us powerful lessons like these below.

Mistakes teach us to clarify what we really want, and how we want to live happily. The word mistake derives meaning only by comparison to what we desire, what we see as success. Noticing and admitting our mistakes helps us to get in touch with our commitments–what we really want to be, doing, and have. Mistakes wake us up and focus our attention like a flashing sign that says "fix this". The urgency created causes us to focus on issues or problems that make us feel off track. *Working on possible solutions, redefining what we want or expect,* or *re-examining our values or goals can lead us to more clarity about our path.*

Mistakes teach us to accept ourselves and that we can be flawed and be loved. *–Husband still loves me, when I comment about the mistakes I made… We can fully appreciate ourselves, even while acknowledging our screw ups. It is possible to laugh at our mistakes and then work hard to correct them. Most of us have a long history* *of putting ourselves down when we blow it. But it's a self-defeating habit we must break, so that we can start appreciating ourselves, with mistakes and all. People who really love and care about us will stick with us with all our flaws and floundering. Our not so perfectness is what makes us unique and we are loved for it. So we should give ourselves a break.*

Mistakes teach us to admit imperfections and face our fears. *Sometimes even our best efforts just don't work out. We might do everything possible to achieve a certain result and still fail, again and again. When this happens we can admit that we're stuck. Facing mistakes often takes us straight to the heart of our fears. And when we experience and face those fears, they can disappear. When we are stuck and admit that we can't do it alone it sends a signal and opens the door for help to show up. People, resources, and solutions will appear, especially when we ask for help.*

Mistakes teach us about ourselves and how to tell our truth. *It is natural to want to cover up our mistakes or be embarrassed by them.* To feel like we wish we had a handy mistake eraser or remover. But *being honest about your failures and limitations offers us opportunities to practice telling the truth. Admitting the truth allows us to enlarge our knowledge of self-to know who we are.* And therefore, *increases our capacity to change.* It is like holding up a mirror to us and really seeing our self. *When we tell others about our mistakes, to let them really see us, it allows us to let go of the embarrassment, shame and blame we may feel, so that we can concentrate on learning and growing.*

Mistakes instruct us, through analysis and feedback, about what works, *and what doesn't. It's a reality check. When we experience the consequences of mistakes, we get a clear message about which of our efforts are working–and which are not. The feedback we get from our mistakes can be the most specific, pointed, and powerful feedback we'll ever get. Many times we can trace mistakes to* *recurring patterns of belief or behaviour–things we do, say, and think over and over again. When we spot and change a habit we may find that other areas of our lives change for the better. One way to gain maximum benefit from mistakes is to examine them through the filter of powerful questions: "How can I use this experience?"; "What will I do differently next time?"; "How will I be different in the future?" Questions like these lead to an inquiry that invites solutions.*

Mistakes impart us responsibility. *Sometimes our instinctive reaction to a mistake is to shift blame elsewhere: "It's not my fault." "You never told me about that," Or the classic "I don't see how this has anything to do with me." –It is more empowering to look for our role in the mistake. Taking responsibility for a failure may not be fun. But the act of doing so, points out what we can do differently next time. Exploring our role reminds us our choices and actions have a huge influence on the quality of our lives. Be fair with others, remember what Jesus said to the multitude condemning Mary Magdalene "Who is free of guilt, throw the first stone."*

Mistakes teach us about integrity. *Mistakes often happen when we break promises, over-commit, agree to avoid conflict or fail to listen fully. Big mistakes often start as small errors. Over time, tiny choices that run counter to our values or goals can accumulate into breakdowns. Even our smallest choices have power, so it is important we pay attention to the integrity of the choices we make every day. Mistakes can be a signal that our words and our actions are out of alignment. In that case, we can re-examine our intentions, reconsider our commitments, and adjust our actions.*

Mistakes educate us to engage in our lives –to live fully. *We are not our behaviour and we are more than our mistakes. We can remember our history does not have to predict our future. And then remember that we have an opportunity to go all in—to participate fully. Many people, when faced with a big mistake, begin to pull* *back–to retreat. Instead, we can use the failure as evidence that we are growing, risking, and stretching to meet our potential. Mistakes help us to remember that we are not content to play it safe. That we understand that without risk there is sometimes no reward.*

Mistakes allow us to inspire others to be courageous*. They may be inspired when we are brave and make our private struggles public. They might decide to live differently. When a lifelong smoker who's dying of emphysema talks about the value of being smoke-free, we're apt to listen. The same kind of contribution also occurs when we speak candidly about less serious mistakes. As parents we can teach our children it is OK to fail because we are willing to let them see our failures and mistakes. This gives us opportunities to talk about what we could or would do, differently. These are great lessons for all of us.* ***We had to learn the lessons!***

I made the decision to bring my kids to the United States, as legal residents; and, with determination got education, secured their future; they got married, and raised their children, and grandchildren with principles... –As adults– not even one succeeds, but the ones who do give exceptional opportunities to other generations to get to the top in life!

We know that throughout life we have possibilities to learn and correct our mistakes... Think that through life, we had been experimenting to the maximum, and we still have curiosity. Death will end the postponements, but before that, we still want to continue being productive, giving seminars, and writing positive books, leaving a legacy to other generations to never spend. Each day we learn the importance is to arrive at old age, very happy, since this action makes an example by our living by helping others and our society.

In the winter of life, at 87 years old, it still feels like spring, I keep my confidence... admire nature, still feel optimistic without letting my mind be destroyed by human indifference that's why I know that I have matured completely. *"I always believe that the old, is the future of the young. Therefore as young person grew without hate, reaching the senility with love. –We do not have to live with anguish, without knowing to live. The stress is the trigger to shot weapon. That shot the arm"* –Words of Gonzalo Canal Ramirez- Colombian Writer.

Following this advice... life will be happy again!

–Did not have to say anything else, and at the end of this second seminar, invited them for the next session. The participants were very happy, had the opportunity to make positive comments, and before they left the crowded place, each promised eagerly to come back to the next one.

–Want to comment about our life... "Living in *Hawaii* with my husband *Michael*, we walk in the woods on a summer's eve, or early in the mornings. At one of our favorite spots, we sometimes take a break from the walking to sit down and absorb the ambience... the birds, – especially the "cardinals" when the sunrise we observe between the trees after going up of the mountains. Summer days in Hawaii are forever, since it rains a lot; almost in all seasons. Across several fields and homes to the right, the sun's brilliance start fire to the mullioned huge trees, and the profuse flowers all around the trees, distract the steps, and my husband reminds me that I have to hold his arm…

Moving forward is the right thing to do; we maintain our balance, poise, and sense of serenity, only as we are moving forward with faith.

CHAPTER 13

Discover the history and secrets of the world, visiting areas of limits to venture, and about rare vantage points in Australia.

"Twenty years from now you will be more disappointed by the things you didn't do than by the ones you did do. So throw off the bowlines, sail away from the safe harbor. Catch the trade winds in your sails. Explore. Dream, and Discover."

– Mark Twain

March 10th, at night, arrived at **Sydney***...* In the afternoon, attended some shows, and visiting the picturesque harbor. Passed sandy bays, attractive harbor, side suburbs, and unspoiled bushland; small islands and construct of all kinds – from tiny sailing boats to colorful harbor ferries – in the water. Observed a magnificent sight that will long live in our memory!

Sydney is the most populous city In *Australia,* with a metropolitan area with approximately 4.28 million. It is the state capital of New South Wales and was the site of the first British colony in Australia, making it both the oldest and largest of Australia's cities.

In 1932 *Francis De Groot*, a retired cavalry officer, managed to be selected as part of the honor guard at the opening of the *Sydney Harbor Bridge*. The ribbon with his sword, declared the bridge open in the name of "the decent citizens of *New South Wales*". They tied the ribbon back together, and the ceremony continued. *De Groot* was carried off to a mental hospital, declared insane, and later fined for the replacement cost of one ribbon.

Sir John Robertson, five times premier of New South Wales, drank a pint of rum every morning for 35 years. He said later, "None of the men who have let footprints in this country, have been cold water men."

Prime Minister Harold Holt went for a swim at *Cheviot Beach,* near Portsea on 17th of December 1967, and was never seen again. In the newspaper the event was titled, *"The swim that needed no towel"*.

Had the privilege to visit *the Royal Botanic Gardens, in Sydney, near by the Opera House.* –This is the most wonderful Park, with miles and miles of all kind of treasures! –Where anyone can walk on the grass smell the flowers, hug the trees and picnic on the on the lawns!

Want to give some data to help my readers, to become acquainted, if you want to visit this great Sydney… –"At 33, 55' south – *Sydney has similar latitude to Cape Town, Buenos Aires, Los Angeles, Casablanca, and Beirut.* If you want to come by air, Sydney is 17,174 km from London, 16.025km from New York, and 7,821 km from Tokyo… *December to February is summer, March to May is autumn, June to August is winter,* and *spring* is from *September to November.* The summer temperature is 22, while winter temperatures average out at 13 centigrade. Sydney boasts an annual average of 342 days of sunshine, the average rainfall is 1200 mm per year, and the *wettest months* are from *April to June"*.

Visited a Garden Shop, railway station, where anybody can travel around on the train; and visit or see… restaurants, parking station, metered parking, drinking fountains, and the Government House. Then, stop at the Vista Pavilion, Greenway Terrace, Herb Garden, and Rose Gardens. Then, the Rathbone Lodge Conservatorium, Old Mill Garden, Rose, and the Pioneer Garden. Walked through the Tropical Centre, The Maiden Theatre, Palm Grove Centre, Palace Gardens, The Codi Jam Ora, First Encounter Garden, and the Succulent Garden… –In other words, we spent all day, walking around, for miles and miles, throughout the wonderful Sydney Harbor in the back grown. –We had been there a few years ago! – And all the time we were fascinated with this Masterpiece in the world! We visited also, a beautiful panoramic place in the High Hills, traveling in a funicular… What a beautiful view!

From the *Royal Botanic Gardens*, we observed the famous *Opera House*, the big bridge, and the fantastic bay, surrounded by spectacular big trees full of flowers! –We got into *Port Jackson* early in the afternoon, and had the satisfaction of finding the finest Harbor in the world, and the amazing *"The Queen Victoria Building"*…

–To tell you the truth, there is no better way to approach S*ydney* than by the sea! The city's magnificent centerpiece – officially *Port Jackson*, but better known as *Sydney Harbor* – offering beaches and quiet bays, beautiful bushland, historic sites, attractive suburbs and breathtaking views.

The *Sydney Opera House* is a multi-venue performing arts center, identified as one of the 20th century's most distinctive building and became a UNESCO *World Heritage* Site on June 28 2007. Designed by *Danish architect Jorn Utzon*, the building formally opened on October 20th, 1973, after a gestation beginning with *Utzon*'s 1957 selection as winner of and worldwide design contest and the government of New South Wales authorized work to begin in 1958 with *Utzon* directing construction. The building and its surrounds occupy the whole of *Bennelong Point* in *Sydney Harbor*, between *Sydney Cove* and *Farm Cove*, adjacent to the Sydney central business district and the Royal Botanic Gardens. We observed The Opera House from different locations and angles; at night, its silhouette reflects on the Ocean.

However, its name suggests a single venue. The building comprises multiple performance venues, which together are among the busiest in a performing arts center –It hosts well over 1,500 performances annually, attended by more than 1.2 million people. We took a guided tour of the Sydney Opera House, and then, we attended the concert. We were fascinated like never before!

In our previous trips, had the honor to applaud The Sydney Symphony Orchestra members, with Chief Conductor David Robertson, and enjoyed the fantastic programs with conductor *Thomas Sondergard*, performing *Tchaikovsky 5*, *Wilhelm Stenhammar, Excelsior Concert Overture*, *Op.13 13*, *Sergel Prokofiev* Violin Concerto No.2 in G minor, Op.63. In addition, had the great opportunity to meet *Bryan Benston*, Emirates 'Vice President Australasia. This is an amazing entertainment for the whole family… You have to join family groups singing, dancing and grooving their way around the world finding lost toys… then enjoyed a delicious meal, right on the edge of the world. A most beautiful harbor-quite simply… and, to tell you the truth, "It' was the ultimate Sydney experience!"

"If we are senior citizens, *Australia* treats us with *tender loving care*… The designated buses routes to travel around are free!

Remember Dale Carnegie's words, "When couples come together lovingly and joyfully, they naturally feel an increase of energy resulting from their union, love, and joy".

CHAPTER 14

Brisbane is the capital and most overcrowded city in the Australian State of Queensland, and the third most populous city in Australia. -We felt enthusiastically and felt fervently.

"We live in a wonderful world that is full of beauty, charm and adventure. There is no end to the adventures we can have if only we seek them with our eyes open."

— Jawaharial Nehru

March 13th arrived to **Brisbane**, the most populous city in the **Australian** state of Queensland. It is a pleasure to continue writing about this fascinating mix of parks, monuments, and treasured 19th century buildings. The Brisbane River runs right through the heart of the city and offers a tranquil way to view the sights. For a different perspective, we visited the Mount Coot-Coot-

that lookout, which presents a panoramic view of the city and its surroundings.

The name of Brisbane came from the *Scotsman Sr. Thomas Brisbane,* the *Governor of New South Wales* from 1821 to 1825. The central business district covers 2.2 square kilometers and is walkable.   Central streets are named after members of the royal family. Queen Street (name after Queen Victoria), is the name given to the main streets and home to Queen Street Mail.   This streets running parallel to Queen Street are named after female members *Alice, Ann, Elizabeth,* and *Mary,* with perpendicular streets named after male members, *Albert, George* and *William*; unlike other Australian capital cities, a large portion of the greater metropolitan area of Brisbane is controlled by a single local government entity. This city is the largest local government body (in terms of population and budget.

In *Australia, Brisbane* has the largest economy of any city between Sydney and Singapore.   -These have been considering economic growth in recent years because of the resources boom and has consistent economic growth in recent years because of the resources boom.

The port of *Brisbane* is the third most important in *Australia* for value of goods. Most of the port facilities are less than three decades old, and some built on *reclaimed mangroves and wetlands.* It is also, a city on the move, where things are always happening. Positioned in the middle of Australia east coast, it is already the third largest city in the country and is well on the way to become *Australia's second largest capital city within the next 10 years.* With a warm subtropical climate year round, *Brisbane* is a dynamic youthful city that greets visitors with a warm and friendly welcome.

Downtown is compact and easily accessible on foot. Taking in the vibrant city, *South Bank* and *Valley* precincts, downtown offers a unique 'out of the box' mix of recreation, retail, dining and leisure experiences all with a few walkable kilometers. *The central shopping on the Queen Street Mall, boats over 650 stores along the stretch of less than one kilometer.* South Bank is always crating new experiences and is the hub of Queensland culture, including the state's art gallery, museum, and performing arts center. The Valley offers diversity ranging from Chinatown to innovative fashion boutiques to bohemian culture and thriving nightlife. Noticed that fresco cafes, and restaurants, are alive day and night in Downtown *Brisbane* at *South Bank, Riverside, Eagle Street,* and *Queen Street,* to name just a few.

Waterways are the lifeblood on the city and *Brisbane,* built around the winding Brisbane River. Dedicated walking and bicycle paths are on both banks of the river making it easy to take in the views. The fast catamaran ferries known as City-Cats are *Brisbane* icons and an essential experience for every visitor and local alike. Testament to the outdoors way of like that *Brisbane* is famed for, it's the only city in Australia with a beach right in the heart of the Downtown area at South Bay, which is a blue water playground for dolphins turtles, and from June to October, the majestic humpback wales.

Located in the heart of Southern Queensland, Australia's best beaches, the Gold and Sunshine Coast are on *Brisbane*'s doorstep. So are the subtropical sand islands of *Moreton Bay,* lush rainforests, mountain hinterland, country attractions, adventure experiences, excellent theme parks and some of the best shopping, dining and entertainment in the country. Adding to the individual style of the city is the unique Queensland architecture, with timber walls, lattice screen, shutters, and corrugated iron roofs.

I was impressed with the engineering marvel, the new purpose built pedestrian and cycle bridge with its imposing arch, straddles the *Brisbane River* to join the city *Botanic Gardens*, and *Queensland University of Technology* to *South Bank* near the *Maritime Museum*; credited with being the world's largest pedestrian bridge at 450 meters. The ridge is name after the successful sporting spectacle hosted by *Brisbane* in 2001, the Goodwill Games. People are very impressed by the *Sir Thomas Brisbane Planetarium*, which operates afternoons and evenings, Wednesday-Sundays.

At the bottom, observed is on *George Street* the *Renaissance style Parliament House*. Next door, in the grounds of the *Queensland University of Technology*, we found the very grand *Old Government House*, home of the National Trust of Queensland.

City trains provide regular air-conditioned services in commuter cars around the city and to outlying suburbs. -The network includes stops at many major attractions, such as *South Band,* and to *Brisbane'* domestic and international airports. –I was shocked to this splendor!

§

March 16th, at sea in route to *Yorkeys Knob*, Australia, **and the great day to present our INTEREST CORNER *Seminar Program 3*, Theme, "*If we want to be happy, Move Forward.*"**

The morning was so bright! At the arrival of the great place, the crowd again showed an extraordinary eagerness to participate with our program… As in previous seminars, husband Michael introduced me to everyone all of whom were eager to start. Was excited to meet the group again, which by then I consider to be in my network as well as friends…

–"Before I start this subject, I want to remind all of you, *if we admire ambiguity, we misplace illusion as well… Let us arrive at clarity, since clarity creates a change. – "Let's keep in mind the words of William Baziotes, "Each painting has its own way of evolving… When the painting is finished, the subject reveals itself."*

–During life, had noticed, that many of us tend to neglect or abandon the issues, whenever an unpleasant piece of clarity is about to emerge. –Please, no matter how angry or disappointed we are, admit it.
"Extreme emotions of any kind are the usual prompts for avoiding the issues themselves.

–After strong failure, we don't know what to do, saying I felt Overacted … I am Jammed! Other times, we fight with this kind of feeling… If we are struggling, it is time to go beyond. There are many things we can do, to change these feelings.

–We have the power to move forward no matter what difficulties obstruct your path. We have the power to live up to extending your own way from bottom to top. We have the power to be wise, and make significant improvement on our important goals, opening to see it is possible. We have this power to make CHOICES. In each moment you can choose what you think, what you do, and who you want to be.

–If we had being pulled in different directions beyond our control, we have to take time to restore what we value the most in life.

–If we admire ambiguity, we misplace illusion as well. If we arrive at clarity … clarity creates change.

–Start building happiness as a daily priority… let go of self-limiting behaviour. –In other words, make life simple again.

–We don't have to insist doing things the same, all the time, like we had been doing before… We don't have to be detained as a prisoner by our old usual ways or expectations; we have to decide to move forward, if we want to accomplish wonderful goals.

–Do you want to be always a student! You have to keep moving forward to reach being a master.

–Let's keep in mind all these wonderful incentives; remember, keeping moving forward we reach the high peaks, no matter how difficult will be, when we achieve the highest of the mountain, we fee absolutely great!

–Just remember Buddha's words,

"What you need to do won't be easy, but it will be worth it in the end. –If you've been asking the same questions for a long time, yet you're still stuck, it's probably not that you haven't been given the answers, but that you don't like the answers you were given. Remember, it takes a great deal of courage to admit that something needs to change, and a lot more courage still, to accept the responsibility for making the change happen. Growth and change may be painful sometimes, but nothing in life is as painful as staying stuck where you don't belong.

– Keep in mind, dear friends, Today is a new day, filled with new opportunities.

–Before the end of this encouraging seminar, *made a positive remark, Time has a key for each door that closes… Has a solution, for each problem… Has the light, for each somber… Has a relief, for each pain… and, has the plan for each tomorrow.*

Of course, I was very happy to observe that everybody left very joyful with the promise to come back to the next seminar on April 15.

Whatever we think, we can do, or believe we can do, go and Start it! Action has Magic, Grace, and Power in it.

—It took six days at sea, and on March 16th, we arrived to *Yorkeys Knob, Australia. Think to give you some details about this place, Knob, Australia. This is one of the beach-suburbs of Cairns,* the regional capital of *Far North Queensland.* "This suburb got its name from *George Yorkeys Lawson,* a Yorkshire-born."

He built a homestead adjoining the Mount Buchan estate near what is now *Yorkey Knob.* During the off-fishing season, he and his boys farmed pumpkins, sweet potatoes and paddy melons, but not very successfully, whatever the bandicoots and pigs did not eat, the crocodiles devoured. He used the mangroves near his homestead to obtain the firewood and water needed for his *beche-de-mer's* smoking station on Green Island. (The *"knob'* is a term for *"small hill'). Overexcited, and happy to visit this great sight, we went back to our own transportation, The Cruise Ship going around the world!*

Locals attached to the name, despite the reaction it sometimes gets; *and recently, successfully stopped by the developer advertising, the new development is call "Yorkeys' Beach".*

According to the story, Aboriginals had been here for thousands of years, it was not until the 17th century that Portuguese and Dutch adventurers began to explore Australian coast.

Later *James Cook* first sighted *Australia* on April 19th, 1770, and landed a few days later at Botany Bay. Then, he continued northwards, forced to land in northern Queensland for essential repairs to the Endeavour after hitting a reef. He remained at Cook town – 215 miles north of Cairns – for seven weeks.

Eighteen years later, the first convicts trod in Cook's footsteps and landed at Botany Bay; the penal settlement of New South Wales was in business. However, it was not until 1824 that Queensland became a penal colony. Free settlers soon followed and in 1859, Queensland became independent from New South Wales.

They called the original settlement *Trinity Bay*. At first, the town served as a port for the goldfield, 60 miles inland, on the Hodgkinson River. –Later, it washed away by a flood in 1879. Further competition came from Port Douglas.

A few years later, they rebuilt the railway, from Cairns to the tableland. The farming of sugarcane began at the same time, and *Cairns* became the main exporting center. The settlement grew rapidly and achieved status in 1903 and city status twenty years later.

–*Queensland* is seven times the size of the UK.

–The Great Barrier Reef stretches for more than 1,200 miles down the Queensland coast.

–All the northern Queensland, the Sunshine State is within the tropics.

–The state's symbol is the Koala.

–*Brisbane* the state capital is 1,063 miles from Cairns.

Today *Cairns* has a population of about 160,000 and is the capital of the far north of Queensland, as well as being the most northerly town in the state. Its recent growth has been encouraged by the expansion of tourism – the Great Barrier Reef is a major attraction.

The city has palm-fringed streets, charming parks easy to walk everywhere. The old port is around Wharf Street and the Esplanade – the latter continues for three mile along the bay and makes for a very pleasant walk. The center of the city has some interesting pubs, plenty of shops, a museum, and a gallery. The Cairns Museum is open 6 hours a day. Visited The Flicker Botanic Gardens, with some 200 species of palm and other tropical plants.

To keep the passengers entertain for five days at the see, the Program Director, organized several platforms, as concerts and celebrities presentations... We chose the award-winning Zeitgeist Classical Concert Zeitgeist Duo UK, with their musical journey through Spanish music. Angelika Low-Beer, violin, and Marina Lieberman, piano presented a program of light-hearted Latin-American tangos by Spinazzola. The first night at the ship, after this wonderful program, we went happily to sleep.

Each day, we walk a few miles on the promenade... then, sat on a comfortable chair, reading a book, newspaper, or a daily program; some-times we just rest and enjoyed the view. Other times, visit an elegant bar, where we enjoy the wonderful music by a professional pianist, interpreting usually romantic songs. At the same time, we observe the strong waves, or far away, mountains, glaciers, or other gracious ships...
Then, we go to the big theatre to enjoy different entertainments, extraordinary movies, or great speakers about an

infinite number of subjects... -There are always very interesting programs, so no one gets bored!

–The hardest part of life is just getting out the door! And the path in front of you is rarely a straight line... It is full of bumps! Embrace the bumps in the road, first; then go!

–Learned this easy way to get the good side of kind people, with manners"... Show a modicum of respect to them, and their culture... You will be, blown away, by what you get back: kindness, consideration, and attention. Try picking up a little of the local language, or take time to learn other languages; but if you do not have time to do so, just learn how to say thank you, gracias, or mahalo (Hawaiian for Thank You) this can make an impact in you showing them kindness.

In Hawaii children learn how to make LEIS (worn around the neck), since nearly everyone loves fresh flowers with leis made of ilima or orchids... We wear them on most special occasions, and since today was a special occasion for all of us, we enjoyed some with beautiful the colors and fragrances.

–Just, remember, the words of *the **French novelist, Marcel Proust,** "The real voyage of discovery consists not in seeing new lands, but in seeing with new eyes".* –He realized *by working with other people that we learn about their cultures and become able to explore new ideas and prospects. Options that would not have occurred to us before stand out as obvious if we understand how other people experience the world.* This is why I believe, it is so important for students to have a deeper global awareness and understanding of other cultures.

We can choose, Short gratifications, or go after Long Term Goals!

CHAPTER 15

In Kota Kinabalu in Borneo's remote Sabah, province, you will find tropical rainforests filled with exotic plants, miles of sandy beaches and warm clear waters and warm people.

"All journeys have secret destinations of which the traveler is unaware."

— Martin Buber

It took six day sailing, arriving on March 22nd, in the Port of **Kotta Kinabalu, Malaysia**.

Kota Kinabalu is the largest city in the State in *Sabah*, and is the main gateway into the Island of Borneo. It lies by the coast overlooking South China Sea on a narrow flatland and occasional hills bordered by Crocker Range with hosts *Mount Kinabalu*. *Kota Kinabalu*, known as *Jesselton* was under British colonial rule from the late 1800s until 1963. When the British left, *Sabah* became part of *Malaysia*

Kota Kinabalu refers as the Central Business district (CBD) or simply *Downtown KK* and is located on the narrow coast overlooking *Gaya Island*. Most of the city center lies on reclaimed land, due to shortage blocked by Signal Hill.

Saba – Borneo's Paradise is only in comparatively recent years that tourist have discovered the virgin charms of the world's third largest island, Borneo and particularly of the northern territory now known a Sabah. The jungle and rainforests, the exotic flora and golden beaches, the animals and the spectacular mountain scenery, are merely some of the attractions on offer. –This was very surprise about this beautiful and delightful place.

Much of *Borneo* remains unexplored, but at northern part, the visitors are so welcome to what was once the British Crown Colony. Sabah is about the size of Ireland, but there the similarity ends. Just of Equator, Sabah lies under the typhoon belt, sold to Sulu sailors as the "Land below the Wind". The climate is tropical, but pleasant. There are short bursts of torrential rain and the atmosphere grows very humid in the monsoon season, but the temperature at the coast ranges between 22"C (72"F) and 32"C (90"F).

Saba has neighbors on three sides by sea, the South China to the west, the Sulu to the east, and the Celebes to the southeast. It covers an area of 29,000 square miles and has a total population of around 2.89 million, though the figure must be approximate owing to the Inaccessibility of some of the tribal villages.

During World War II, the Japanese took over Sabah and colonial rule ended. *American bombing toward the end of the way destroyed Sandakan and Jesselton* and the region lost many lives in the resistance movement.

Since the war, things have been peaceful and independence came to Malaysia on 16th of September 1963. Two weeks later, Sabah joined the Federation of Malaysia and in 1968, the town of *Jesselton* was renamed *Kota Kinabalu* or KK, after the highest mountain in South East Asia; and became the next capital. Today the town has around 300,000 inhabitants. Light industries include truck assembly, woodworking, and the manufacture of furniture, soap, and plastics, and tourism is the fastest growing industry.

There are over thirty ethnic groups with eighty different dialects In Saba; the *Kadazons* are the most numerous, living largely in the coastal areas, growing rice and trading for a living. KK has a predominantly Chinese population who are involved in business and commerce. The *Bajous* are anglers and farmers. –They are the "Cowboys of the East" due to their natural aptitude for horse riding. The *Muruts* live in the mountains and cling to their past more tenaciously than other tribes, since they are more remote from modern civilization. Sabah State Mosque holds 5,000 worshippers; this is a splendid example of contemporary Islamic architecture, keeping in mind of its gold-inlaid dome and its pencil-slim minaret in Ottoman Turkish style. The serenity and peace of Islam, the country's official religion, is reflecting in the prayer hall. They permit visitors to see the corridors of the mosque, but dress appropriately covering knees and arms.

–Husband Michael was feeling energetic, and decided to climb very, very high for the view, taking the road going east from Town Padang and enjoyed the panorama of KK from the top; I was not so brave, and waited for him at the near area sitting comfortable in a chair under some trees, and took wonderful pictures.

We visited the white sand beaches and clear warm water, of "Tanjung Aru" lined with casuarina trees, and Prince Philp Park – a delightful garden with recreational center-ways, built to commemorate the visit of Her Majesty the Queen.

On March 23rd, upon clearing the northern coastline of Malaysia, the ship steered a series of North and North Easterly curving into the South China Sea, and in the morning cleared the *Balabac Strait* to *Starboard,* before later in the day passed the *North Danger Reef* to port and the island of Palawan to starboard. This morning visited and enjoyed a cup of cappuccino coffee and some delicious pastry, with *Shyla* and *Tom* friends; then, went to listen to a piano concert; and before lunchtime, we walked a few miles in the promenade. Next night, we had the chance to join Art Director on a trip around the world, as he delved into the portfolio to discuss the inspirations and techniques of some of our cityscape artists. Among them, were Brazilian born *Henderson Cisz* the 2007 artist of the year in the UK and had been ascribed the moniker of the "master of the modern cityscape".

Next evening went to join our resident Port Lecturer *Graham Howell,* for an informative talk on *Hong Kong.* Next knight we went listened to Danny Elliot an Australian premier multi-instrumental and vocal entertainer. He was a multiple award winner for "Vocal-instrumental" and "Versatile Variety". While in board at sea in route to *Shanghai,* we attended to the main theater, to enjoy the Featured Entertainment o Philip Browne, who has starred in nine West End shows including the Lion King, Anything Goes, Show Boat and Porgy &Bess. He took us on a musical journey with songs of Paul Roberson, Nat King Cole, Elton John, Lionel Richie an many more.– We enjoyed the fantastic show very much, then, we went to rest. ***This phenomenal entertainment always kept us very happy***

CHAPTER 16

This fascinating village of Shanghai began as a fishing village and grew during a period of 1,200 years into a township, ultimately becoming an Imperial Chinese Colony.

I let myself go into creative mode today... Drift into a whole other world. Escape present reality and explore my fantasies through artistic endeavors. Dream, as big as my mind will allow, with no limits to the things I can realize, on a day like this; pushing boundaries to taste frontiers; I may be able to soar much higher than I think.

On March 26th at 7 p.m., we arrived in the *Port of* **Shanghai**, *China*.

By 1700, international trade had started to develop, and cotton finishing had become a big industry

Through that next century, the owners boomed while the general population grew poorer and poorer. Conditions for many citizens were primitive, while foreigners accumulated fortunes. Ultimately, revolution became the result.

The European name given to *Wai Tan Road* (along Huangpu Park) was "*the Bund*". It signified the kernel and center of old *Shanghai* and geographically meant "up the river" (from the sea). The river in question is the *Huangpu* and the city radiates from its banks. Along the waterfront, the wide Bund is once again a place where multimillion dollars deals are common. The modern city rivals *Hong Kong* and Tokyo.

Let us talk about *Shanghai*; this is one of the Worlds' most fascinating cities, bursting with ancient tradition, culture, and modern technology. This fabled port on the Huangpu River has played a pivotal role in the history of Modern China. –Originally, the chief of seven "treaty ports" visited the by the west to Imperial China. *Shanghai* had been famous for the Bund, and elegant section of riverbank lined with at first modest Merchants' houses, and later as they prospered pleasant Merchants' mansions.

Let us talk more about *Shanghai*! *The People's Republic of China's* largest city is located on the coast of the *East China Sea*. *Shanghai* is a major port on the *Huangpu River* near its confluence with the *Yangtze River*, and is an important mega industrial and commercial center. The municipality covers almost 2,400 square miles and has a population of around 20 million, of whom some 8.8 million live in the city. Unlike some Chinese cities, Shanghai has a strong foreign influence being the second Chinese port to open itself to the foreigners from the West.

An agricultural community undoubtedly existed in the Shanghai region some 5,000 years ago, but as late as the 7th century, Shanghai, then called *Hu Tu* or *Shen,* was little more than a small and insignificant fishing village.

The town -designated as a countryseat- in the late 13th century, but it was not until 1553 that building the city wall was started to protect the population against marauding Japanese pirates. By the mid-18th century, *Shanghai* had become the center of a major cotton-growing area. –With the wall destroyed in the 20th century and expansion necessary, they expanded the city.

The city flourished quickly in importance when the Chinese surrendered Shanghai to the British in 1842, after the first Opium War. The British destroyed the city, opening it to the outside world, and the British were able to live and trade without being subject to Chinese law. The Americans and the French also took an active interest in *Shanghai* and its trading and commercial potential. Each had a selected part of the city and the "French Concession" was under the direct control of the French government. *Shanghai* soon became China's leading port and an important banking and trading center, in 1895 the Japanese defeated the Chinese in the Sino-Japanese war, and they received a "concession" in the city. They were well established by the end of the 19th century.

Foreign domination in the city was unlikely to last forever and the rise of the *Chinese Communist party in the 1920's* was the end for Britain, France, Japan, and the United States. After World War II, during which the Japanese occupied the city, the four foreign powers returned the entire city back to China. In 1949, Communist troops entered *Shanghai* and *Mao* became the leader of China when the People's Republic of China started building there on October 1.

During foreign domination, people considered *Shanghai* as the *"Paris of the East'*. Naturally, the second half of the 20th century had changed it, – industries again flourished, the feuds between rival factions during the Cultural Revolution are now part of history, and much of the city has been re-developed and modernized.

Tourism is still in its infancy, but each year the city attracts more and more visitors. One question remains, "will *Shanghai* be a rival?" – Or, even "replace *–Hong Kong* as China's city of the future?" – Bearing in mind, "the total population of 1.4 billion realizes more than one-fifth of mankind is Chinese"!

–The 3,900-mile-long Yangtze River is the longest river in Asia and enters the sea just north of Shanghai…*–Shanghai* is on the same latitude as *Alexandria in Egypt* and *New Orleans in the United States of America.*

We visited another *Buddhist Temple*, it was the original temple on the site, built in 1882, first destroyed in the 1911 revolution, and re-built between 1918 and 1921. However, the main attraction is the tall, seated Buddha, in white jade and encrusted with jewels, donated by a monk from Burma in 1882. -We can observe several other gold-plated Buddha's in their Great Hall.

In complete contrast to the city's older buildings, is this very modern and stunning museum in a 1990's building shaped like an ancient Chinese food container. If the outside is impressive, then so are the collections of Chinese scrolls and ceramics, Ming Dynasty 1268 – 1644).

The pace of economic change in China has been extremely rapid since the start of economic reforms just over 25 years ago. According to official statistics, economic growth has averaged 9.5% per year over the past two decades and seems likely to continue at that pace for some time. National income has been doubling every eight years. Such an increase in output represents one of the most sustained and rapid economic transformations seen in the world economy in the past 50 years.

On March 27th and 28th at sea in route to _Hong Kong_.

At night, we had great entertainment. a) _"Music & Memories" with Jeff Hughes in Concert._ b) _"Showtime" with Virtuoso Cabaret Violinist Ian Cooper from Australia..._ c) _"Classical Concert" with Zeitgeist Duo from the UK... "Beauty Meets Talent"_ as titled by the BBC, the sophisticated yet contemporary performance of the award-winning _Zeitgeist Duo,_ with violinist _Angelika Low-Beer,_ and pianist _Marina Lieberman;_ for their final recital featuring works by _Debussy, Kreisler, and Gershwin._ –That means we had a lot of wonderful entertainment, that night!

On March 29th, we arrived in **_Hong Kong_**...The first settlers came to Hong Kong, we believe arrived in the third millennium BC, but for the early part of its history, Hong Kong saw only nomads. _Hong Kong_ primarily consists of _Hong Kong_ Island, Lantau Island, Kowloon _Peninsula,_ and the New Territories. The Kowloon Peninsula, to the New Territories, which eventually connect with mainland _China_, across the _Sham Chun River_ (_Shenzhen River_). _Hong Kong_ encompasses a collection of 262 islands in the South China Sea. _Ap Lei Chau_ is the most densely populated island in the world. The name "_Hong Kong_", literally meaning "fragrant harbor", is derived from the area around present-day _Aberdeen_ on _Hong Kong_ Island, where fragrant wood products and fragrant incense were once traded. There is evidence that anglers many thousands of years ago inhabited the islands of _Lamma_ and _Lanta_ and in the _Middle Ages, pirates lived in Aberdeen._ Regular trade between _China_ and _Britain_ began in 1700 and the _British_ traders operated from _Macau_, a _Portuguese_ colony near _Canton._ Hong Kong was mostly under-developed up until the mid-19th century. Due to rapid trade expansion _Britain_ needed a _Chinese_ base to operate from and in 1841, Captain _Charles Elliot occupied Hong Kong_ for this purpose.

At that time, trade in opium was flourishing and the British were making huge profits from its sale to the Chinese, much to the disgust of the Emperor of China, and as a result, the banned opium. Trade continued, however, until General *Lin Tse-Hsu* demanded that all opium supplies be surrender and then destroyed. *William Jordine* and James Matheson, the most successful opium traders, persuaded the *British Government* to use force and resist the ban. *General Lin* had the opium factory in *Canton* surrounded and eventually the British surrounded 20,000 chests of opium. *General Lin* hoped that normal trading (other than in opium would continue between the two countries, but this was not to be. Opium trade was also big, and colonial leaders made sure the drug kept flowing into China from India. The first Opium War broke out in 1840, leaving Britain in control of Hong Kong and the Shanghai political economic "concessions".

In 1860, Britany gained the Kowloon peninsula and in 1898, the New Territories released to Britain for 99 years. Huge foreign-owned industries were established. Since then, Hong Kong has become an important Far East trade and financial center and a popular tourist destination, the only interruption to be growth being the Japanese occupation during the Second World War.

The narrow body of water separating Hong Kong Island and Kowloon Peninsula, Victoria Harbor is one of the deepest natural maritime ports in the world. Since reunification with China, Hong Kong has been a "Special Zone", operated according to a "one country, two systems policy" to help ease transportation and to keep the economy thriving. *Hong Kong* is a Special Administrative Region of the People's *Republic of China*, lying on the southeast coast of *China*. The Chinese sovereignty started July 1 1997, under a unique arrangement referred to as "One Country, Two Systems"; the Hong Kong Special Administrative Region (HKSAR) of China enjoys a degree of autonomy. The total land area is 424 square miles (1,100 square kilometers) comprising *Hong Kong Island, Kowloon* and the New Territories, plus 260 outlying islands. -The territory's official languages are Chinese and English.

This is a personal opinion about *Hong Kong*... "It is vivid and vibrant! Since 1 July 1997, Hong Kong has been an autonomous territory of mainland China. A thriving community devoted to business with amazing contrasts, mirrored skyscrapers, paddy fields, luxurious shopping mall, and colorful street markets.

If you did not know, *Hong Kong* is undoubtedly one of the most exciting destinations in the world! A truly impressive skyline of modern skyscrapers outlines the busy harbor, which is full of sampans, ferries, and foreign cargo ships. The streets are always crowded and full of color, with people going about their daily business. There are so many sights and sounds to take in, on any particular day in Hong Kong, and is sure to be simply unforgettable...

–Hong Kong enjoys a subtropical climate: Summers are hot and humid, while the autumn months are much cooler with very little rain. –And, the average temperature on winter is 16 C (61 F), with humidity at 73 percent...

Hong Kong Special Administrative Region of the People's Republic of China established as of 1st. of July 1997. Under the Sino-British Joint Declaration on the future of Hong Kong, signed in 1984 and registered with the United Nations, the reversion of sovereignty bring very little change.

Hong Kong's capitalist system will remain unchanged for at least 50 years. The territory will be free to continue its own political, social, and economic systems, and will enjoy a high degree of autonomy, except in foreign affairs and defense matters. *Hong Kong,* is now run by Hong Kong's own people... A Chief Executive, who, is a *Hong Kong citizen,* selected by a Selection Committee comprised of *Hong Kong people,* rather than a *Governor appointed, by the Queen, in the UK head the government.*

Hong Kong will keep its own laws (*British* common law system); the judiciary will remain independent with a Final Court of Appeal based in *Hong Kong.* They maintain its existing border and its own immigration controls. In addition, this entire area, is maintained and controlled by Hong Kong, regarding the movement of people from China and Hong Kong. We visited the Cultural Center, which is along Kowloon's waterfront and comprise of a Concert Hall, a Grand Theatre with a revolving stage and an electrically operated Orchestra. The studio theater is use solely for dance and drama production; the central Business district has modern high-rise blocks housing international banks, hotels, and up-market shopping malls.

The oldest place of worship in *Hong Kong,* which faces Hollywood Road, is The Temple full of burning joss sticks and incense coils. The statue at the main altar represents *Man* and *Mo* and the gold plated used for carrying statues of the temple's gods around the streets. Located on a hillside west of *Sha Tin* railway station is the *Buddha Monastery* which has 12,800 statues of *Buddha* lining, its walls, and there is a nine-story pink pagoda.

Keep decorating mind and memory with all of these real treasures giving pleasure.

CHAPTER 17 ★

According to some researches, the name Neha Trang derives, from a false Vietnamese spelling, of a geographical name in the Cham language, of the site Yak Trang–lit or Red River.

If you are an American looking to go travelling in Vietnam, do not worry about getting a frosty reception, because of the legacy of the war. – Do not worry… the Vietnamese have abiding warmth for American visitors that will soon make you feel right at home! – Yes, I was delighted with their charm, personality, and enjoyed very much their shows.

March 30ᵗʰ… After clear of *Hong Kong* last night, at sea, in route to *Nha Trang*, during the afternoon, we attended a Classical Concert with *Naomi Edemariam*, including pieces of *Chopin &*

Liszt, and at night, we had a luxurious dinner while we transited the *South China Sea*. We passed west of the *Parcel Islands*, and continued on the southwesterly heading toward the cost of *Vietnam*.

On March 31st, we arrived at Nha Trang, Vietnam. A long time ago, when my husband Michael and I, were selecting the tours around the world, I had my doubts about visiting *Vietnam*… since it came to my mind the time when my oldest son *Herb* enrolled in the US Marines, and was assigned to go to *Vietnam*… The memories came back… "My darling son… decided to be patriotic, got the training and the sad day arrived!" – I did not cry, to avoid me showing sadness. He was wearing his *Marine* uniform… I gave him a hug… hopping, his future will be fortunate...! With his determination, he said to me his Mom, *"Mother I am an American Citizen, I am loyal to my new adopted country, and now I am going to defend my nation in need!"*

Without tears, we said good-by! –Went back home and meditated for him, accepting his firm purpose and faith. When he whispered "Mother, do not worry … I will be back"; then I said "Thank you, son, for choosing to be loyal to your country… doing the best, God will protect you, and you will be back to my arms –Go in peace!"

(I remember many years ago, (he was only eleven years old when we arrived at this blessed country of the USA, with faith in the future; son *Herb* was very happy, and with determination he wanted to succeed in life. –Besides he attended a some years at the Catholic School where he regained his faith; also now he also had loyalty to his own new adopted country).

With faith, remembered the words of the Master *Paramhansa Yogananda*, **"The great man doesn't think he is great!** *Those who say they are great, are not. In addition, those who are great are too* *busy being great to think being about their greatness. Besides, no matter how wonderful you think you are, as soon as you proclaim it, everyone wants to prove you otherwise. The point is being sincere. Live it in your life. Never try to deceive others. A fake rose can never be a real rose. In addition, a real rose will shed its fragrance no matter how much is crushed. So never, pretend to be what you are not. If you egoistically display yourself before others, the world will eventually cast you aside. Moreover, do not try, in any way to deceive God, for in the false notion that you can fool Him, you only deceive yourself. He is behind your thoughts. If you are not sincere with him, He will fly away. He comes only to those who are humble and true devotees. When you love Him, you will know Him; and you will know He is present in every soul. It does not matter whether a charcoal or a diamond personality covers that soul; God is equally present in both. However, the diamond mentality of the saint more fully reflects God. There is no joy comparable to that joy which comes when you have earned the friendship of God. In addition, it is most wonderful to share that joy with others. When we have the cup filled with milk, and you pour more into it, it overflows. You can't help it."*

Many years back, when my sons were attending elementary school, they were great! Besides, having lovely memories from the two sons… later attending high school in Los Angeles, California, always taking a daily shower, combing their hair, and dressing in a decent manner, we got into the car, and before leaving the vehicle, they always gave me a kiss. Very happy, they ran crossing the school's gate, and after classes, waited for mom, in the study room, they were eager, informing how they advanced in all the subjects, learning also English very fast.

When son *Herb* was at the war in *Vietnam*, he corresponded every time he had a chance, and those treasure letters I kept, all the time. Always thought, "*Doors of happiness are always open, when we think life closes*". *Even with the sad occurrences, every time, I received his correspondence from Vietnam, I regained hope and happiness, thanking the hidden light always present to illuminate my life.*

Wrote, next poem my dear son *Herb*, so I read it every night, before praying for him, asking God to return him to me... *Knew then, and know now, there are advisers, lights, teachers at every moment of our life, offering the chance and the opportunity to learn; we just have to pay attention and have faith for good results. This poem affirms my beliefs,*

MY HERO, (for first son Herb) © By *Nohemi*

A young man went to war... It was dear son Herb
Lie awake each night drifting into fantasies
Where I saw him steering the tanks around a corner

Rifles thrown on the floor, helmets in a pile
Guns silent for the first time after many sad months
Were empty, but the ground keeps moving backwards

Envision him in the jungle, water around his neck
There were canoes everywhere
Taking Marines to a town with wooden fences

The letters sent to him some came back unopened
Went to the post office near our home
Where the old mail carrier still remembers

One stool was empty nearby
Sat drinking water, while waiting for the mail,
One letter, found from a pile of envelopes...

Recognized the envelope, rapidly opened
"Mom, please, be calm... "Hundreds of children
were killed in seconds, after we left the tent."

"Nights drained away from me
Lifting the room toward morning light
Heard helicopters going by"...

"Tried to sleep and I had a dream
There were melted bodies, still smoked...
This time I observed the roof in flames."
Saw son's face in the corner of the tent,
His teas were rolling down looking at his empty hands.
"We have to keep moving, or we will burn as them."

"Helicopters left the territory,
Burned bodies were everywhere
Dirty shirts and boots, were left behind"

"The enemy lies hidden on the other side of earth".
—Oldest son, who I adore, was there, that is, all I know.
Months went by... Stopped reading news about the war

Sent him some wine and cheese for Christmas,
This way, he could drink with friends
Hoping one good day, he will return, safe.

—One early morning, was cleaning home
Felt body strongly clutched... —Tried to see his face...
He embraced strongly...

He was going around, holding mother.
Shouted the loudest! Could not excel the breath!

A great kiss, I received, and then, a big hug!

Tears of joy went down my startled faced
Saw my hero! –He came back from the war
With dozens of gold and silver medals,
For being so brave, courageous and heroic

He was the darling son, and he still is
He finally returned from the Vietnam War.
Waited years, drying tears rolling down,

"Mother," –He said- "I had left the war,
However, the war does not leave us ever,
It will be in our mind, the whole life!

That is all I can say! Sadness is eternal
Horrible experiences and Happiness will
Govern our mental attitude."

"The sad experience with blue issues we had so many years ago, I tried to leave behind, where they belong. – Many years after, told husband, "I think, this issue made me see the reality of leaving the past in the past…" –Let us go back to the present…

This time, we arrived at **Nha Trang, Vietnam**, on *March 31*, at 9 a.m. This is wat I learned about this place we visited in Vietnam…According to research, the name *Nha Trang* derives from a false *Vietnamese* spelling of a geographical name in the Cham Language of the site *Ya Trang (Red River), the name of the now Cai River* as referred to by the Cham people. From the name of this river, adopted to call what is now *Nha Trang*, which was officially name *Vietnam's* territory in 1653. From 1653 to the 19th century, *Nha Trang* was a deserted area rich in wildlife such as tigers. After just two decades in the 20th century, *Nha Trang* underwent a rapid change.

Modern *Nha Trang is* a city of two parts. One takes the form of a small *Danang* – a bustling *Vietnamese* city humming with commerce, but blessed with access to a beautiful beach, the *Hon Mun* marine protected area is one of four first marine protected areas in the world admitted by the *IUCN*. The other is a peaceful Western resort town encompassing several blocks of hotels, tourists, shops, bars and international restaurants. Entering the sheltered enclave you could be anywhere in the world. The city is beautiful, bordered by mountains, with the beach tracing an impressive long swoop along a bay dotted with islands... Topiary and modern sculpture dot the immaculately manicured foreshore. A recent addition to the tourists industry is the *Vinpearl* complex on *Hon Tree* Island (Bamboo Island), a luxury resort accessed via a newly constructed cable car that crosses the bay. We visited Long Son Pagoda, the largest in *Khan Hoa* province, outside of the city and we reached by taxi.

We were informed that the destruction of the original pagoda in a storm in the early 20 century and was rebuilt in 1940. We admired the huge, seated white Buddha, erected on the hill behind the last pagoda. There were 152 steps, with an excellent bird's-eye view of *Nha Trang* from this viewpoint. We observed thousands of bicycles as regular transportation. We detected hundreds of motorcycle taxis, running all around the streets, but the traffic police informed us, that this method of transportation was potentially dangerous, and not recommended. The National Oceanographic Institute and Aquarium, contains live fish and turtles and, there is, also a large collection of stuffed fish and sea birds, together with a 60-ft long skeleton of humpback wales.

Citizens are very cordial, treating the American tourists with kindness. Husband wanted to buy a beer near the Buddhist Temple. Not sure, what to do because of possible local laws, and the military police also having coffee at the coffee stand, asked a very elderly woman about it. He thought she was old enough to maybe know some English (perhaps learned some from the G.I.'s who were there during the Vietnam War). She said *"Sure! These military police are my children having coffee with me at my coffee stand... "No problem",* she said, *"Enjoy some beer!"* She then got a very large beer out from hiding - behind the soda pop cans behind the glass door in the refrigerator and then she said, *"We love to have Americans on these tours, since they were very kind with us".*

Husband Michael had the occasion to ask about the war, and a young man said, *"We understand that President Kennedy was assassinated the day after he gave his executive order to pull out of Vietnam, because he said 'We were supporting a corrupt regime. We are fighting on the wrong side' he said." –Since then, the young man said, "We consider the United States our faithful friend."* Very happy with his words, we gave him a hug.

Something darling happened that afternoon, when the weather was so hot… husband wanted to find a fresh glass of water to cool his throat; he asked the head of the tour, – who was a relatively young man, about the place to buy something cool… He said, "come with me, I will take you to the right place, where you won't be disappointed. I observed both of them walking down the street, and then, they entered a place… –According to my husband's comment, "This kind gentleman took me to a humble, but nice place, to buy me a bear; I accepted, and then, asked him, "How much do I own? Moreover, with a great smile he said, "This is my treat!" (we knew the salary of these people were very low). Therefore, at the time of leaving the bus, Michael gave him ten dollars for "his kind service". He looked at the bill and we observed tears in his eyes!

We had the chance to admire different shows, in which everyone was very friendly, treating us with love and care. In addition, since I learned years ago that Vietnam was one of the countries that take great delight in the dance of TANGO, we were able to find a wonderful Concert Hall to enjoy this professional dance, with grace and quality.

On April 2nd, we arrived at Port of Phu My, Vietnam... Ho Chi Minh City is the largest city in Vietnam and is located near the *Mekong Delta.* Under the name *Prev Nokor,* it was the main port of Cambodia, before was annexed by the Vietnamese in the 17th century, under the name *Saigon.* –It was the capital of the French colony of *Cochin China,* and later of the independent state of *South Vietnam* from 1954 to 1975, when Saigon merged with the surrounding province of *Gia Dinh* and renamed as *Ho Chi Minh City. Sai Gon,* is written in two words. Some people however write the name of the city as *Sai Gon* or Saigon in order to save space or give it a more Westernized look.

(Remember Aunt Angie, with whom I lived a few years after my dad was assassinated, when I made a "bubo" (a small mistake) she used to punish me with this expression, "Vases a la Cochin China" (Go to the Cochin China.)

Hochi Minh City (Formerly Saigon) is the largest city in the Socialist Republic of *Vietnam,* with a population exceeding seven million people. It is located on the Saigon River, near the Mekong Delta in the southern part of the country. –QM2 is too large to navigate up the river to *Ho Chi Minh* City, therefore it docks on the coast, from where the city is about a two-hour journey by coach.

This is part of the story… In 1859, the French captured Saigon and then the rest of *Vietnam*, and *Saigon* soon became celebrated as the "*Paris of the East*". Later the Viet Minh, under *Ho Chi Minh's* leadership, declared independence from France in 1945. This war resulted in a French defeat at *Dien Bien Phu* in May 1954.

Their government divided Vietnam into two zones, *Saigon* and *Hanoi* as two capital cities. A second Indochina War, usually called the Vietnam War, was inevitable, as North Vietnam and the Viet Cong, a communist movement operating in South Vietnam, were determined to unite North and South Vietnam. The United States was initially only involved in training the South Vietnamese army, but larger numbers of US combat troops began arriving in 1965 and the war escalated. Saigon was the headquarters for US military operations, the Viet Cong targeted the city on many occasions during 1960, and only in 1968-70 during the *Tet Offensive*. The Viet Cong attacked the Presidential Palace and the American Embassy. After a disastrous campaign, the last US troops returned home in 1973 and left the South Vietnamese to continue the war alone. Finally, a *North Vietnamese* tank smashed through the gates of the *Presidential Palace in Saigon on April 30 1975*, and then the war was over. North, South Vietnam became one country, and Saigon government renamed it as *Ho Chi Minh City*.

Can you imagine? *Ho Chi Minh City attracts more tourists from the United States than any other country! –Shanghai and San Francisco are Ho Chi Minh City's Sisters Cities. A French influence is the Neo-Romanesque Notre Dame Cathedral on Paris Square, in the heart of the City.*

"God created war so that Americans would learn geography."
—Mark Twain

"*Father Ray Children's Charity Foundation*" *now encompasses a Children's Home, vocational school for People with Disabilities, especially Children'*

Visiting Thailand... The weather is good throughout the country in January, February or March... This time of year, it is very pleasant... There is little chance of rain, while cooler temperatures in the north make conditions more comfortable and all the west coast beaches are likely to be bathed in sunshine. I personally enjoyed this gorgeous place the most!

This foundation has, on numerous occasions, been one of Cunard's World Voyage chosen charities providing basic care and education for children of the Foundation where they are encouraged to develop advanced cultural skills through various means, such as traditional *Thai dancing*, *Thai boxing*, and musical performances. It has also become a tradition on these vessels, to have children perform on board during ship visits to *Laem Shebang*. Therefore, it was with great pleasure that we welcomed the children of the Father Ray's Foundation on board. —All I can say, is "We, thousands of passengers and crew were touched by their skilled performances, and graciousness, and their happy faces." *Laem Chabang*, —is the gateway to the wonders of *Bangkok*! This enchanted city on the *Chao Phraya River* is a fascinating place where everyone finds temples with gold leaf spires and graceful statues of Buddha.

Its population of about 62 million is slightly more than that of France. —And it is roughly the same size as Spain. The neighboring countries are *Myanmar* (*Burma*), *Laos*, *Cambodia* and *Malaysia*.

—Looking at their happy faces, I remember, that at the time I was teaching college courses in California I had the great opportunity to have Thai students in some of my classes. They are a smiling young people, eager to learn English. —And, by the way— all of them were thanking me with a great smile when they pronounced their sentences very well!

(–By the way, in 1939 the country was officially renamed **Thailand**, instead of *Siam*). Found out also, the highest point of Mt *Inthanon* has 8,484 feet in the highest point, almost twice the height of *Ben Nevis*.

In addition, something else impressed me… *Thailand* has the world's only hospital for elephants! In addition, I remember, "*Good Morning Vietnam*" and "*The Man with the Golden Gun'*, were partially filmed in *Thailand*.

Since 1945 on, Bangkok has grown dramatically and its present population is approaching 8 million. The city is a crowded and fascinating place, with severe traffic congestion and a pollution problem; even though, there is so much to see and enjoy!

After steaming overnight on a South Easterly course, on April 5th, we anchored in the Port of *Sihanoukville, Cambodia*, also known as *Kampong Som*, named after King Norodom Sihanouk. After many harsh years of rule under Pol Pot, the port city of *Sihanoukville* is now a popular tourist resort; located at the tip of the rolling hills of a peninsula at the Gulf of Thailand. To the North-West and at its center it rises up to 15 meters (49 ft.) above sea level, Sizable economic sectors of the city are fishery, aqua-cultures and frozen shrimp processing; the garment industry, food production (the Angkor brewery), the vast tourism industry with its constantly growing service branch and of course the resulting boom of the real estate market.

In 1863, the French entered Cambodia and, together with *Laos* and *Vietnam*, formed a French protectorate known as French Indochina. *Sihaoukville* only came into existence in 1950's when the French built a port in the coastal area known as *Kompong Sam*. The small town a few miles inland and named after *King Norodom Sihanouk* was soon a popular place for *Cambodians* wealthy to escape the heat of *Phom Penh*.

French rule ended in November 1953 and *Cambodia* declared its independence. The country then prospered for a few years until becoming involved in its civil strife and the Vietnam War. The United States bombed *Viet Cong* camps in northern *Cambodia* and *Sihanoukvile* on one occasion. Worse was to follow in 1975 when Saloth Sar, better known as Pol Pot, and the Communist *Khmer Rouge* took control of the country.

During brutal regime, intellectual and professional people were executed, temples destroyed, industries closed down, and urban dwellers forcibly moved to labor camps in the countryside. Rouge attempted to turn *Cambodia* into a Communist state, based on agricultural production. At least 1.5 million Cambodians died from starvation and disease, or murdered, during the Khmer Rouge's barbaric time in power.

Eventually, a large Vietnamese army, sickened by the atrocities, invaded *Cambodia* in late 1979 and entered Phnom Penh on January 7, 1979. They withdrew ten years later, but the Khmer Rouge continued to be a powerful influence for many troubled years. It was not until Pol Pot died in April 2998, that Cambodia began to achieve some degree of stability. Modern *Sihanoukville* is booming and it is now the country's second largest city after *Phnom Penh*. Tourism is rapidly becoming one of *Cambodia*'s leading industries and building several, luxurious resorts. The port expanded to cope with cruise ships… That is why we are here….

We enjoyed eating *fish* in *coconut milk* with curry, wrapped in banana leaves, and steamed, called *amok trey*; and rice cake wrapped banana leaves… Cambodia has 69,905 square miles… its population is 14.9 million… The people called *Khmer*, as is the language… Neighboring countries are Vietnam to the east, Laos to the northeast and Thailand to the northwest and west….

To celebrate the sail away, we joined the international band Vibz and the Entertainment team at eight pm, before going to sleep.

Enjoy these treasures –A husband who cooks and cleans, is a real treasure!

CHAPTER 19

"Singapore is an island city-state, located at the southern tip of the Malay Peninsula; it consists of 63 islands, including Singapore...

One of the most expensive places in the word is dear Singapore... This is a great spot for snorkeling, especially since it is teeming with biodiversity. Some of Singapore's richest coral reefs reside here... Come and enjoy it, as we did!

Throughout *April 6th*, at sea in route to **Singapore**, steering a series of south-south easterly courses, clearing the Gulf of Thailand, and gradually drawing closer toward the eastern coast of Malaysia; and at early hours we will enter the *Singapore* Strait and encounter the busiest shipping traffic in the world.

In the afternoon, we enjoyed a Classical Concert with the famous pianist, *Naomi Edemariam*, as she returned in the afternoon for her second classical recital of this voyage, including pieces by Tchaikovsky, we rested a little, waiting to enjoy this particular conglomerate of 63 islands, including mainland Singapore.

Then, on April 7th at 7am, we arrived at the Port of Singapore. The Republic of *Singapore* is an island city-state, located at the southern tip of the *Malay Peninsula*. The name of the main island is *Pulau Ujong*. According to history, the name *Singapore* it comes from Malay words *singa (lion)* and *pura (city)*, which in turn comes from *Sanskrit*. Folklore attributes this name to a 14th-century Sumatran prince *Sang Nila Utama,* who, on lightering to the island to see it firsthand after a thunderstorm, renamed it *Lion City* after spotting a suspicious beast identified as a lion.

The national language of *Singapore* is *Malay*, and everybody singing it as an anthem as national holidays, "*Majulah Singapura*". However, the local colloquial dialect of *English is Singlish*, which has many creole-like characteristics, having incorporated vocabulary and grammar from various *Chinese dialects, Malay, and Indian* languages.

In 1819, *Thomas Stamford Rafles* landed on the main island and signed a treaty with Sultan Hussein Shah on behalf of the British East India Company to develop the southern part of Singapore as a British trading post.

Singapore declared independence from Britain on August 31, 1963, before joining the new *Federation of Malaysia* in September, along with Malaya, Sabah, and Sarawak, because of the 1962 Merger Referendum of Singapore. Tunku Abdul Rahman separated Singapore from the Federation two years later, after heated ideological conflict between the ruling parties of Malaya and Singapore.

The island republic at the top of the Malay Peninsula, *Singapore* has come a long way since Sir Stamford Rafles, founded in 1819, once symbolic of the mystery and romance of the Orient; it retains its Eastern flavor.

People call Singapore "A city of colors, cultures, cuisine, and contrasts". A wealth of attractions and a warm welcome await us in one of the cleanest, greenest cities in the world! From the moment we arrived in the world's busiest harbor, we found that Singapore has all the ingredients for an action-packed day ashore.

Singapore lies 85 miles north of the Equator on the tip of the *Malay Peninsula* the most southerly part of Asia. Within its 227 square miles lives a population around 3.8 million and its position in the main trade routes from Europe to South Asia and the Far East has meant *Singapore* has become the commercial capital of South-East Asia and one of the world's greatest ports. It is a relatively young country, which is pristine clean, reassuringly safe and joy to explore. –We were very impressed!

Singapore became an English Crown Colony and by the beginning of the 20th century, the island was filing up with people from neighboring China, Indonesia, Malaya, and India, as well as many Europeans.

For many years, *Singapore* is considered Britain's key defense base in the Far East, but during World War II *Singapore* was occupied for the most part by the Japanese and the Singaporeans, suffered much brutality and hardship during these turbulent times. On 1st. April 1946, it became a separate colony and on first of June 1954, it has self-government as part of the Malayan Federation.

In 1965, *Singapore* left the Federation and became on Independent Republic and a member of the Commonwealth. Since then, this great *Singapore* has grown in leaps and bounds. It is now a weighty financial center (with more than 130 banks), and oil refining … and distribution center, a leader in shipbuilding and a major supplier of electronic components. Despite the rapid growth and the elevated skyscrapers, Singapore has retained and restored its most enchanting areas – the evidence of its popularity lies in the fact that it is one of the few countries in the world to receive more tourists (six million a year) than its resident population. *It is amazing. – Isn't it?*

Singapore is home to people of many different races and creeds, speaking 54 languages, *who all live together in harmony.* The majority of the population is Chinese (76%), and then there are the Malays (15%), the Indians (6.5%), the Europeans and smaller Arab, Armenian and Jewish communities. This multi-cultural mixture has meant that *Singapore* has a blend of unique traditions, remarkable cuisine, and varied costumes.

The street scene in *Singapore* is one of the most colorful and international in the world and is symbolic of the secret of Singapore's development. There are four official languages – Malay, Mandarin, Tamil and English… English being the language of administration and most people are proficient in at least one other language.

The climate is tropical, due to *Singapore's* proximity to the equator, and the weather is warm with little change between the seasons. *This is a marvelous temperature! –We can compare it with beautiful Hawaii… –Do you agree?*

Then, we took the Mass Rapid Transit to *Bugis* to visit the National Museum and Art Gallery... we visited the greatest *Chinatown,* The *Arab Street, The National Museum,* and Art Gallery. On this last wonderful place, after 3 years of extensive restoration, this museum was reopened in 2006 after being closed for a very long time; found more than hundred years of Singapore's treasures, such the mystery-shrouded Singapore Stone and 14th century gold ornaments unearthed from nearby Fort Canning Hill.

The Sultan's Mosque is a local point for Muslim Singapore, and makes a stunning landmark of the area with its huge gold dome. According to history, people built, according to history, an original mosque, on North Bridge Road, built with the help of a $3.000 grant from Sir Stamford Raffles. They completed this mosque in 1928. When we visited the Mosque, we observed the dress code, removing our footwear.

Noticed that the street was full of shops selling leather goods, brass, perfumes, and jewelry; also observed a lot of basketwork, the wonderful insight of the Muslin lifestyle.

Also, visited The Asian Civilizations Museum' core collections, which are used to show the rich multi-ethic heritage of *Singapore* and the South-east Asian region, explored the ancestral cultures of Singaporeans, and stopped by for a few hours at the old *Too Nan School,* where we donated candies to students,

Enjoyed the brief stop at the *Alam Shan Palace* and finally rounded off the day with a stroll in Little India.

We found Singapore at the heart of the River; and the most exciting thing we did, was to take a cruise on a *twakows* (bumboat).

I was fascinated with so many different places, like the *Parliament House* build in 1827. Also, to finish our tour, before taking the transportation back to the cruise-ship, observed The *Merlion*, which, according to them, "it is the tourist symbol of Singapore "– *A mystical beast said to be half lion and half fish.*

Now understand the meaning of this great perception! "It takes every color to make a complete rainbow!"

CHAPTER 20

An important part of the navigator's job aboard a large vessel, is planning the voyage: Assembling the charts, calculating tides, currents, laying out track-lines; weather and draft, pay attention to depths, aids to navigation, hazards like rocks and shoals and traffic separation schemes… –Very similar as planning our future.

We learned about elephant conservation and met elephant orphans at the Kuala Gandah, then, the Elephant Sanctuary; climbed to the world's second tallest Hindu deity at Batu Caves, and observed the fireflies of Bukit Melawati, not too far away from Kuala Lumpur.

On April 8, we arrived at Port Kelang, Malaysia… **Kuala Lumpur** is the capital and the largest city of ***Malaysia*** and is one of the three

Malaysian federal territories. It is an enclave within the state of Selangor, on the central west coast of Peninsular Malaysia; known as KL *Kuala Lumpur* is located at the confluence of the Kiang and Gombak River. Mostly surrounded by forest and hills, it is the only city in the world to have a million-year-old-primary forest within the heart of the city. There is no sea adjacent to Kuala Lumpur… The Golden Triangle, the commercial hub of the city, contains the *Petronas Twin Towers* and has a distinctive nightlife.

These are among the tallest towers in the world and stand adjacent to one of the busiest shopping malls in *Malaysia, Suria KLCC, and Kuala Lumpur* enjoys year round equatorial climate, which is warm and sunny, along with plentiful rainfall, especially during the southwest monsoon from April to September.

A scenic drive from *Port Kelang* gets you to *Kuala Lumpur*, known as *Malaysia's Garden City*. From a tiny huddle of thatched kampongs surrounded by trackless jungle, *Kuala Lumpur* has grown into one of Asia's most fascinating cities. We spent about five (5) hours visiting *Kuala Lumpur*, and the scenic drive through contrasting images from minarets and mosques to colonial style clubs and Victorian houses. Visited Independence square, the Cathedral of Saint Mary the Virgin… –Discovered the colorful Sri Mariamman Hindu Temple, one of the most ornate in the country.

Malaysia offers the best of both worlds; the individual comforts intrinsic in a well-off country, as well as the natural wilderness of its tropical rainforest. *Kuala Lumpur*, the capital, is 25 miles (41 Km) inland. *Malaysia* has a tropical climate and humidity is often high. The average temperature in January is 26 Centigrade (79 Fahrenheit. Much of the country is mountainous and about 80% is still covered by rain forests. This country has a mixture of people with most of the population living on a near the west coast, especially in an around KL.

It is possible that the earliest setters probably came here about 5,000 years ago, and 2,000 years ago, there was a strong Hindu-Buddhist influence. However, Islam had become the principal religion by thee early 14 century.

The Portuguese were the first Europeans to take interest in what is now modern Malaysia. Then the Dutch, but it was not until the early 19th century that Britain became the dominant power, with bases in *Melaka, Penang,* and *Singapore.*

In 1965, became independent... *Singapore* united to form *Malaysia.* Today, the country is constitutional monarchy with one of the nine sultans elected for five years by his fellow rulers. Kuala Lumpur became a Federal Territory in 1974.

Malaysia is the world's leading producer of rubber, tin, and palm oil; industries that continue growing. More than 15.7 million tourists visited in 20004 and Britain is still one of the top markets in Europe for tourists to Malaysia. By the way, the country celebrated 50 years of independence in 2007.

Modern *Kuala Lumpur* (KL) is now known as the *Garden City of Lights,* has a population of 1.3 million and is not only the capital, commercial and social life, it is primarily a rapidly expanding business and commercial center.

We admired the *Merdeka Square,* the 100 meters high flagpole –the tallest example in the world – marks the spot when the Union Jack was sank, people raised the Malaysian flag on August 31, 1957.

Visited also, the *famous temple*, near the Central Marked and close to Chinatown, *Sri Mahamariamman Temple*, built in 1873, and it said to be the most ornate and elaborate temple in Malaysia; with invariable crowded and bustling, full of activity and noise, and not to be missed… At night, the area becomes one big market.

From the Navigator, at this great ship, people informed, "the departure from Port Kelang took place around 6 pm. – Started the 215 nautical passages overnight to Langkawi, setting various Northerly courses, leaving the Malaysian coast on her starboard site throughout, arriving at 7.30 am the next day. **April 9** at the Port of ***Langkawi, Malaysia***.

We learned that "*Langkawi* is an archipelago of 104 islands in the *Andaman Sea,* some 30km off the mainland coast of northwestern *Malaysia*. The islands are part of the state of Kedah, which is adjacent to the Thai Border. By far the largest of the islands is the eponymous *Palau Langkawi*, with a population of some 64,792, the only other inhabited island being nearby *Pulau Tuba*, The total land mass of the islands is 47,848 hectares, while the main island of Langkawi itself has a total of 32,000 hectares".

The forest covers two parts of the island… including mountains, hills, and natural vegetation. The island's oldest geological formation, *Gunung Matchincang*, was the first part of South-East Asia to rise from the seabed in the Cambrian period more than half a billion years ago.

We took the *Langkawi Cable Car* to go up to the peak of *Gunung Mat Chinchang* to observe the *Langkawi Sky Bridge* Was hesitant at the beginning, but marveled, once made the decision to climb, admiring the beauty or the area.

Our tour-guide said to us, "Remarkably little is known about *Langlawi's* early history, although a Chinese dynasty record reveals that the kingdom of *Langgasu*, which would have included the island, had its origin in thee1st century AD. The following centuries are something of a mystery and only at the early 19th century people learn more about *Langlawi*. – That was a popular legend...

"The beautiful *Mahsuri* was falsely accused of adultery in 1819, found guilty and sentenced to death. "When she was stabbed with the *kris*, (a Malay dagger) white blood flowed from the wound as sign of her innocence. With her dying words, *Mahsuri* cursed Langkawi for seven generations. A few years later, the curse seemed to work as a Siamese army invaded the island in 1821. People burned the rice granary and the paddy fields, around *Padang Matsirat* (Field of Burnt Rice) to prevent the rice being a source of food for the invading army. Nevertheless, the Siamese took *Langkawi*."

Langkawi, like the rest of the country, was under British rule from 1909 to 1957 – apart from a brief period during World War II when the island was under the Thai monarchy, and during the Japanese occupation. After the war, pirates used *Langkawi* as a hideout, but life continued in the old-fashioned way for the local people. In 1987, *Langkawi received* "duty-free status" and they opened the airport. Three years later, the authority created a *Langkawi Development Authority (LADA)* to transform the island into a major tourist destination and to raise standards for the local people. Doctor and politician credited with modernizing *Malaysia* during his 22 years in office from 1981 to 2003.

Now, modern *Langkawi* has excellent resorts, golf courses, marinas and a developing eco-tourism industry, with the International Airport to handle more than a million visitors a year.

The island is the venue for such international events as the Maritime and Aerospace Exhibition, a Motor Show, and the Cruise ships are traveling around the west coast of *Malaysia*.

The *Langkawi* Cable Car runs from *Oriental Village* to the top of *Gurung Machinchang,* the second highest mountain on the island. The very steep and exhilarating 1 ¼ -mile ride over the rainforest and some interesting geological formations takes about 15 minutes. On the way up there are magnificent views of the Seven Wells Waterfall, some of the neighboring islands and even southern Thailand on a clear day. They built shops and restaurants on Oriental Villages around a lovely lake, against a mountain background. –We found out other places of particular interest in the north of Langkawi, the Ibrahim Museum and Cultural Foundation and the Crafts Complex. We were impressed with the extraordinary art of *Ibrahim Hussein,* one of Malaysia's acclaimed artist, whose work is renowned throughout Asia and further afield. The Crafts Complex at *Teluk Yu's* displays a wide range of Malaysian handicrafts, including weaving, batik, woodcarving, glass, and silverware. Likewise, we observed at the museum local myths and legends through dioramas.

Many areas of considerable interest are now in *Eastern Langkawi,* including *Langkawi Crystal*. We observed *Langkawi* own many smaller islands, including the very close *Pulau Dayang Bunting* (Island of the Pregnant Maiden), this scene has a local legend, and *"A Childless couple is believed to have drunk the water of a small lake on the island and was later blessed with a baby girl"*.

We sacrifice our greatest treasures, to give each other the best possible Christmas present.

CHAPTER 21

Colombo, Sri Lanka's capital city is located at the crossroads of the great spice routes, where many cultures and races have combined and collided for centuries resulting in colorful bazaars, vibrant temples, and colonial buildings.

On your safari drive, kept your eyes peeled for the two native species of crocodiles that breed there. It was hard to miss the wandering elephants and—the highest concentration of leopards anywhere; our chance of spotting an elusive big cat was good. In addition, we had the chance to observe the skies; 215 species of birds inhabit the region and nest in a variety of plants in this colorful environment. -It was a wonderful experience!

Happily, on April 12th, we arrived at Colombo, Sri Lanka. The pear-shaped island of the Democratic Socialist Republic of *Sri*

Lanka (previously known as *Ceylon*) rests in the Indian Ocean and is totally within the tropics. It is only 18 miles from the southern tip of India.   *Colombo's* population is 680.000; the country's largest city principal port and commercial capital is on the west coast. The majority of the country's earliest residents (Sinhalese) came from northern India; their recorded history stretches back some 2,500 years.

The sacred city of *Anuradkapura*, the country's first capital, was founded in about 4th century BC. It remained as the capital and home of Buddhism, until Dravidian *(Tami)* invaded southern *India*; Various places, then served as the capital of the *Sinhala* kingdom, notably *Polonnaruwa*, the medieval capital, *Kotte*, near present-day Colombo, and Kandy.

In 1505, a Portuguese fleet arrived in *Ceylon* and soon had control of the west coast. *The Sinhalese, a word meaning "a port of ferry", then called Colombo Kalamba.* The Portuguese developed the port and by the early 17th century had extended their control over much of the island Kandy remained as a separate and unconquered area. The threatened *Kandyan* kingdom asked the Dutch for help to ours the Portuguese. The Dutch were pleased to oblige and by 1660 were Ceylon's new rulers, again with the exception of the area around *Kandy*.

In 1796, the British established themselves in Ceylon, which became a crown colony in 1802... Colombo was the new capital; however, it was not until 1815 that the last King of Kandy ceded his territory to the British. Coffee was the leading export until destroyed by disease.-Many things happened through the years...It was only February 4, 1948 *Ceylon* became an independent state, and in 1972 the country's name was changed to *Sri Lanka*, a traditional name for the Island.

More problems as racial tensions between *Sri Lanka's Sinhala* and *Tamil Communities* erupted into violence in the 1980 when the *Tails* demanded a separate state in the north of the island. The fighting between government forces and the *Tamil Tigers* took place mainly in the north. –But, terrible problem, affected by the suicide bombing in 1990, then, the country collapsed.

It was not until May 2009 that the long-running war ended. The violence killed at least 70,000 people –many of them innocent civilians- and severely damaged the economy, especially the all-important tourist industry.

Hope that Sri Lankans can now enjoy a permanent peace!

Sadly, the tsunami of December 2004 devastated coastal communities and killed more than 30,000 people.

Luckily, Sirimaya Bamdaranaike became the world's first woman prime minister in 1960, and Sri Lanka is the world's fourth largest producer of tea after China, India, and Kenya.

Happily, the hill country town of *Kandy* (1,526 ft. above sea level is the UNESCO World Heritage Site)... 72 miles from *Colombo* and again the route is full of interest – paddy fields, rubber and coconut plantations, beautiful mountain view and small tea states.

We noticed the high temperature during summer... –The things about seasons are that they always come and go... here today, gone tomorrow, and back again in their own time. If we are talking about good times, naturally we could wish that the season of happiness would never end.

On April 13, in route to Cochin, India... we decided to enjoy the afternoon, listening to wonderful music! A Classical Concert, *Michal Wesolowski,* and *Malgorzata Czapor...* for the second of their classical recitals... this time, include pieces by *Gershwin, Debussy, and Rubinstein.* After the concert, we went to rest, since the next day we were in Cochin, India, and we already had our plans to be busy and happy.

§

On April 14, we arrived at Port of Cochin, India... As a surprise, we received this information, "Upon arrival in *Cochin,* it is a requirement of *India* Authorities to inspect all guests face to face against the passports! As part of this inspection the Indian Authorities will be collecting your passports from you at this time." We were surprised, but we complied by the immigration request, and got our guide to visit *Cochin...*

"Formerly known as *Kachi,* the large city of *Cochin* is in the state of *Kerala* in southwestern *India...* This cosmopolitan city is only 170 miles from the southern tip of India. It is often called the *Queen of the Arabian Sea* and even *The Venice of the Orient*".

Learned that *Cochin,* or *Kochi* means in Malayalam, a rather misleading name for a city with more than 1.6 million inhabitants. –The date of the first settlement is uncertain, although the Romans, Greeks, and even the Phoenician may have visited this part of India...

History, "Occupied by the Portuguese in 1503, Kochi was the site of the first European colonial settlement in India it remained the capital of *Portuguese India,* until 1530, when Goa became the capital. The Dutch, the Mysore, and the British later occupied the city. *Kochi* was the first state willingly to join the *Indian Union,* when India gained independence in 1947. As of 2009, Kochi had a metropolitan area population of 1,355,900 and a literacy rate of 94%. Scheduled castes and tribes comprise 14% of the city population. *Kachin*'s major religion is *Hinduism, Christianity* and *Islam, Jainism, Judaism, Sikhism,* and *Buddhism,* with small groups practicing *Kochi.* Tough 47% practice Hinduism. Christianity's large followers 35%, make *Kochi* a city with one of the largest *Christian populations* in India.

Some of the earliest settlers may have been Jews, and there is still a *Jewish community* in *Cochin.* The *Chinese* also took on interest in this area and *Arab* traders arrived here, at least a thousand years ago. –Spices have always been the great attractions.

It was not until the mid-14th century that *Cochin* changed from an *insignificant fishing village* to a *potentially important port*; the *Periyar River* burst its banks and found a new outlet to the sea, thus creating the almost landlocked harbor at *Cochin.*

Cochin was the first European settlement established in 1500, when the Portuguese explored the Indian coastline. Three years later, *Vasco da Gama established the first Portuguese trading station and a fort was built a year later by the Portuguese viceroy, Alfonso de Albuquerque.*

Many European powers were anxious to exploit the riches of India and in 1663; the Dutch ousted the Portuguese and remained at Cochin until 1795. Under the Dutch, trade expanded and the city prospered. Pepper, cardamom and other spices, clover and copra all passed through the port.

The British started with the powerful British East India Company, ruled from 1795 until 1947, when India became independent. The present port – one of the largest on the west coast of India – dates from the early 20th century. Material dredges from the harbor was used to create Willingdon Island in 1920's,

Cochin has a large naval base, on important deep-water harbor and good transportations by rail and air. Tourism is growing in reputation, although the total of visitors is small when compared with Goa. The city is also famous for its coir products made from coconut fibers.

The Southwest Monsoon season is from June to September; and June has about 30 inches of rain.

I found out that *Cochin* consists of a number of islands, including *Willingdon*, the mainland town of *Mattancherry*, and the town of *Emakulam*. –Each part has a different character; *Willingdon* Island has the *docks*, *A Naval Airport*, and the *Government of India Tourist Office*, which is next to the Taj Malabar.

It also observed… the most historic buildings are in the part of *Cochin; the most fascinating mixture of European-style buildings, mainly Portuguese and Dutch; British cricket pitches, Chinese fishing nets, Jewish synagogues are everyday life in modern India.*
Unbelievably, Saint Thomas, introduced Christianity to Kerala, probably 20 years after the death of Christ.

There is no question about uncovering the old cities, revealing the beauty, I would never have known otherwise. In addition, life has taught me how to reveal a far greater beauty in people –especially the most unlikely people. What a story they all have to tell! What hidden beauty they all have to share!

CHAPTER 22

Let us have the inner wisdom and vision together, because people rarely learn in isolated aloneness. When we utilize Inner wisdom and Vision together, we can truly understand intuitive knowledge!

Charles Dickens, and J. R Tolkien found out that "making a long walk" (without your phone), as part of your daily routine, people who went on daily walks, scored higher on a test, that measures <u>creative thinking,</u> than people who did not, and that people who went on outdoor walks came up with more novel, imaginative analogies than people who walked on treadmills.

April 15th, at sea in route to Dubai... INTEREST CORNER, Seminar Program #4, - By Nohemi Lewis, We possess the Inner Wisdom to make our dreams come true.

We all have had experiences with our natural "***Inner Wisdom***" making our dreams come true. *–Such as an inspired solution, seemingly out of "nowhere!" …The unexpected gift of meditation, or a dream, to guide us, or an intuitive inspiration, apparently out of "nowhere." To be happy, to create a poem, write a good article, make a business deal, deal with something we have been struggling, we get or help by doing a daily walk, or doing something which allows us to be inspired, maybe by admiring the trees, flowers, and the birds, happily chirping! –This is one of our routines every morning, my husband, and I walk a few miles; and when we come home, with intuitive inspiration, we write articles for magazines, newspapers, or books, about positive subjects, which inspire.*

This "***Inner Wisdom***" happening on the inside, as *a private feeling,* in our minds, a quiet interior source that opens our inner connection, toward something we need to examine closely, thought about to be seen by us or understood. This ***Inner Wisdom*** had many names, including *God, The Unconscious, God/Goddess, Great Spirit, Primal Energy, Divine Inspiration, and Intuition.*

The name "***Inner Wisdom***" has special significance, because this "*body intelligence*" or "*intelligence*", or "*aspect of the Divine*", *seems to always know exactly what our total being needs to evolve and heal,* and *how* and *when to manifest in the most perfect, simply and efficient ways. –Sometimes* humor frightens, scares; and sometimes is, eloquent... *It is so simple, perfect, and present, that it is often difficult to notice and acknowledge; and thrives*in an atmosphere of love, happiness, patience, acceptance, and openness.

Inner Wisdom's vehicle goes through the body or mind. *Inner Wisdom* is like coming from *Special Space or Supernatural Being.* All we have to do is quiet the mind and allow the *Inner*

Wisdom to express itself in or through the body. – Often, *Inner Wisdom clearly shows up in dreams*, visualizations, and visual creations depicted in the form of a mysterious dream, or a face or figure with a powerful presence, or even a concept or message.

Common practices that actively invite **Inner Wisdom** are *Yoga, Meditation, Breath Work, Drumming, Athletics, Chanting, Being in Nature…* All these experiences bring us to sensations and feeling, to *Inner Wisdom*, to our Soul. Wish, that all of us:

Have the inner vision that we all want to make a difference in the world, and that we *do the things we do, is just as important as why.*

Have the inner vision that families work not from a point of control and fear, but *a place of connection and collaboration.*

Have the inner vision that we stop asking people to follow the status quo, but allow them to be curious and creative, and that we recognize all ideas as potential stepping-stones to something much greater…like in brainstorming, where nothing is wrong only a stepping-stone to another thought.

Have the inner vision that we treat money as something to work for, but not something we just accumulate.

Have the inner vision that when fear shows up, we stare back at it courageously.

Have the inner wisdom and vision that we replace, trying to please each other, caring for each other as caring for ourselves.

Have the inner wisdom and vision that we communicate with meaning and purpose, saying what really matters, and not what we think people want us to say.

Have the inner wisdom and vision that we commit to lifelong relationships that stretch across the boundaries of geography.

Have the inner wisdom and visions that we open to connecting on a deep level, so we can mutually benefit and enrich each other's lives, instead of away from us

Have the inner wisdom and vision that we become a universe that shares our collective intelligence and inner wisdom… That together, we create such creativity, strength, and insight, for future generations, to look back at this time, as the beginning of the world, to grow up.

As life would have it, and we have the inner wisdom and vision together, we can change our families, friends, and the whole world, leading from Inside!

Let's have the inner wisdom and vision together,—*making our dreams come true, because nobody really does anything alone— when we ensure the Inner wisdom and Vision together, we can truly have the inner vision abundantly and synergistically! We all have the will to win, desire to succeed, urge to reach our full potential… these are the keys that will unlock the door to personal excellence. Let us give you some smart advice from sages, so you always have with you the Inner wisdom and vision.*

—Everyone smiled during and after the seminar, invited all to the next session. Smiling, they left with promises to come back. — *In the mean-time, we shared some words of the Masters*

"He who knows all the answers has not been asked all the questions."   – Confucius

With chocolate and an Ice Buffet, we celebrated in advance, the next visit to one of the places that had attracted world-wide attention through innovative real estate projects, sports events, conferences and many Guinness records...This is the great Dubai!

Dubai is an impressive place that mixes modern culture with history, adventure with excellent shopping and entertainment. Admire a show at the Dubai Opera, Observe downtown from atop the Burj Khalifa, and spend an afternoon along Dubai Creek exploring gold, textile, and spice souks. You can float above the desert dunes in a hot air balloon, climb aboard a high-speed ride at IMG Worlds of Adventure, or skydive over the Palm Jumeirah.

On *April 15th*, we started leaving *Cochin*, this gorgeous ship started her 3 day, 1600 nautical mile sea passage towards *Dubai*. Overnight, and throughout our passage, we will head North West through the Arabian Sea, with a passage speed of 19 knots.

April 16th, –We had the chance to admire a mix of familiar operatic and classical material, performed by New Zealand's leading Tenor, Benjamin. He had performed concerts to audiences around the world, including New York, Tuscany, Barcelona London, Sydney, Melbourne, Brisbane, and the Pacific Islands, with the Royal Court Theater Orchestra under the musical director Bill Gibson; and as usual, we had a wonderful time!

Next day April 17th, –beside walking, resting and having wonderful meals, we attended another night of show-time with Virtuosic Piano Entertainer *Maria King*. She revealed her unique style, personality, and humor, as she skillfully entertains at the piano many different styles of music such as Billy Joel, David Brubeck, Peggy Lee, and Gershwin's *"Rhapsody in Blue"* and more… –Of course, we did not want to miss this wonderful show!

April 18th, Read, the amazing advance information about **Dubai**… *"Dubai* refers to either, one of the seven emirates that make up the *United Arab Emirates* on the *Persian Gulf*, or that emirate's main city. Although, *Arabic* is the official language, *English* is very widely spoken by residents; besides *Urdu*, *Persian*, *Hindi*, *Telugu*, *Bengali*, *Tamil*, *Tagalog*, *Chinese*, *Malayalam*, and other languages are also spoken in *Dubai* by its many foreign residents. Besides, Dubai has the largest population and is the second largest emirate by the area, after *Abu Dhabi*.

That night, as guests, joined Captain Christopher Wells, for a continued World Voyage itinerary relaxing leisure time, with a great celebration to visit Dubai, with a cocktail party with music and delicious "empanadas".

Dubai is a place of fascinating contrasts. A distinctive blend of modern city and timeless desert, east and west, old and new, Dubai has something for everyone, as this is one of the world's fastest growing cities. Its evolution from a collection of Bedouin settlements around a creek to a modern city full of skyscrapers has been dramatic.

Dubai is the second largest of the seven emirates of the United Arab Emirates (UAD). It is on the southern shore of the Arabian Gulf in the southeastern part of the Arabian Peninsula. Dubai City is the main commercial center of the UAE, the rest of the emirates is desert with very few inhabitants.

Small fishing communities have probably existed on the coast for thousands of years… The natural harbor of Dubai Creek was undoubtedly a port-of-call on the trade route between Mesopotamia and the Indus Valley.

It was not until the late 18th century that the small pearling village began to change. The Al Faheidi Fort built around 1799 to defend the city from invaders: some 40 years later Dubai broke away from the influence of the more-powerful Abu Dhabi. It was then that the Al Maktoum family moved into the village and this family was to play a most important part in the development of Dubai.

In the 1830s, *Dubai* depended on fishing, dhow building, and pearl diving; neighboring Sharjah (now also part of the UAE) was the main center of trade. However, by the late 1870's *Dubai* had been principal port on the Gulf coast and one of the Trucial States – various truces signed with Britain. By 1920, more than 400 ships had been base here, and the souks (markets) were developed.

Pearls continued to be the mainstay of the city's prosperity, until the industry collapsed after the introduction of cultural pearls, in 1930's. Gold then became the dominant influence, even if the trade with some countries was often illegal; it remained a major money earner. In addition, they discovered offshore oil field in 1963. Then, exports boosted the already considerable wealth of the city. At the same time, *Dubai* built up a re-exports to Azerbaijan and Russia have expanded dramatically recently.

In 1971, the British finally left the area and the emirates of *Abu Dhabi, Dubai, Sharjah, Ajam, Umm Al Quwain, and Fujirah* solidified in 1971. Then, *Ras Al Khaimah* formed the federation of UAE.

– "The United Arab Emirates (UAE) is a federation designed in 1971 by the then Trucial States after independence from Britain. Since then, it has grown to one of the Middle East's most important economic centers. Although each state *–Abu Dhabi, Dubai, Ajman, Fujairah, Ras al Khaimah, Sharjah* and *Umm al Qaiwain –* maintains a large level of independence, a Supreme Council of Rulers made up of the seven emirs, who appoint the Prime Minister and the Cabinet, governs the UAE. We got the story about the economic crash of 2008 that left *Dubai* with large debts to foreign investors who were trapped during the prosperous years, and accepted assistance from Abu *Dhabi*. In December 2009, Abu Dhabi gave Dubai $10bn handout to pay off the debts of the government-owned company Dubai World".

Today, the city is flourishing – the airport handles over 3,350,000 guests monthly, the deep water harbor at *Port Rashid* opened in 1972 and is nowadays exclusively for cruise ships and small pleasure crafts. They also finished the supertanker dry dock, seven years later; then, opened the deep-water port in 1979, with the world's largest man-made peace of art, in the Middle East. In addition, they finally, inaugurated the *The Jebel Ali, in South of Dubai.* –Isn't it marvelous?

The city has also superb sporting facilities, including championship golf courses and important horseraces. Also, have 274 hotels, for the growing number of visitors. –Many of which, are of the highest standard.

One of the most famous and luxurious hotels in the world, is the *Burj Al Arab*... Fortunately, personnel is widely English spoken and understood, for visitors from UK, English is widely spoken.

We found out the longer-term assessment of *Dubai's* property market; however, showed depreciation, some properties lost as much as 64% of the value from 2001 to November 2008. The largest scale real estate development projects have led to the construction of some of the tallest skyscrapers and largest projects in the world, such as the *Emirates Tower*, the *Burj Khalifa*, which raises 828 meters (2,717 ft.) and contains 160 floors. The tower has stood as both the tallest building in the world, and the tallest manufactured structure of any kind in the world.

The second-tallest building in *Dubai is the Princes Tower*, 414-meters (1,358 ft.) which also stands as the world's tallest residential skyscraper of *Dubai*. The land along *Sheikh Zayed Road* was the first to develop, followed by the Dubai Marina neighborhood and the Business Bay District.

Overall, *Dubai* has 18 completed and topped-out buildings that rise at least 300 metres (984 feet) height, which is more than any other city in the world. Dubai has 73 completed and highest buildings that rise at least 200 metres (656 ft.) in height, again which is more than any other city in the world. Based on the average height of the ten tallest completed buildings, Dubai has the tallest skyline in the Middle East and the world. As of 2012, the skyline of Dubai is ranked sixth in the world with 248 buildings rising at least 100 metres (330 feet.) height.

The history of skyscrapers in Dubai began with the construction of ***Dubai World Trade Centre*** in 1979, which is usually regarded as the first high-rise in the city. At the time of its completion, it also stood as the tallest building in the **Middle East**. Since 1999, and especially from 2005 onwards, Dubai has been the site of an extremely large skyscraper building boom, with all 73 of its buildings over 200 metres (656 ft.) tall completed after 1999. In less than ten years, the city has amassed one of the largest skylines in the world; it is now home to the world's tallest building, the world's tallest residence, and the world's second tallest hotel. As of 2012, 363 new skyscrapers are under construction in Dubai; additionally, there are over 640 active high-rise developments that have been proposed for construction in the city.

The Tower, which will form the centerpiece of the 3.7 square mile (six square-kilometer) *Dubai Creek* redevelopment project, will be "a notch taller" than *the Burj Khalifa, Mohamed Alabbar*, the chairman of Emaar Properties (the same company behind the *Burj Khalifa)* revealed this April when the plans were first announced. The developers are aiming to complete its construction before the Dubai World Expo in 2020.

Highlighted features of The Tower include The Pinnacle Room, a slender, streamlined structure with a needlepoint-like tip, as well as several "garden" observation decks, decorated with trees and other greenery, which will offer 360 degree views of the city.

The building will also have glass balconies that rotate outside the wall of the tower, as well as a luxury hotel and 18 to 20 floors of shops, restaurants and other tourist facilities, the company said.

They also have in mind, to build in the same area of downtown a 63-story luxury hotel.

Note… The third major skyscraper fire in Dubai since 2012 raised renewed fears about the use of highly combustible materials on the exterior facades of hundreds of skyscrapers throughout the UAE. *Let's change the subject of great construction in Dubai, who places it in the most fantastic subject!*

Dubai's population is about 3,000,000 people, including the present ruler His Highness Sheikh Mohammed bin *Rashid Al Martoum.* The diversity of cuisine in *Dubai* is a reflection of the cosmopolitan nature of the society. Arab food is very popular and is available everywhere in the city, from the small shawarma diners in *Deira* and *Al Karama* to the upscale restaurants in *Dubai's* many hotels. Fast food, South Asian, Chinese cuisines are also very popular and are widely available.

Within easy walking distance, we found the narrow alleyway of *Dubai* Old Souk (silks, cottons, lace, wool, and chiffon) *Al Juma Mosque* and the *Grand Mosque* are between *Dubai Museum* and the *Creek*; nearby *Al Faheidi* Road is the place to go for textiles, electrical appliances and photographic equipment.

The *Dubai Creek –Khor Dubai–* splits the city in two; and another amassed fact, when found out the government's decision to diversify from a trade-based, oil-reliant economy to one that is service and tourism-oriented. The decision also made property more valuable, resulting in rapid appreciation.

We admired the *Miracle Garden* with over 45 million flowers over a 72,000 square meter site and, as well as traditional flowerbeds, it features topiary-style displays with booms fashioned into the shapes of hearts, stars, igloos, pyramids and much more.

Floral displays changes each season so that repeat visitors will have a new experience each time. We also enjoyed the western side of the Creek, and the *Jumeriah Mosque,* a lovely example of modern Islamic architecture and particularly impressive when floodlit after dark. By the way… during our fantastic cruise, Captain Christopher invited us for dinner at the *Armani Hotel (6 Six Star),* the most fantastic Hotel in Dubai (Remember the table number was 22. We had all kinds of Champagne, all kinds of wines, (in moderation) and all kinds of delicious appetizers, and a succulent dinner with an international sensational show.

We all admired the amazing water fountains, raised from the first to the 20th floor, like dancing in all kind of colors and lovely music! At our table we had the surprise to be with people from Latin-American countries and Spain; we all shared the same language of Cervantes; some-times mixed with English. This was one of the most fantastic experiences, during the cruise!

After spending the late afternoon, as well as the night steaming towers Muscat, transiting the straits of Hormuz once more, before setting South Easterly courses through the Gulf of Oman towards *Muscat,* we arrived at *Muscat, Oman,* at 8 a.m.

This visit to Dubai inspired, without discouragement by anything in the future… Was motivating, to set my dreams in motion again… –The time has come once more to listen to the music; remembering that we are the only ones who act in our best interest.

CHAPTER 24

It was a dream, visiting this strategically located port of the Arabian Peninsula from ancient times, since Muscat is now the capital of modern Oman; a picturesque, medieval structure with contemporary quarters.

Oman is a fascinating country located on the eastern tip of the Arabian Peninsula. To us, Oman is a mysterious nation since we do not hear many people speaking about it very often. Visiting Oman is very easy, because it is very safe and full of very friendly and hospitable people.

*On April 20, we arrived at **Muscat**...* The capital and largest city of the *Sultanate of Oman* is an independent state in the southeast corner of the *Arabian Peninsula.* The city is located on the Arabian Sea and the financial and economic center of the country.

In 1932, *Sultan Said bin Taimur* became leader of the country, then known as Muscat and Oman. His regime was harsh, the country had little contact with the outside world, and the economy crashed and ended. –The glory days of the former *Omani Empire* were a faded memory… A rebellion was crushed in the north only with the reluctant aid of the British.

Problems began in the 1960's when a guerrilla movement in the southern mountains, aided by Marxist forces from the Yemen, rebelled against the sultan. Oman soon declined in wealth and influence.

(The new Sultan had attended the *Royal Military Academy at Sandhurst,* and then served with a *British infantry* regiment in Germany for a year holding a staff appointment. His father called him to take over, after his son had studied local government in England. Before the country descended into total anarchy five years later, he was the ruler of his country; and soon he was the *Sultanate of Oman* because on July 23, 1970, the sultan's son, Qaboos bin Said, overthrew his father in a bloodless palace coup.)

The Sultanate made outstanding progress sin 1970, without losing sight of its traditional values. During that time, he ordered to build modern hospitals, improved the antiquated road system, upgraded the country's ports, and opened a new international airport.

–The facts reflect the positive changes made in those recent times; the average life expectancy in 1970 was just 47 years; today it has risen to 71 years for men and 76 years for women. They built several high-class hotels to encourage the development of tourism and cruise ships now regularly visit *Muscat.*

Something good happened in 2006, *Muscat* was named the "*Arabian Capital City of Culture*". They completed the magnificent *Al Alam Palace,* located between the two forts of the waterfronts, in the early 1970; –this was the palace and official resident of *Sultan Qaboos bin Said. Then, they built The National Museum, the Oman Museum, also, the Natural History Museum.*

–At night, we were in route to Salalah, Oman, anticipating beauty and happiness.

On April 22nd, early in the morning, we arrived at the Port of Salalah, Oman, the capital city of the government of *Dhofar* in the South of Oman, and the second largest city in the country.

Salalah is the capital of the southern region of *Dhofar* in the Sultanate of Oman, and independent state in the eastern part of the Arabian Peninsula. The Republic of Yemen, Saudi Arabia, and the United Arab Emirates border Oman. Guests land at the recently developed deep-water berth in Port Salalah, formally known as *Port Raysut*, ten miles from Salalah.

The Omani civilization dates back many thousands of years. The *Queen of Sheba* may have had a palace in *Dhofar* and the earliest known settlement in the region dates back to the 13th century BC. *Salalah* was famous in ancient times for its frankincense in the 13-century AD; *Marco Polo* described it as a prosperous city. It was not until the early 1800s that *Salalah* came under the rule of the sultans of Oman.

They signed the treaty of friendship with Great Britain in the late 19th century, The Dhafari rebellion of Marxists from Yemen was not crushed immediately, until 1975 with British and American help peace finally came to the southernmost part of the country now called the Sultanate of Oman. It maintains good relations with the

West especially with the United Kingdom, and with the Arab states. They transformed the brown landscape of *Salalah* into a beautiful and lush green, and locals and tourists alike congregate to Salah during this time.

This place is very famous or its ancient frankincense trade, with the UNESCO including several ancient settlements (*Al Balid, Sumharam, Shisr,* and *Wadi Dawkah, in Dhofar,* which is in the *World Heritage* List appropriately name it the "*Land of Frankincense*". For thousands of years *Salalah* is still the first one, for the quality and quantity of *frankincense products.*

Want to remind to all of us, "We are always students, never masters, so let's keep moving forward to see the results!"

The 23rd of April, at sea in route to Aqaba and Limassol, we had the "International Corner "–our last Seminar Program #5, "With Belief and Creativity we live in, and Keep Happiness."

The place of the Seminar over again filled the capacity, with people standing or sitting on the floor! – Nobody could be happier! – And all of these many –now friends–, attended to all five seminars! The participants were very grateful to "Cunard" for being very perceptive in recognizing their needs as human beings… by providing this services to them… The contributors, –at all times–, were very thankful for this innovative and successful program about "Happiness" so, also, feel grateful to them.

After I started the Seminar, Observed sad faces, and then, heard comments like this: "It is so sad that the good thinks have to end sometimes! " We hope to have the chance to see you again in future trips..." –Let us hope for the best, since we all enjoy discussing together, getting good results!

Let us talk about our last subject, **"With belief and creativity, we live in, and keep happiness**... "As we make our way, throughout life, our purpose is to make our burdens light, allowing us to live happily. "

The one thing we all have in common as children is our desire to be happy. –Remember, after dad and uncle's death, I asked Aunt Angie "Is it possible to live happily when confronted with the challenges of daily life?" –Her answer was, "Try and keep trying... Do always your best... Don't give up... and one of these days you will obtain happiness".

"When I was a very young adult, was already a mother, I wanted to watch my children go through elementary school, serve missions, attend college; but I did not have the chance to get a job since I was pregnant! To survive I had to get a job! Since their husband/father abandoned us. Of course, I had to seek employment to pay for baby-sitter... to pay rent... to get food... send children to private school... –In other words, to raise and support them, totally! –Do not forget, that there are unknown circumstances, which detour us from living our youth, but at the same time we learn responsibility! "

Was wondering how I could raise my kids... being able to be close to them... and, at the same time, have the resources to help them along the way!

Mother, after the death of our father, supporting her five kids, and later had another seven, –all without a daddy … did not have enough to feed all of them; was working at all time! Yes, she had a Master Degree in Philosophy… However, living in a small town, what kind of job could she seek? Her only solution was to work at the Notary, eight hours a day, and sewing clothes for dozens of shops; and this was not enough! Also at night, she was balancing accounting accounts for local business! She had more than enough to do!

–Sure, at young age, we all wanted to be happy. However, for many reasons, happiness was an elusive, fleeting state, that we captured only for brief moments, before floated away like dust in the wind!

The truth was, and still is, that as human beings; almost all of our forward momentums are to pursue happiness. Even the desire to socialize, to love, and to connect with other human beings is driven by our desire to be happy. We pursue to get a better job, higher status and wealth. – *The root of everything was and it is, to chase happiness. This certainly does not mean that everything we chase will bring us happiness.* In fact, a big part of our struggle with life is figuring out what makes us happy, and more important, what makes us consistently happy. We can learn about the nature of happiness by reading quotes about happiness from the wise men and women who came before us. Here are some quotes about being happy to help you find your own path to joy and satisfaction in life.

"If you want to be happy, be."
                                – Leo Tolstoy

"We all live with the objective of being happy; our lives are all different and yet the same."
                                – Anne Frank

"Don't cry because it's over, smile because it happened." - Dr. Seuss

"For every minute you are angry you lose sixty seconds of happiness." — Ralph Waldo Emerson

Anybody can read thousands of quotations to analyze and to learn. You will read them; you will agree, but *the right approach is, to follow them, every day of your life. -Here is the right approach!*

-Release negativity or disapproval, totally from life.

-Learn to forgive and forget… to let go…-Exonerate your adversary forever.

-See every trial, every judgement, and every verdict, every conclusion, as an opportunity for further growth.

-Express appreciation, and gratitude, for what you have.

-Be more optimistic, and confident about the future and your ability to accomplish life goals.

-Open up to success and identify failures or mistakes that happen along the way.

-Know that nobody is perfect; we are all here to entertain and be entertained.

-Don't worry about little mistakes. -Take plenty of "worry escapes" where you clear your mind of upsetting, for a certain lengths of time.

-If you want to be positive, surround with positive people… Develop positive relationships that help uplift your life.

-Accept and love yourself, for the exceptional gifts and talents that you bring to life.

-Devote less time trying to please others; and spend more time trying to please your higher self. ...Take life less seriously and learn to laugh at yourself.

-Be kind to others.

-Treat everyone with kindness. Not only does it help others to feel better, then, notice that you too feel good after having a positive interaction with others.

-Speak well of others. When you speak negatively of others, you will attract more negativity to yourself, but when you speak positively of others, you will attract more positivity to yourself.

-Truly listen. Be present and mindful to what others are really saying when they speak. Support them without bringing yourself into it.

-Be careful with your words. Speak gentler, kinder, and wiser.

-Respect others and their free will.

-Practice generosity and give it without expecting anything in return. Get involved with service opportunities and offer what you can for a greater cause.

-Smile more...to family, to neighbors, to strangers. It not only changes how you feel, but how they feel too.

-Live in the present. – Try with all your power not to replay negative events or worry about the future.

-Be grateful for your life, for every day. Observe the constant and natural flow of change.

-Work on your reactions to outer circumstances and learn how to approach life harmoniously.

-Choose a healthy life style… –medical doctors, psychologists, and writers recommend this practice….

-Keep a daily routine… Get up if possible at the same time every morning, preferably early. Setting to a natural rhythm, will make it easier to wake up and feel energized.

-Get enough sleep. Proper sleep is linked to positive personality characteristics like optimism, self-esteem, and even problem solving.

-Exercise daily to the point of sweating. –It helps to purify the body, and help to prevent stress, relieve depression, and positively improve your mood.

-Laugh more. This is the best remedy that fights the negative effects of stress, and stimulates a sense of well-being and joy.

-Practice deep breathing. Periodically yawn and you will feel air go directly to your brain. The body and mind are connected. Emotions affect the physical systems in the body, and the condition of the body affects the mind. By relaxing and releasing tension through the breath or yoga practice, you feel calm and centered throughout the day.

-Be creative. This will not only challenge you to learn new things, but will also help to keep your mind in a positive place. Practice living in the present moment and being a channel for the divine flow of creativity.

-Practice meditation. Even as little as 10 minutes of meditation a day can lead to physical changes in the brain that improve concentration and focus; calm the nervous system, and help you to become more kind and compassionate, and even more humorous. Then bring joy and peace into your daily life. (Try this exercise…Periodically raise your eyes upward as if slightly looking upward toward the space in between your eyebrows. The yogis call this living in your spiritual eye or third eye.).

-Be authentic. Telling the truth keeps you free inside, builds trust in relationships, and improves your will power and the ability to entice success.

Do you want more advice? -Always, try doing your best!

Made copy of these pages, My Dear Readers of this Program, about *Happiness* I advise you to keep them handy, and read them, if possible each day to remind you to try the best.

Know we can follow the most important and positive advice, and eventually, we will live a Happy Life, which make our existence more peaceful and cheerful. Doing this, we live a happy long time.

Remember, nobody is perfect! Just keep trying your best, to live happily and healthy.

Looking back is not going to help us, either… Moving forward is the right thing to do. Also, remember… The best philosophy in life, no matter what happens, is, to move forward!

At the end of this incredible program about HAPPINESS, I requested a "volunteer" from the group to read my poem "A *WILLING PASSENGER*" which I wrote for my new dear friends on this Cruise. –Happily, *Mr. Hegarty*, an American Attorney at Law, read it with all his appreciation, to the participants… and at the end, they collected a copy to take with them as a remembrance from these lecturers about Happiness.

– "Hope everybody read the poem, and follow the advice to keep *Happiness* in their life!

On the next page, you will find a very special poem…

A WILLING PASSENGER
© *By, Nohemi*

From youth remember pain and grief
I was an unwillingly bird without bulky wings
Flying under strong wings of insecurity
Through rainstorms, flowing gloomy
Fallibility throws anybody down the cliff

Through waving and agitated seas
Ups and downs bent and split
Over time, became an abiding sense of peace
Flying, soaring started lifting higher,
Faith and Happiness let forget the cliffs

Fears of seclusion and lonesomeness
With heartaches of broken spirit,
Tears of defeat wore out the virtuous heart…
It was then, when had let go of everything.
Then, faith and happiness glided to lofty peaks.

Realized had no fears to cross the seas
Or, to do anything, or to hold back,
Taking sure steps, actually reached the great hills
Allowing me true new freedom and peace
To breathe, take heights or frightening peaks…

Now, I have baskets full of treats…
Accepting Happiness, Very Happy, and Free!

April 27th at sea in route to Limassol, Cyprus… Arrived April 28th

The 28ᵗʰ of April, we are in the Port of Limassol, Cyprus. This city is renowned for its extensive cultural traditions, and is home to the Cyprus University of Technology.

This famous University was founded by law on December 2003 and welcomed its first students on September 2007. CUT aspires to develop into a modern, pioneering and internationally recognized university, able to offer education and high level research in leading fields of research that currently have a great impact on the economic, technological and scientific sectors of humanity.

Limassol, on the island of Cypress is the third largest island in the Mediterranean, lies tucked away in the northeast corner, 40 miles from the nearest point of southern *Turkey,* 60 miles from *Syria* to the east, and 240 miles from *Port Said* to the south.

About a hundred million years ago, the area bed of the Eastern Mediterranean cracked under the crushing strains of the great landmasses to the north and south, and mountains of molten rock broke through to become islands, one of which became Cyprus. The coastline of 486 miles is indented and rocky, but there are sandy beaches and peaceful covers as well. The total area is roughly equivalent to that of Norfolk and Suffolk in England combined.

The *Kyrenia* range of mountains runs parallel to the north coast and at the eastern end forms the "panhandle", the peninsula that, to the British, gave the island the appearance of a frying pan. Rising to nearly 3,500 feet, these mountains help shelter the interior plain, the *Mesooria* –literally "in between the mountains"- creating extremely hot conditions in the summer months. The Troodos range in the south-west rise to over 6,000 feet; both ranges still have plenty of forest consisting of oaks and pines, cedars and cypresses.

Around 2,500 B.C. the discovery of copper amounted to an industrial revolution on the island, and due to the Bronze Age (swords), Cypress assumed the position of great commercial importance in the comparatively civilized Mediterranean world.

Before the time of *Tutankhamun, Cyprus* came within the orbit of *Egypt,* and the tribute paid in return for protection appears to have been copper.

Cyprus is wealthy in other ways, where Man has assisted Nature... Citrus fruits, cereals, potatoes, carrots and other vegetables are cultivated with bananas, figs, strawberries, melons, avocados and pomegranates. Olive and carob trees – the fruit of which, the locust bean, John the Baptist ate in the wilderness – predominate in the valleys and lowland areas. They planted Vineyards wherever grapes will grow, but their main concentration is the south-west. Here they produce the famous "Commandaria" dessert wine dating from the occupation of the islands by the crusaders of the *Knights of St. John.*

Mentioning of the Knights brings us to a brief historical survey following the early Egyptian period...

Around 800 B.C. Greeks from the west and Phoenicians from present-day Lebanon started colonizing *Cyprus*; they looked with favor on its climate and natural resources, its harbors and forests. Swallowed up by the empire of *Alexander the Great*, the island later became a very small cog in the vast machine of the Roman Empire, in fact due to the Iron Age (again swords) it becoming a small part of the province of Cilicia on the Turkish mainland to the north. When the *Roman Empire* was split in half at the end of the fourth-century, *Cyprus* was ruled from *Constantinople*, and though the Arabs attracted twice, it remained *Christian* under *Byzantine* rule and naturally played a part in the Crusades, being the last port of call in route to the *Holy Land.*

Richard the Lionheart married Berengaria of Navarre in Cyprus before he did battle with Saladin. He had recently seized the island on his way to the Holy Land, because the Byzantine ruler had insulted his fiancée. However, when Richard left to continue the Crusade, he sold Cyprus to the Knights Templars for 100,000 gold bezants. After the fall of Acre near Haifa in 1291, these Knights of St. John of Jerusalem made their headquarters in *Limassol* and stayed on the island until they moved yet further west to Rhodes in 1309. Even so, they retained an outpost at *Kolossi in Cypress.*

In the 15th century, by means of intrigue, bribery, and murder, *Cyprus* came into the power of the *Venetians*. Shakespeare set "Othello, the Moor of *Venice*" partially in *Cyprus*. After a century, the *Turks* stayed for 300 years, until *Britain* bought the island in 1878. Cyprus achieved independence in 1960 after Greek Cypriot guerrilla fighters had harassed the British forces for years in the name of freedom and political union with *Greece*. However, the British retained two sovereign bases, *Episkopi-Akrotiri* and *Dhekelia,* as they do today.

In 1964, a U.N. a peacekeeping force arrived in *Cyprus* because it was clear that more trouble than usual was brewing between the Greeks and the Turks. An uneasy peace was maintained for ten years until the mainland Greeks attempted a *coup d'état*, thus giving the Turks an excuse to invade the north to "protect" their own minority. They divided the island with the Turkish community occupying the northern part after expelling the resident Greeks, most of who fled to the south, which is now officially the Greek-Cypriote side. At present, the population is 740,000, which includes 88,000 of native Cypriot Turks living in the North, which make up 13.5% of the population. Whereas for almost 30 years, travel between the South and the Turkish occupied North part of the island, are not allowed to do so unless via certain official checkpoints, with minor formalities.

Compared with other cities on this island, *Limassol* was a latecomer on the scene, attaining prominence only after the decline of Amathus to the east and Curium to the west. Interestingly enough the even though the town became a Crusader base, it did not permit the previous owner *Richard the Lionheart* to marry *Berengaria* in the Castle.

Racked by earthquakes and attacked by the Saracens, burned by the Genovese, sacked by the Egyptians, and devastated by the Turks, Limassol has not enjoyed a happy history. Five hundred years ago a traveler remarked: "One dismal church remains standing, but it has no bells. A few Latin priests still inhabit the place, but their manners are not edifying". The artist J. Turner spoke of 150 mud houses in the early 19th century, but he also mentioned the considerable export of wine and carobs, a trade that has gone on to financially strengthen the area.

Since 1974, the population has increased so rapidly that Limassol is the most important seafront city in the Greek sector; it has a busy harbor and is an important maritime center in the Eastern Mediterranean.

The Venetians restored a Castle and Old Carob Mill, set with a view of the town, so now it provides a faithful and interesting example of military architecture from that time. Apart from the *Great Hall*, there are other rooms and passages, cells and a chapel, everything tastefully arranged now as a museum with exhibits ranging from early pottery to Crusader silver. You will be happy to climb the spiral stairway to the roof, to have the picturesque view of the town as we did.

The *Limassol Museum*, at the east of the main town by the public gardens, holds artefacts gathered from as far away as *Paphos* and starting with the earliest period of the island history. You can appreciate handmade seals, glass, alabaster, and gold among the exhibits.

Limassol has developed about four kilometers of the waterfront… We observed pathways for walking near the sea, and they installed benches to sit and enjoy the sunshine and sea view. We had the chance to visit *The Knights Hospital* of *St. John of Jerusalem*, who made their headquarters in *Limassol* when they were finally driven from the *Holy Land* in 1291, and when they left *Cyprus* for *Rhodes* a few years later. They kept a post at *Kolossi*. Only the retained walls of the castle remain.

At nearly 6,500 feet, radar installations and a TV tower have usurped the site of *Aphrodite's temple*. From the summit of *Mount*

Olympus, there is extensive view over the *Mesaoria* toward *Nicosia* and down to *Limassol* on the south coast.

They declared the mountain range "A *National Park*" with a number of nature trails, to view the beautiful landscape and its flora... We took a trail starting at *Troodos Resort,* and explored the 1951 meters of *Mounts Olympus,* a*nd the Persefoni trails range, from 3km to 9 km.* Admired beaches on the east and west of *Limassol; Akti Olympion* starts opposite the Orthodox Catholic Church, extending for several miles to the east. An *Aki Olympion* local informed us that other beaches in *Limassol* do not have permission to display the special Blue Flag.

This information alerted our curiosity... *"Foreign settlers and traders over the past 3.000 years have brought their recipes and many of these have been introduced into Cypriot cooking. These foreign flavors have combined with the food produced on the island to give Cyprus its own traditional cuisine. The island cooking is still wonderful if you avoid the more obvious tourist's establishments".*

These have been favorites "Mezes d'oeuvres" (Humus and a peace of chicken with oil), "Taramasolata" (Cucumber with smoked cod's roe, Jougher with garlic are served with pita bread), "Tzatziki" (Cucumber in Joughur with garlic are served with pita bread, chicken, as an omelets is served)!

Since we started getting sweet tooth's, at times we ordered Backhaba...it's on thin pastry stuffed with nuts and doused in honey, or Loukoumades...it's fried puffballs in honey, complemented by the rich Commandaria desert, and wine of the Knights of St. John. In addition, it is a refreshing drink after 10 in the morning. —This sour brandy, soda water, lemon juice, and angostura bitters are Michael's favorite at any time. Because I am a diabetic, I only had little tastes. **-After all the hors d'oeuvres, we felt in paradise!**

CHAPTER 28

We set a South Easterly course through the Eastern Mediterranean Sea, until we arrived on the Cost of Israel, at the Port of Haifa on the 29th of April at 7am.

Haifa is the third largest city in Israel, with 250 thousand people. Haifa is one of the largest industrial centers in Israel and a hub for transport, trade, shipping, and tourism. The city has institutions for higher education and scientific research, theatre, auditoriums, museums and many varied cultural and recreational facilities. The city sits at the foot of the Carmel Mountains, on its Eastern, Northern, and Western slopes on the top of the range round the top of the bay area.

Theodore Herzl predicted this town would be "the city of the future" how true his words were.

Where "Carmel Touches the Sea", lies the city of **Haifa**, flanked by the Mediterranean, and crowned by *Mountain Carmel*, it is Israel's third largest city and entry port to the Holy Land.

Haifa has changed hands many times in its troubled history. It was in existence during the Moslem conquest of Palestine in 636 A.D., and by 1100, when the Crusaders conquered *Haifa;* the place had grown into a fortified town of some importance. The town continued to thrive under the Crusaders and by 1154 also served as the main port for *Tiberius*, the capitol of *Galilee*. The fortress was destroyed when the famous *Saladin* conquered *Haifa*.

The Crusades' rule finally ended in 1291, with Mameluke *Sultan Qualawun of Egypt's* capture of the *Kingdom of Acre*, which forced the Crusaders to withdraw to *Cyprus. Haifa w*as destroyed, and a traveler going through the town in 1350, found it completely in ruins.

During the 18th century, Haifa remained a squalid little hamlet, but gained some renown as a pirates' lair. Its doom, however, was near. In 1750 *Zahir el Omar*, the great *Sheikh of Galilee,* quarreled with the people of Haifa and razed the then village to the ground. Eight years later, in 1758, due to the whim of the same *Zahir el Omar*, they rebuilt the city, just to the east of the former Haifa. The population increased slowly. By 1815, it had reached 1,000 and by 1913, it had reached 15,000.

The First World War temporarily halted the development of Haifa, and after the conquest of the town by the British in 1918, the Mandate was established and the *Ismailia-Kantara-Gaza-Haifa* railway constructed. *The Damascan* rail link had already established its trading viability,

After the erection of the first electric power plant, it was a steady influx of Jewish immigrants... By 1023, the population grew to 24,000 and the figure rose to 100,000 by 1936. Today the residents have grown to around a quarter of a million.

The creation of the State of *Israel* in 1948 gave once again a new impetus to the growth of *Haifa*. It is now the premier port of Israel and a mayor industrial as well as a holiday center, being also the home of *Technion* – an advance Technology Institute – and University. The city has established international standards with its theatre, symphony orchestra and other cultural institutions.

Later, they divided Haifa into three main parts. Downtown, which is the commercial area for banking, shipping and wholesale trade, contain the two Railway Stations and the Bus Terminal. *Hadar Carmel* a residential and commercial area located in the middle, hallway up *Mt Carmel*. The third district is *Mount Carmel*, which is the main residential and shopping area. The mountain rises quickly from the Port to a height of 300 meters. *Hadar Carmel*, the main shopping area with its three lined paved boulevards and cafes, is about halfway up. *Mount Carmel* itself provides an excellent vantage point from which to view the whole area. The 550-meter-high summit of this impressive landmark also boats a Nature Reserve.

Exploring *Haifa*, we found *Baha'i Shrine and Gardens* on the slopes of *Mount Carmel*, which is a local landmark, and the Shrine of the *Baha'i Faith*, where they buried the Bob (*Siyyid 'Ali-Muhammad*) founder of the *Baha'i religion*. The golden domed mausoleum is set in beautiful formal gardens. Open from 09.00 – 1200 hrs. The gardens are open from eight to five, admission free.

We admired the Elijah's Cave, the most sacred Jewish site in *Haifa*. Tradition holds that this grotto gave shelter to *Elijah* in his fight from *King Ahab*. –This the site where *Christians* believe the *Holy Family* sheltered on their return from *Egypt*. Hollowed out of rock at the foot of the steep Cape Carmel, the Carmelite Monastery stands above it, as does the Stela Maris Lighthouse. A cable car runs from the corniche to the Stella Maris observation point. The inside of Elijah's Cave is open on Sundays – The areas hours are, open from Monday to Friday, from nine to noon; closed on Saturday; and admission is free.

The Haifa Museum of ancient and modern art is located at *Rehov Shabbetai Levi*. There is a large collection of Greco-Roman artifacts recovered from the Bay of Haifa as well as items found in the vicinity.

The Prehistoric Museum and the Zoo was near the top of *Carmel Gan Ha Em*. The museum is adjacent to the *Zoo of Haifa; and The Railway Museum* is located in the old *Haifa-East Railway Station*. According to information stamped on the wall, "This was site was established in 1882.

–This is perhaps the most authentic and evocative part of the country from the New Testament point of view. This spot 700 feet below sea level, the water forms Israel's chief reservoir and is renowned for the catch known as *St. Peter's* fish. However, this beautiful stretch of water, bordered by the Galan Heights on the east, can turn in a trice from an azure millpond into a green and snarling demon, as the disciples discovered.

We passed the Jordan River and the area of *Tiberius*, which are biblical names. –We were fascinated with all these treasures, but we had to hurry up, to go back to the ship.

Later we visited *The Garden of Gethsemane*, when were in Jerusalem. –According to the New Testament and history, Jesus spent His last hours here, before Roman soldiers arrested Him.

CHAPTER 29

After a late departure from Haifa yesterday evening, we dropped off the local pilot, then, set North Westerly courses overnight, through the Mediterranean Sea towards Kusadasi, Turkey, passing between the islands of Rhodes and Karpathos.

Kusadasi is known as the "Bird Island" located in the Aegean region of Turkey. This is a magnificent and perfect place for an unforgettable vacation. Since we love History and Culture, we did not want to miss another chance to see these wonderful historical attractions. We were happy to have further opportunity to visit these historical places, Ephesus, The House of Virgin Mary, The Temple of Artemis, Priene, Milestos and the Temple of Apollo in Didyma; then went back to the ship, very satisfied!

On May 1, we enjoyed the Entertainment *"Appassionato"*. Featuring the *Royal Cunard* Singers and Dancers, –Want to explain to all of

My Dear Readers, what did they mean by an "Extravaganza". It is an exciting style dance from around the World.

By Glenn Miller's Swing to the tantalizing *Argentinian Tango*, this show featured some of the most incredible dances ever seen at sea. With the Royal Court Theater' Orchestra, under the director Bill Gibson, presented by our entertainment Director, Paul O'Loughlin. –We really enjoyed the wonderful show… Walked around, saying hello to some friends, rested in a coffee shop, had some tea; and then it was time for dinner…Then, after, we enjoyed the most elegant and powerful production directed by acclaimed directors Moshe Leaser and Patrice Courier, featuring a supremely talented cast, superbly performing this gripping drama to Puccini's haunting score. *3D glasses* were available at the entrance to the Illuminations Theatre 30 minutes prior to the star of the show, and were collected at the end. It was fantastic!

On May 2, we arrived at the **Port** of **Kusadasi, Turkey**… This historical place is a beach resort town on Turkey's western Aegean Coast. A jumping-off point for visiting the classical runs at nearby *Ephesus* (or *Efes,*) and is a major cruise ship stop. Its seafront promenade, marina, and harbor have hotels and restaurants. Just offshore on Pigeon Island is a walled Byzantine castle that once guarded the town, connected to the mainland via causeway.

Remembered many years ago, we visited *Kusadasi*, a lively place, where old-fashioned alleys and whitewashed stone houses, rise in tiers behind the market district to the remains of the medieval walls. –Commented to my husband, "Turkey is a land of the unknown, cloaked in mystery and shadows." We found-out that famous Romans such as *Mark Antony*, Brutus, *Cassius,* and *Cicero* roamed the country, visiting its many great cities! Anyway, Turkey was and still is the home to one of the *Seven Wonders of the Ancient*

World – The *Temple of Artemis* – where tens of thousands of people came from around the world to worship.

One of the most important forms of ancient tradition is the art of carpet weaving, we learned that Turkish carpets date back over 3,000 years; they wow each carpet by hand, and each unique masterpiece lives forever! *Yes, yes, we can certify that! Since we are still adorning their covering our floors at home, for more than twenty years... and yes! We are still admiring them with all designs and colors! Unbelievably, we choose these perfect treasures to enhance our own home in California, then in Texas and now in Hawaii.*

Before making the purchase, a friend recommended this place... At the entrance, they offered a cup of apple tea, and while sipping the wonderful liquid, the store staff provided us with a brief lecture on the history and art of Turkish carpets! We appreciated the wonderful Turkish hospitality! This time, during our visit to Turkey, they encouraged people to learn more about carpets... – By-the-way, *Turkey is a shopper's paradise* and the art of carpet making, is still very strong today; same as a jewelry industry with beautiful designs.

Now, we want to be discreet, confessing to you, this incident! Went with husband to experience the traditional Turkish bath, – recommended to us "to get rid of the tiredness from our long trip"... After paying the fee for the service, at a little window, a kind woman directed us to separate dressing rooms... The woman ordered us to remove the clothes. –Of course, we each received a big white towel to cover our bodies... Then the woman guided us to different areas...

I was laid down on top of a big-round moving surface, turning slowly... then a naked woman, –the masseuse, massaged my body, after pulling the towel completely from my body. –I was shocked! –Tried to communicate with her, but she did not speak

English, or Spanish!   Tried to explain the embarrassing situation with signs, using hands; but she did not pay attention.

– I was very happy she was only interested in giving a hand massage, and using some cream to exfoliate my skin In the meantime, the big warm moving platform, did not stopped going around, until the lady, took me to the shower, and then to the dressing room to get clothed. At last noticed the skin and hair were very soft, as a baby's skin! At the end of the service, she conducted me to the dressing room. A few minutes later, my husband came out and we left! What was the lesson I learned? –Ask all the questions in advance!

(I only found out, at the end of the session, when someone who spoke English, finally explained the "good service" to me.)

–In the mean-time I would like to say, *"Find out if anyone speaks your language, otherwise you could be embarrassed with the episode!)*

–The name *Kusadasi* comes from *Kus*, a bird, and *ada*, an island. This fascinating little Turkish town lies not far away from the Greek island of *Samos*, about 55 miles south of Izmir. The coastline here was civilized when the *Britons* were painting themselves with ashes from burnt wood.

This exquisite place dates back to *Pre-Ionian* times when the *Carian's* and *Lelegians* lived in a wide plain near the temple of the *Mother Goddess*, later to become the Temple of *Artemis* or *Diana*, one of the Seven Wonders of the *Ancient World*. In the 11th century B.C., The Ionians landed and set up a new city further to the west. During the next three or four hundred years Ephesus became a prosperous center of trade and banking. In the 6th century, *Ephesus* fell to *Croesus* of *Lydia* and later to *Cyrus* the *Persian*. In 334 B.C., Alexander the Great established democratic government in the city and on his death *Lysimachus* gained control and founded a new city further west. In 190 B.C., the Romans defeated *Antiochus, King of Syria*, and his ally *Ephesus,* which to *Eumenes gave it to him, King of Pergamum*. In 133 *B.C., Ephesus* and *Pergamum* became Roman cities. The latter is how the city got its name.

In the early days of Christianity, *St. Paul* spent three years in *Ephesus*, at times in jail, while founding the first *Christian community* there. *St. John* also came and wrote his *Gospel* there. According to local belief, *Ephesus was the last home of the Virgin Mary*.

In the first century, A. D. *Ephesus* was the largest city of the East after *Alexandria*. In A.D. 262, *the Goths destroyed Ephesus and the Temple of Diana*, and although the city revived, its former splendor it was never restored. The *Ecumenical Council* of the Church met at *Ephesus* in 431 and condemned the doctrines of *Nestorius*. *Ephesus* lessened in importance and by the 15th century, it had declined to the status of a village. Today the town of *Selcuk* is steadily developing.

We visited the ruins of *Ephesus, The Aqueducts, The Basilica of St. John, The Mosque of Isabel*, and *The Temple of Diana*. Most of them are stones and debris surrounded by marshlands. Then we visited the ruins of the *Church of Virgin Mary…* During the second century A.D, they erected a building, 883 feet long by 98 feet wide, and first used it as a meeting place for doctors, professors, and as an exchange. They later transformed the western part into the first *Christian Basilica* and dedicated it to the *Virgen Mary*. Then, they used the eastern part as a domed church and named it the Double Church.

It was there that the *Ecumenical Council of 431 A.D.* met, attended by 200 bishops, and proclaimed the three dogmas of *Christianity*. The most impressive of the ruins in Ephesus, which final construction began during the reign of Claudius A.D. 41–54 was completed at the time of Trajan (A.D. 89-117) It is incredible that at this time, 2016, we were walking on Marble Street, built in the 4th century A.D. with a perfect drainage system in the middle.

The Temple of *Hadrian*, built about A.D. 130, in the interior of which people found armaments, representing scenes such as *Androcles* hunting and meeting of the Gods and Kings, all relating to the foundation of Ephesus... The Temple of *Serapis*, 2nd century A.D., had a façade about 90 feet long decorated with eight Corinthian columns each consisting of a single piece of marble 50 feet high. Parts of the Temple were unearthed during the excavation of 1913 and 1926. Its dedication to an Egyptian god was no doubt due to the close commercial relations between Ephesus and Alexandria at that time.

The most important structure of the third group, about four and a half miles further south, is the ruins of the HOUSE OF THE VIRGIN MARY, ON THE ALADOG OUNTAIN, 1377 FEET ABOVE SEA LEVEL... According to tradition, MARY came to Ephesus with ST. JOHN between the years A.D. 42-50. On the walls of the Domed Church dedicated to the Virgin Mary mentioned earlier was the inscription "On the cliff above is the home of the Virgin Mary who lived out her days until she died". This plaque discovered when archeologists, were excavating the Domed Church below, which had not previously been dugout and coabartes the location of her home on the cliff above. Only the perimeter of the foundation of her home is left. We meditated in that place. We both received the same special feelings we received when we had previously meditated a few years earlier in Fatima, Portugal.

–Sat with husband Michael on the ground and meditated there for quite some time; during these minutes, we both felt incredibly peaceful! –At that point, we happily left this very special place.

CHAPTER 30

May 3rd, in route to Naples. On May 4th we arrived at the Port of Naples. The second most populated In Italy, and one of the largest in Europe.

Naples is one of the most beautifully cities in Europe. It is also one sparking and colourful with a flavour on its own. Rising from the sea and spreading to fill a splendid natural amphitheatre, its mazy, crazy streets disclose historic treasures on every corner – and there are a great many corners! Naples, they say–"never goes to sleep, and the spirit of this great, vibrant place is hard to resist".

On May 4th, we visited Naples (Napoles). The beautiful city is located on the *Bay of Naples,* opposite to the *impressive Mount Vesuvius. Naples* is the perfect doorway to visit, with charming towns swaying on the edges of cliffs, and nestled into deep canyons.

–We were fascinated with the ruins of *Pompeii* or *Herculaneum*, – the enchanted Island of *Capri,* and much, much more.

Make your own way from castle to castle… from cathedral to palace… through bustling streets… –some narrow and paved with lava, others wide, modern and lined with the smartest shops – and you are sure to be caught up in the cheerful atmosphere.

Whichever way you cut through, you will find *Naples* as with many-layers, from the sea to the mountains and from the times of the ancient Greeks to the present day. You find gorgeous buildings from each period of its long and wealthy history. Many of these, as well as being of great interest, also serve as museums or galleries displaying a dazzling range of art and artifacts from near and far.

As at today, Neapolitans, one and a half million of them, exist In their homes, shops and workshops right next-door to ancient arches, palaces and frescoed churches, and also pizza; since this is the place where they invented it; so make sure you don't leave before trying their wonderful pizza!

You probably remember that *Naples* was founded by the Greeks, more than two-and-a-half thousand years ago, retaining a decidedly Greek character even after the Roman occupation. The city later suffered during wars with the Goths and did not achieve full independence until the 8th century.

After four hundred years of independence, they incorporated into the greater *Kingdom of Naples*. The city's position as the seat of this kingdom, continued until the middle of the 19th century, and it was ruled in succession by Europe's most powerful dynasties –the *Hohenstaufen's*, the *Angevins, the kings of Aragon, Spain, Austria,* and the emperor *Napoleon*. Finally, under Garibaldi – the liberator of Italy – it became port of the kingdom of *Sardinia*.

Naples was under bombardment during World War II and nobody rebuilt it. The newest industries of computers and electronics, have sprung up alongside the existing, motor vehicles and steel, which themselves have never completely replaced the old wool, linen, silk, wine, perfume, porcelain, jewelry, and olive oil industries.

We found great collections of Greek and Roman antiquities; many finest pieces from Pompeii and Herculaneum; mosaics, frescoes, coins and paintings, as well as bronze and marble sculpture.

Was fascinated with the National Museum and Gallery of *Campodimonte*, set in beautiful gardens with splendid views on the slopes of the *Capodimonte*; it displays a fest of the finest paintings with many Renaissance masterpieces. Artists include *Simone Martini, Maraccio, Botticelli, Colontonio, Lotto, Parmigianino, Correggio, Titian, Caravaggio, Breugel, and El Greco!* This great museum and gallery, also has *porcelains, cameos, tapestries, ivory and the Farnese Armoury.*

We had the change to visit the Duomo of the Cathedral of San Gennaro... –This story really impressed. According to the story, "He was call "St. January: –to give him his English name, – He was martyred and beheaded in the year 305. They kept his skull in a chapel at the cathedral. –More famously, so is his congealed blood, sealed in phials... Three times a year, on the First Saturday in May, the 19th of September and the 16th of December, this blood returns to its liquid state in one of the most celebrated of all miracles.

Changing the subject, went to visit *San Carlo Opera House*, dating from 1737 in the reign of Charles of Bourbon, with an interior of stupendous luxury designed by *Ciccolini* in 1816... the greatest singes down the ages have performed here – and they still do! The season runs from November until June, but it is possible to tour the building during the off-season.

Having some extra time, before returning to the ship, we looked out for the *Galeria Umberto*; (Umberto's Gallery) located opposite the Opera House…The interior of this great glass-roofed arcade, begun in 1887, which is the grandest in southern Italy.

–Although today *Naples* is a large city, its ancient center is for more compact and much of it lies within an area bounded by three of the castles and the central railway station. *Castel Deli'Ovo* and *Castel Nuovo*, both stand guard at the bay, while Castle *Sant'Elmo,* commands higher ground inland.

The Mount *Vesuvius*, is the great presence of the life of the city and has presided over the history of the entire region. It has two peaks, Mt. *Somma* -3,713 feet- and Vesuvius itself -4,189 feet- with the main crater between them.

There were many famous castles, piazzas, and temples, and squares, destroyed by catastrophic eruptions of 79 AD. We, for sure will comeback in the near future to Visit *Pompei* and *Herculaneum*, to spend there more time to admire.

When, visited those wonderful historical places, recalled when I left my old country full of history, pain, sadness, anger, and grief… I could hardly describe the ache in my heart! Then, realized I was so very glad I had followed my determination, and the heart, coming with my darling children to a much better land.
–The United States of America-

On May 5th and 6th, in route to Cadiz... On May 7th we were glad, we arrived in Cádiz, Spain... Felt the sparkle in the air and the glittering ripples of the sea...

We really enjoyed visiting Cadiz, called "The Cup of Silver". It is an ancient port city in southwest Spain, on a strip of land, surrounded by the sea... A 16th century base for exploration and trade... It has enormous amount of watchtowers, including the iconic Torre Tavira, traditionally used for sporting ships... The 18th-century waterfront cathedral has a golden dome, with views of the city ad sea. We enjoyed visiting this delightful and beautiful place!

The Spanish coastline of CADIZ stretching from border up to Gibraltar known as *Costa de la Luz* (*Coast of Light*), capital of the province of the same name, is the oldest inhabited town in the western world with 3,000 years of history. Standing at the top of a long peninsula, which makes it virtually on island, its position has entirely shaped its history.

The metropolis, with 140,000 inhabitants, is one of the largest ports on the Atlantic coast of Spain; it is a major shipyard and naval base, as well as being the port of shipment for the *brandy* and *sherry* from *Jerez* and the olives and olive oil from *Seville*.

Far back in the mists of antiquity, the Phoenicians, great traders from the Lebanon, who even reached Cornwall looking for tin, founded *Gadir*, meaning castle. This would have been around 3,000 years ago. Tin, silver, and hides changed hands and the city knew its first period of prosperity. *Cadiz* experienced the passing of other civilizations including *Greeks*, *Romans*, *Visigoths* and *Moors*, but maybe the most remarkable chapter in the contemporary history of Cadiz are her links with American continent. At the time, men discovered America and treasure began pouring into *Spain*, *Cadiz* became a haven for the fleets. The cultural and commercial exchanges appreciated the old city, where the 18th century treasures are preserved.

By 1770, because of peaceful trading with the American Colonies, *Cadiz* was a wealthier city than *London*. The comparison was not prolonged, however; thirty years later it was bombarded by Nelson and its final claim to historic fame lies in the fact that from *Cádiz* sailed *Villeneuve's* fleet on the eve of its near-total destruction off Cape Trafalgar. The year 2005, marked the 200th anniversary of the famous battle of *Trafalgar*.

Later in the 19th century, *Cádiz* acted as the capital of Spain with its Constitution of 1812. Since then, Cádiz deteriorated to some extent; there, are few great historic monuments and the paint is peeling in the narrow streets of the 17th century town, but the main attraction for visitors is the authentic Spanish atmosphere with regard to daily life and the friendliness of the people. Spaniards usually come for holidays here –you can see the many hotels along the peninsula, which was once a sandy waste.

We walked around and observed through the park and along the promenades, which are very pleasant places. Some of the trees and bushes are native, but the majorities are from different corners of the world, mainly from America. The nickname of the town is *"the cup of sliver"* since it sparkles with a radiance. -Certainly, the combination of white houses and the sea with its salty smack gives the impression of crisp, perfect freshness.

Walking through the green *Plaza de España*, then the gardens of *Alameda de Apodaca* and the *Alameda Marqués de Comillas*, we felt at home.

Further round we observed the more extensive *Parque Genovés* –Genovese Park, before we reached the rather gloomy Fort of *Santa Catalina*, guarding the little harbor used by the Romans, but now there is a rocky beach and at low tide, we may see some of the foundations of the ancient port.

Continuing walking we observed the picturesque quarters of *La Viña* toward the old *Cádiz*.

Asking about the Beautiful Cathedral, people informed us that its construction began in 1722 in *Baroque style,* and was finished in the mid-19th century in *neoclassical style*; –No wonder we observed that it really need restoration. This treasure is considered to be the third most important in Spain and holds some interesting and valuable pieces, including a 13-foot-high silver monstrance, and another twice as high, which is carried in procession through the city, once a year.

We perceived also the beautiful church of Santa Cruz… This is the old 13-century cathedral, destroyed and rebuilt in *Renaissance* style, that contains some paintings and a neo-classical altar.

We also observed the *Museum of Cádiz*, located in a Neo-Classical building at Plaza de Mina, was a fusion of the *Provincial Archaeological Museum, the Fine Arts Museum, and others*; divided into three parts...   There is an archaeological section with fifteen rooms with an interesting collection from the *Roman necropolis* of *Cádiz* and *Phoenician anthropoid sarcophagi.*

One of the top attractions and is well worth a visit, is *The Tavira Tower, that offers a bird eye view at the city.   This 18th century "watch tower" has been renovated and now offer an interesting attraction —The Dark Camera, —The Cámara Oscura which projects a moving image of the surrounding town as if you were standing inside a photographic camera.*

We wanted to visit Arcos de la Frontera, 38 miles east; one of the White Towns, Arcos, which is highly picturesque for its Moorishness – the whole layout and atmosphere speak for themselves. (This was the information given to us by other visitors; but we did not have the time to visit it, due to a change in schedule.

The next places to visit was Seville, at 80 miles from the border; but remember... we did not have extra-time, but then, we recalled, we visited this city a few years ago, and witnessed the most fascinated dances of *flamenco*; remembering *Seville* seems to *encapsulate the idea of the throbbing soul of Spain.* In reality, *Seville* is a large and busy city with three-quarters of a million inhabitants; it takes time to visit these points of interest with enough time...to do it right!

"Don't cry because it is over, Smile because it happened."

...Dr. Seuss...

CHAPTER 32

May 8th and 9th at sea in route to Southampton…
The World Cruise was almost over.

…We all had mixed emotions.

IT IS OVER… by – Nohemi

To staying up and sailing up with you, Dear Queen…
Now we are slipping near the edge of sea…
Holding something, we do not need to see.
Oh, this delusion in our heads and dreams
is going to bring us to our knees.

So come on, just, let it go!
Just, let it be!
Why do not you be you…
and I will, be me.
Everything that ends, -like this cruise ship…
Leave it to the dear and soft breeze.
Why do not you be you…
and I will, be me.
Thank you, Dear Beautiful Queen…
Thank you, Dear Breeze…
and Thank You, Dear Magnificent Sea.

These were the ways we described our emotions! This wonderful cruise, reminds us about the elements throughout our lives that are very important, even at old age. Start with the meaning of *appreciation…* to be able to be grateful for the little things in life! Appreciating the little things in life, involves focusing our attention on what is pleasurable, nurturing, and sustaining in our lives, and away from those events that are *annoying, frustrating,* or *hurtful. —It means, practicing gratitude for those everyday things that are easy to take for granted or to miss altogether.* Adopting this attitude will not stop negative events from occurring, but it helps to prevent us from over-emphasizing their importance in our lives! Did you get it?

Just remember what gratitude is

Let's keep a *gratitude* record… People who kept *gratitude journals,* compared to those who didn't can feel the difference… a) *some recorded their daily blessings, and found doing better. Like more optimistic view of one's life, experiencing a more positive disposition, showing a greater inclination to help others. How else will this build character and resistance to negativity and stress? Gratitude…* Develop skills in expressing gratitude can help us connect with others. When we take the time to *appreciate an act of kindness* from a loved one, or even a stranger, we become more fully aware of our universal connectedness, or having something in common, with that person, and positive regard for all of us. Interchanging these kind actions we have as a resource to draw on, in times of need.

How does positive emotion relate to our mental health?

Positive emotions have been shown to be connected to good physical health, also. People who experience positive emotions are likely to live longer, enjoy better resistance or even developing a immunization toward disease or biological mal-functioning, and recover more effectively from treatment for heart disease.

(I have a good example!) It's not just our physical strength that is affected by positive emotions… Our *psychological wellbeing* can be assisted also. Just remember… *"–When we experience positive emotions, we are able to think and behave more creatively and flexibly, than when we experience negative emotions. "* This way we enlarge the range or magnitude of positivism, or become wider in range or magnitude of the way we think and act, building resources for us that we are able to use in more difficult moments.

I have experienced that strong individuals experiencing positive emotions use these emotions to help them to cope with difficult situations. –There are many things we can do to enhance and increase the presence of *positive emotions for us*! *Learning how to appreciate the little things in life is one good way! I want to share positive things with My Dear Readers… From negative experiences, I lost vision in my left eye! … From negative-cruel experiences, I had heart attacks… From negative experiences, it was very difficult to have normal blood pressure… That's why we need positive emotions and positive experiences, to improve physical and also mental health!* –**What can we do, to appreciate the little things in life?** Here are some ideas you might like to try… to develop the ability to appreciate little things. One of them, is keeping a *Gratitude Journal*, another *sharing Gratitude Cards to people*, remembering that it doesn't cost much, and it contribute to health and happiness to someone else.

Again keep a Gratitude Journal. Spending ten or 15 minutes each day, *writing down three to five things you are grateful for, is a great way to boost your psychological immunization against negativity which helps us develop an appreciation* for the little things in life. Think creatively – the little things could be a text message from a friend, hearing a joke that made you laugh out loud, a wonderful meal, or even the experience of spending 15 minutes doing something nurturing just for you. –*This was how I started a Gratitude Journal… –Since I am a writer and journalist, I write*

–I walk with my husband, every day under wonderful areas – most of the time surrounded by aromatic or colourful flowers or trees… admiring and listen the gorgeous vibrant birds… When I find anybody walking alone, I start asking a silly question or making a funny remark about "the surroundings" and the person, does not have other alternative that to smile, and most of the time, she or he engages in a friendly conversation, and most of the time at the end, he/she is very happy.

We are generally pretty good at marking the big moments in our own lives; 'He said to me yesterday, let's celebrate your birthday today, Dear Wife!" –"But my birthday is not today!" "It doesn't matter, let's go to the Island of *Maui* tomorrow or let's do this or that (usually something inexpensive)." –I smile very happily, and immediately he starts packing or we do some little thing, which we just cooked up to be a pleasant distraction and sometimes these turn into wonderful memories. It is not how much you spend, but that you chose to something interesting together…that you gave to each other by making quality time together. Husband and I have the habit to celebrate these little things**…** After completing these positive exercises for a number of weeks, I learned to spend quality time writing in my journal or in my books, about how this daily discipline has changed my outlook and perspective in my own life.

In a few hours we are swimming in another beach, happy and relaxed. He does the same thing about our wedding anniversary… "Do you want to celebrate our wedding anniversary, eating Hawaiian food in Kauai?" – Again, I replied, "our anniversary is in November, – "What is the difference, dear? Weddings, graduations, and birthday's we could celebrate at any time… What would happen if we gave ourselves permission to celebrate little things? "The how or what and when, of any celebration will depend on what's important is to you and me!" –Let me share with you, dear readers this imprint of my personal life… "I met *Michael*, many, many years ago, after I came back from the funeral of my dear brother Gus, who was shot in Colombia... I was very, very sad! I went to a Rosicrucian Lodge to meditate, that at that time he was a member. –He said "why are you so sad". He dried my tears *we went into the meeting room and listened to the Head Master's motivational talk... After a few weeks of Michael visiting me, took care of me by being a friend. We visited beaches on the Pacific Ocean near in San Francisco, and other places to meditate…(I learned from both the Rosicrucians and Hindu Yogis, and Buddhists that meditation greatly develops our Intuitive Side which helps us in life regarding knowledge, and our decision making. A few weeks later, he invited me to a Cheerful restaurant. –Out of the blue, I heard him talking to the Chef, "I want to be seated at the window where we can appreciate that beautiful beach.., and then, out of the blue, he continued... "Today we are celebrating our anniversary!" –Very surprised, I looked at him, "What anniversary are you talking about?" – "Just one month since the time I met you Dear Nohemi." –he said. – And again, surprisingly, a year later, I accepted being his wife!" Many, many, years we have been husband and wife, and also, very happy, good friends!"*

By the way, here are some simple ideas I developed with my friends and students, when I was teaching College…

– *Always kept* gold stars in my desk… Give one to a student when he or she mastered a new skill or completed a challenging task.

– The Sun finally appeared after a week of grey skies, I asked a friend to go for a walk to celebrate the good weather and regenerative effects of rain.

– Pampered myself after getting through a tedious task, such as cleaning my room or writing a report, by doing something I enjoyed, like creating a poem.

–Keep a souvenir of the experience, to prompt your memory later.

–Share the experience with others, either as it happens or by reminiscing later on.

–Slow down and taste… –This idea falls into the *'take time to smell the roses'* tradition. Try these tips to get even more out of positive emotions when you are experiencing an uplifting event.

Now, let's come to the present… We are at the cruise-ship, on May 8, at sea in rote to Southampton… The pilot setting Westerly courses, before turning to the North and transiting various traffic separation schemes off the coast of Portugal. These schemes are designed with safety in mind and organize traffic flow in areas where the traffic density is high. Other such examples include the Dover Straits and the Singapore Straits. Once clear of the separation schemes, Queen Mary 2 continued her Northerly course toward Cape Finisterre. In the meantime we were entertained by the "Broadway Rocks" featuring the Royal Cunard Singers and Dancers.

May 9, still at sea, in route to Southampton… Tonight's variety group Showtime, back with brand new shows, *The Patriot Girls.*, and at the Queens Room, celebrated the almost the end of World Voyage Party with Vibz. Yes, I was right! Now, we are celebrating the end of the World Voyage for this year, with an international band in the Queens Room for an evening of party tunes to keep us dancing all night long. We couldn't miss our famous ballroom, so we started the party at 1:30 p.m.

"Keep in mind that "Every Day is A Mindset." – It is a plain issue, – yet, extremely powerful! – It is the way in which we live our life. What is a Mindset? – Simply, it, reminds us that this day we are currently living… – It only ever happens once and therefore encourages us to make the most of it".

CHAPTER 33

On May 10th, Queen Mary 2 sets sail on her Westbound Transatlantic Crossing.

The Captain, his officers and excellent crew, welcomed us on board as we began our westbound transatlantic crossing; announcing *"Cunard ships* had spanned the mighty Atlantic Ocean since 1840 embracing aboard those seeking adventure, style and sophistication.

We had the chance to admire parks, castles, gardens, famous streets in South Hampton; took wonderful pictures, and then, went to the ship. At May 11, after *Southampton* we were in route back to *New York.* Queen Mary made her familiar passage down through the Silent, the Island of Wright on her Starboard side, before going by the Nab Tower and dropping off her local pilot. Steaming West overnight in the English channel and throughout the day, she left the South coast of England, on her starboard side heading out towards the North Atlantic Ocean.

An International television-recording artist Stuart Gullies, who has sung with all the BBC Radio Orchestras, throughout the UK for BBC2 Easy Listening, and was a regular guest on the QM2 on Friday Nights, entertained us. According to entertainer, he won the opportunity Knocks Talent Show seven times as well as winning the Songwriters Competition with a song called "Amanda" that reached Number 9 in the Charts, culminating an appearance on Top of The

Pops with *Engelbert Humperdinck* and *Paul McCartney*. He had also the honor of singing before several members of the Royal Family, with the Royal Court Theatre Orchestra, under the musical direction of Jeff Hughes.

On May 12, we celebrated with another *Captain's Cocktail Party*, having excellent entertainment. Remember during that time, the speaker mentioned, "The American Presidential Election and the State of the U.S. Presidency". Divided America; The Presidential Election of 2016, The current presidential campaign in the United States is one of the most turbulent, divisive and ugly in modern history. Moreover, the prospect is for it to get even worse as front-runners Hillary Clinton (for Democrats) and Donald Trump (for the Republicans) collide. Award-winning White House Correspondent Ken Walsh analyses the situation in this fact-based and anecdote-filled presentation".

At night, we attended to the Grandiose Royal Theatre, with charming vertical cloth choreography with a touch of Arabian music. The duo presented poetic pictures and passionate movements that merged with one another to create harmony, power, and elegance in full development. The mysterious worlds of fantasy and reality combine to become scenes of spirit and seduction.

May 13th. Before we went to sleep, attended the Opera Presentation, "*Carmen* 'in 3D: passion, jealousy and betrayal take center stage at London's Royal Opera House in a spectacular production of the world's most popular opera "Beautifully filmed in 3D by Julian Napier, Seville is brought to life with ranks of soldiers, crowds of peasants, gypsies and bullfighters.

May 14, 15, 16, we were in route to New York. We had a wonderful entertainment, with Virtuosic Violinist, *Cateryna Sychova*, her show included a variety of styles and genres of violin music. Enjoyed classical and jazz in combination with Ukrainian, Moldavian,

Armenia, Irish traditional music, and American Country, all successfully bound together into one fascinating performance. Her mesmerizing state presence, beauty, and bright personality captivated the audience and left an unforgettable impression in our hearts.

Then, very happy, and in the way, very sad, we said goodbye to all our new friends, with the promise to get together at another place, to share more experiences…

Left the ship… – *a wonderful fortress* – and took a taxi saying good-by to the last place, *New York*; where the QM2 was slipped, and the next day, was very happy to fly Hawaiian Airlines, to go back to our home, on the great *Oahu, Hawaii*.

We enjoyed the escape for four months, with wonderful entertainment, stimulating visits to historical places around the world and had the chance to share with members of the cruise, how to get, and keep happiness. This marvelous segment on the voyage made us realize how delightful it is to share these worldwide adventures with pleasure, and coming back home with inspiration from our expectations to share.

Assure you, the best things in life are the people we love, the places we discover, and the memories we create along the way.

The same about taking photographs, they are proof that once, even if just for a heartbeat, everything was perfect.

This enjoyable cruise had been so great, leaving us all kinds of experiences, and wonderful times… Even, if it was so fast. -I wish everybody in this land would get some beautiful time to share life with many people, in many places.

Remember, Yesterday is gone; however we can try to do something positive now, to enjoy tomorrow! – Past is gone, it was mystery. – Our inner light is shining brightly now, we can use it to illuminate the path for us, and others. Today is a gift!

"Every Day well-lived makes Every Past a Dream of Happiness and Every Tomorrow a Vision of Hope."

…From the Sanskrit…

WITHOUT FEAR

© Nohemí

We thank Life, for giving us life
For the surprises, happiness and sometimes grief
To be able to hear, talk, think, and appreciate the sun's light
For our inoffensive childhood, growing, even with fear

For having innocence, kind heart and sound mind
To be able to appreciate music, art, beauty and love
To poses compassion and to perceive honesty
With those who share our life with happiness, without fear

For the dreams we forge toward our marriage,
For illuminating our minds, to act with reason
To see our children grow without anguish, with courage
for opening the door to love ones, without fear.

With humility, we thank Life again, and again, without fear
Giving us occasions to form and grow with our children
With humility, modesty and compassion
Observing, them succeed, confident, happiness, without fear.

CHAPTER 34

I leave the best for the end…
My humble personal life…

When I was a little girl, sat near the front door of our home in the small town, at probably five or six years old, felt the wind blowing, remembering it's renewed energy slowly, observed the plaza full of street-dogs, rejecting the insects from their bodies…it was the tropics.

Guiding the vision across the road, looked at a local old woman walking slowly, – carefully avoiding a hole on the dirty road; then, watching her, paused down until she reached the old church, at the other side of the square. As observed her before, she visited that place to collect some food from the priest.

After she accommodated the goodies in her basket, continued walking slowly, until reaching the corner; and then, came toward our home, located in the heart of the small town, slowing her pace on the dark street, where we, as children, had fun, before going to sleep.

The night' air was a little warm… –Then, I noticed, after we were already in bed, that we forgot to shut off the gas lamp, so one of us hurrying up, did it, and then went back to bed. We used to remove the covers to cool off our bodies from the humid heat and in no time at all, we were all sound asleep.

The next morning, very early, before the sun showed his rays, we eagerly jumped from our beds anticipating that mom, in a few minutes, will come with a cup full of water to sprinkle our faces. One by one, went to the back yard to bring wood for the stove, and came back to the patio where the tank was full of water from the rain, to remove the sleepers from our eyes. —This light cleaning, changed on Sundays, when we have to wash our whole bodies, before we got dressed and then go to church, to listen to the Priest, who always officiated the mass in Latin, and unfortunately, we did not understand a thing.

—According to Mom, Dad was already in heaven, after his assassination, while trying to vote two years ago during election time…

Observed mother, being very tired from working at the sewing machine every night; so we, —her kids— tried to help her with all kind of chores, to make her life less wretched. —Among the duties, I was in-charge of preparing the dining table to eat a simple breakfast of a cane-sugar hot beverage, with a piece of corn-bread. (*We called arepas*). Then, taking the bag with the books, we went through the front door and started running to school.

There, in the small village school patio, we pledged allegiance to the Colombian flag, prayed to God for a good day; then went to the classroom to start catechism class. Then taking the chalk, went to the black-board, started our arithmetic session; next, after taking a small brake, went back to the class-room to learn about the life of Virgen Mary; then it was time to have lunch. — Remember, later I continued on my own to read other kind of material, like *Don Quixote De La Mancha*, or *Federico Garcia Lorca*, —*Great writers!*

Let us go back to more stories of childhood… After returning from the play-ground, dried the sweat, started a new class;

this time it was our turn to learn geography of our state, gather the name of the mountains, rivers and oceans; then, we had to learn about patriotic history, paying allegiance to the flag, and other things.

Afterward, we said good-by to our teacher, in no time we went back through the park, jumping, playing with the street dogs, following the cats; and minutes later, we got home. Leaving the books on the near-by wood bench, went to the room where mom was busy with the sewing machine, making lots of dresses as a seamstress, doing accounting for local businesses, and also serving as the town's notary; I gave her a kiss, and started studying the lessons for the next school day. —This was the daily routine, during the week days; keeping in mind that later we made time to entertain ourselves, playing in the back-yard, before it was time to have diner.

On Sundays, unfortunately, we had to take a shower, cut our nails, brush our teeth; wear a white clean dress and clean shirts and pants for the boys, comb our hair, and immediately went to church. —The sad part of being in church was that again we could not understand the sermon of the Priest, since he celebrated the mass in Latin, and we only spoke Spanish.

Later on, after we moved to the nearby city, to attend high school; at that point, I had more brothers and sisters; and by the time, was finished high school, the family grew to twelve kids. —Unfortunately, since I was the older sister, became *Cinderella*, (helping was not an accurate description substituting for mom) to raise that "Army" of kids was my prime duty.

In the mean-time, during summer vacation, I was lucky to spend time with Aunts and Uncles, until Dear Uncle Richard, was assassinated also, when he was on his horse going back home. —I used to ride with him in front of his saddle, but that sad day, I chose to spend some time with brothers and sisters, to show my only "beautiful porcelain doll" –uncle and aunt got for me in Europe on one of their trips. –And at the end, it was not, worth it, since in a few minutes they doll was in pieces, going from hand to hand, until it reached the hard cement.

When I earned the reason for mother crying, begged them to take me back to *Aunt and Uncle*; and that afternoon, finally arrived at their home… Rushed, running, under the legs of so many people, was able to cry near uncle's coffin. –Could not see his face – But then, analyzed it was better this way, since his body was without his head! –Went to Aunt, and cried on her lap. He was my favorite uncle. I was only about 4 years old.

For many years, tried to put aside those very sad moments, but still was drawing on the blackboard at school, people without heads! Time went by...

It was time to attend college… so, between working part-time as a typist for a lawyer; and since mother did not have enough funds to afford the expenses of high education, brother Gus, who was working after school as a delivery boy for a drug store, offered to help with part of the tuition, in conjunction with my Aunt Angie.

Fortunately, with my part-time salary, was able to pay for the textbooks. –Studied literature and poetry with *International Professor-Poet Laurate Luz Stella*… –By the way, was very proud to be the Valedictorian, and prepared the dissertation. After graduation, was very proud to present to my Brother and Aunt the graduation credential, thanking them for the opportunity to be a professional. –In the mean-time, continued helping mother, to raise the "Army".

Was very young when I finished College, able to take the main road, and continue growing, building a diversified portfolio, getting more skills, devoted to perform excellence waiting for this glorious moment!

One night coming from choir rehearsal, ten minutes late from the usual time, brother *Charlie* ask, "Where had you been?" –At the conservatory, rehearsing the concert, for next Saturday! –I answered. "You are lying to me, I called the Conservatory, and nobody answered the telephone!" –They disconnect the telephone during rehearsal –I said- Before I continue with an explanation, Cruel Brother Charli, involved my small body with a Whip, and continue with this cruel procedure until blood was running my legs! –Mother did not say anything!

Sometime later, I was raped, and was forced by my Bother Charlie to marry the offender, because he made me pregnant; had two children; he abandoned us since the marriage did not function, ending raising two children by myself… Happily, got a position as an Assistant to the President at the State Penal Court, in this way had funds to raise my dear kids.

Having ambition, remained learning music, educated my voice during lunchtime, – since the Music Conservatory was across the street from the Law Court. –All of this effort, paid off, since I was admitted at the Choir of the famous *Conservatory Alberto Castilla*. After many months, had the opportunity to have some happy moments, as a member of the famous group, of one hundred voices… –Did not miss a class, attending every lunchtime, for years…

Continued schooling at the Music Conservatory; was able to sing in local concerts; and then traveled to the city of *Cali*, to celebrate the *Football Championship* with a musical recital. Next year traveled to Europe, to sing with *"The Little Boys of Vienna"*. – Now at old age, when I observe the pictures, I believe, "It was worth it to be assertive, and never give up, since I Kept Moving Forward on My Journey to Happiness life, always gave me the opportunities to succeed and be happy".

Years later, since mother moved to Bogotá, Capital of Colombia, I followed my intuition to relocate there, also; looking for better perspectives for my kids and me. A few months later, received invitations to sing with groups in different organizations. Spirit was helping during my consciousness.

Was proud to past the test, among many candidates, and immediately, started working for *Nestle,* an international company, as an Assistant to the Personnel Department for four years, under the direction of *Dr. Charry*, a famous Writer, and Poet.

Then, I received the offer to work at *Schering Corporation, –* a pharmaceutical company from USA, as an Assistant to the Vice-President, *Mr. Roger Arnoe;* this company gave me the opportunity to know about the potential market around the world...— He was also the Director of a choir at church, and was I singing there.

Had a dream to raise my darling kids in the United States... and that dream came true! After work, learned to be a beautician, opened a beauty salon at home using the living room, to be near my kids. This way, saved some pesos to buy dollars, for the project to raise my darling kids in USA. Having a full-time job, worked at night in a beauty salon, also, during the weekend, vaccinated chickens at the near-by farm. Years later, life gave the most wonderful trophy as a mother of a beautiful girl; she was indeed, like receiving an absolute magnificent gift, despite the fact that her father also abandoned all of us.

With determination, feeling all the requirements, even saving thousands of pesos to buy a few dollars, applied for the resident visas –It was not easy! It took many, many years. With patience and determination arrived at Los Angeles, California with my little girl.

Got a job as a bookkeeper at *Pasco Industries*; three months later, the President of the company, proud of the work well done, offered a check to process the visas and buy the airline tickets for my two kids to bring them to USA. They were temporarily in Colombia living with Brother Gus, and the other, other at a boarding school, until I proved myself to the United States a responsible immigrant... In the meantime, I temporarily traveled to the USA with my little girl. After a few month, sent the funds to brother and he processed the American visas for the other two kids, based on the certificate from my employer. Very proud of the commitment that all my children came legally to USA, about half century... After all, my children raised beautiful children, now have grandchildren, and I, Nohemí, have the blessing to have gorgeous grandchildren and great grandchildren!

"Going to bed with satisfaction... Woke up with faith and determination, fulfilled the dream to come to USA with my three darling kids; now, all successful and free!" ...Nohemi

Keep Moving Forward...On My Journey

Ready to take the Main Road

– Remembered, what *Aunt Angie* used to say, *"Perseverance is the tool to get happiness." Also, during the following academic positions worked 2 and sometimes 3 jobs concurrently...*

Came to USA ... Went back to College, to revalidate my studies, and immediately after, worked *at California Business*

College as a Teacher in Los Angeles, California, *then,* promoted, to *Dean of Instruction*… Keep Moving Forward…

Next, *William C. Smith, President/Director of Academy of Business College, Inc. hired me as* an Instructor; within one year became a *Director of Training*; the duties included, Student Scheduling, Placement, and Instructor. After a few years, before he accepted my resignation, the President, stated", *Nohemí's motivation and loyalty to the Academy are unquestionable. She is a very energetic and hard worker. We have been proud to have her as part of our staff."* …Keep Moving Forward…

Then, had the offer from *California Business College,* where worked four years as an Instructor, teaching *English, Mathematics, and Computer Science.* Before leaving, Got a letter of commendation stated, *"Nohemi has been an active participant in the College Student's and Teacher activities; she was a planning, coordinator, and arranging the entire graduation exercises. She possesses the highest personal character, which emanates among other fine attributes, and has a tremendous love for humankind. Her undying initiative in all her tasks will prove to be an asset to all concerns. She always performed with the highest standards, therefore it is a pleasure to recommend Nohemi in whatever endeavor her quest may be; of course, regretfully she is leaving us. –Signed, Calvin Matsuoka"…Keep Moving Forward…*

Transferred to *South Bay College of Business, –also in Los Angeles, California;* worked for three years, acted as an *Instructor, Academic Dean, and as a Placement Director.* Mrs. *Ella Witska, - The Director, stated, "Nohemi is also bilingual, and this proved to be a help to the students, not only in their classwork, but in placement as well. She is conscientious, friendly, and good worker. Nohemi organized the school's formal graduation, and has become a tradition since then. She was always excellent in the area of attendance".*

In the new endeavor, Ms. *Vivian Hougland, Director of Hill College*, made the interview. After introductions, she asked, "What is the primary reason you want to become a Professor at this institution?" –proudly, answered. – *"Teaching youngsters, is like raising a family, preparing them to look at life with confidence." "Also have the goal to transmit success and confidence."* – Hired me immediately and started working the next week…

Besides teaching Mathematics, English, and Computers, organized ceremonies for graduates at The Grandiose Los Angeles Biltmore Hotel, where I received a standing ovation for the job well done. – Also devoted time as a *Placement Director in-charge of helping graduates to get a good job".* – Remember, after the Vietnam War, the College received many hundreds of young students from *Vietnam.* I got the first group, and, since I was raised in *Colombia, South America, "They learned "English with a slight Spanish Accent".* –This was the funny comment of the President of the College – during graduation, and everybody liked his comment, applauding the remark.

At graduation, they had an excellent command of subjects, as Mathematic, Accounting, and Computer Science. This fact gave them the chance to contact companies willing to hire competent foreigners to function at divisions without contacting the public. – Was proud to do their placement, since through the years their employers promoted them to management positions in their corporations, rewarding them with accolades.

Going back, remember… The first day of work at the College, was very happy, *receiving a bouquet of flowers. "Left the past, and Moved Forward."* – Since then enjoyed every single day of class. – Worked there for years; always delighted from the progress and performance of the students. Fortunately, because of the success, I was called to work for another College, and I accepted the challenge.

Next, *achieved as an Academic Dean* for *South Bay College of Business* in Los Angeles, California, with additional responsibilities; there organized graduation Programs, helped with placement, and some other tasks. –Since then, the college continued the style of the graduation exercises.

Worked for the State of California in various positions, and as a *Dean of Instruction* for *Academy of Business College, Inc.* and at the same time continued writing at the *El Hispano Newspaper and translating at the Court House for an attorney, when he had customers that did not speak English.*

As an Author, Poetess, Journalist, Dean, Professor, Translator, and Spokesperson for the United States Federal Government's FEMA, and the State of California OES, during the earthquake catastrophe and Directing their Television and Radio Program as Anchor and Broadcaster, was also Spokesperson for organizations including The American Cancer Society. Also spent two years in Costa Rica as Anchor, Talk Show Host, and Television Star

– On these endeavors acquired medals of praise and honor, certificates of special recognition, appreciation, and achievement...

– I had finished a second poetry book in Spanish, *Semblanzas y Recuerdos. (Profile and Remembrances) Dr. Santana, Director of the Spanish Literature Class at Sacramento State University, Sacramento, California, and when the head of ETL – Hispanic Press, heard about it... Surprisingly, he came to visit and requested the book; gave him a copy; and next day he came back to make the*

offer to publish it at the ETL – HISPANIC PRESS at the State University.

At that moment, he announced, "This book is a masterpiece! I want to use it in Literature Classes at the Universities all around California."

With my permission, Dr. Santana *informed me that the University wanted to present the poetry book to the Professors, students, and friends, in a public event.*

Then, the Mexican Consul, also a poet, requested the book... He was fascinated with it! "Your book is a piece of art" –he said. "Would you give me the honor to tribute your poetry book at the event? It will be a pleasure to do that!" Then, he wrote the Prologe and read it at the great occasion!

The day came...To my reverence, The Department of Foreign Languages prepared the most wonderful "Poetic Night" at the campus to introduce and honor my Poetry Book.

Not surprised, Dr. Jorge Santana, Director of Literary Texts Program at the California State University in Sacramento, invited Nohemi, to participate as a well-known poet and literary expert, at one of the Prodigious Events and I received excellent media reviews.

Dr. Jorge Santana, Master of Ceremony, welcomed Nohemí –the author of a new book... I Read some of the poetry to the crowd and dedicated this poetry edition to Dr. Santana, President of The Spanish Press of the California State University Sacramento, and to, Dr. Fausto Avendaño, who contributed the final concept of the work; and to family members, husband, kids, and grandchildren.

At the beginning of that great event, very proud directed the speech to the staff and crowd, "My advice to all is, Express yourself in prose, and poetry; besides providing the ability to communicate with others, it serves as your own self therapy. If you are happy, sad, or disappointed about things in life, put it on paper... You will be surprised how energized you will feel."

Amazed, *the General Consul of México in Sacramento, Dr. Humberto Murillo Diaz,* made everybody cry with his dissertation about honoring my Poem Book *"Profile and Remembrances" (Semblanzas y Recuerdos)... –In an emotive voice, he said,*

"Talking about Nohemí's poetry, – I proudly say –"It is entering sensitivity that marvels from beginning to end! Reading this extraordinary piece of literary manifesto, meets all forms of understanding."

Reading each of her poems, means remembering the Sunrise of a Colombian landscape we had already forgotten long ago, but it connects us with a line to romance, returns with the greenery of the countryside, and with the waves of the rivers, plants that sing telluric prayers and rhymes of spiritual people.

'When Nohemi explains the people' idiosyncrasy, out for a day of rejoicing, says, and defines the customs of the different regions. The enchanting musicality of the "bambuco", the lively rhythm of the "joropo llanero", until the fever of "cumbia" and sensuality of "vallenato", we find it in the following lines: "They have left so many moons indicating falls, reminding the time to pick up our crops."

For her, the idiosyncrasy of the "paisa" (farmer of the State of Antioquia) becomes a stanza; the holidays, a poem; -religious anniversaries are unexpected compositions; any birthdays, defines the folklore of their mayors. - This folklore never ends ever; neither destroyed under the influence of imported musicians. Ah 'she remains' –continued in a particular state, without changing – for future generations as expression 'on pop' ethics dun sensitive temperament. Nohemi does not dare to manage the language of beauty, coming in the word of authenticity to tear of what is good and what is true, to deliver it to the reader with care, and sincerity. – Here, she speaks of... "Anita from Bogotá..."

People say she was born for good
With her spirited life...
With craziness in love
"Bambuco" she interprets it
The compass of the music
The cumbia takes her inside...
The skirt's color' too. –"Bambuco" is a folkloric dance.

The literary figure becomes geometric... All in space, drawing from nature, movement undulated of water hidden to the kicking of summer, giving them life crossings immaculate zones and boisterous towns. The images repeated one by one, in a profusion of forgotten symbols. The love of the land, the fondness of home, children, the singing of hope, give the inspiration, the guideline for Nohemi to circulate in and a marvelous poetical ambiance This way she talks about tenderness of a party in June:

"It is the festivity of my land
– that I grieve for"
When the pains had forgotten
"By the rhythm of its swinging..."
When Nohemi speaks about love,
She does it with the sincerity of the natural light,
The Sun, the dawn, the afternoon,
So the human feeling, becomes magnetized

This way she speaks to love
With tranquility
Horizon giddiness, stars,
Moreover, spikes when she says:
"Love... when the afternoon is sunny"
The green of the trees
Invites the birds to sing their melody

And the flowers come-back to life."

Love, at that moment is everything:
Horizon, Stars, giddiness
Moreover, its river and is current.
For this reason crying out illuminated:

You are like the Sun from the horizon
You are like the stars at night
You are like the river and it is current
"You're like the guide of the absent"

Amore is also eternity:
"And you did get to my life"
Like an echo from the distant eternity"
Amore is memory of the future:

"She reminds us that there are other days, other lives...

Nohemi's subjects are so many: "Her home, filled with flowers and trills, now already empty, because "the children, now adults had left" and did not hear their voices. Her own life being "As the moon"... "As the snow." ..."As the rain"... "As the breeze".

Reading Nohemi's work, you feel filled with tenderness, musicality, love, and beauty.

"There are splendid summer nights
That draws a bird in the plain...
There are tropical and radiant nights...
There are nights when we miss the absentees...
There are stormy nights of mystery...
There are night's shadows and mists..."

It seems that we re-read Porfirio Barba Jacob, his compatriot and like her, globetrotting, when he wrote "Song of the deep life"; "There are days when we are so fragile so gloom... as lubricious..."

Humberto Murillo Díaz
Mexican Cónsul, Sacramento, California, USA.
Author of Me dió por ver Octubre, and
The rumor of August hours.
Sacramento, California 1987.

This poetry book went -after that glorious day-, to as many, many places, and continued use in Spanish classes at colleges and universities, through the United States! This fabulous poetry book had traveled through the Spanish speaking countries, and around the world.

§

Now, let us go back to the prospectus of life...

Later, functioned as a Translator for the *Government of California*, in Sacramento, There, also had the opportunity to help in diversity programs on newspapers, radio, and television.

At that time, very sad, we learned of the tragedy of the *Loma Prieta Earthquake* in *San Francisco* and near-by vicinities. *The Governor of California, Pete Wilson,* and the *Federal Emergency Management Agency –FEMA* was looking for volunteers to help Victims of the disaster. Since I was one of the persons speaking Spanish and English, with extensive background translating material for the government; and also, *was the voice of the State of California, to announce news in Radio, Newspaper, and Television, for the Hispanic Community,* I was assigned to help the government to help the most victims of the disaster.

(About a week before, a youngster hit the back of the car, when I was driving to work.) Since I did then not have own transportation,–a young volunteer, rescued, and we both went immediately to San Francisco's vicinities, to help the victims.

It was a sad quandary! We, the volunteers had to work many hours, almost day and night, helping people all around! Mainly, old, and youngsters wounded.... Some children were calling their parents that were deceased during the fatal volcanic activity... Mothers looking for their families also injured!

After the problem subsided, was giving information to survivors about their needs... Also, filled out forms for mainly Hispanics without English Language... also for all kinds of people, about their needs, as shelter, food, health clinics and benefits... Likewise, announcing on radio, newspaper, and television in Spanish and English, about the government programs to help them deal with these tragedies.

We, the volunteers worked with the victims for a few weeks, helping also with shelter and food. –We solved their needs, working together with FEMA to provide temporary homes. –I was tired, but very happy to be able to guide the victims for their recuperation and needs.

I believe the purpose of life, is to be useful, to be compassionate, and to make some difference in someone' life... No one has ever become poor for giving; so, if I have no money, had happiness, making time to help.

On October 17, 1989 received a Certificate of merit from the *Office of Emergency Services, "Loma Prieta Earthquake".*

From The State of California's, Governor, received a *Certificate of Merit,* for the extraordinary service in support of earthquake (August 1.1990) in response and recovery operations. I, received a letter, in which Tom Mullis, Director of Information and Public Affairs, of California stated, *"Please accept the enclosed Certificate of Merit as a symbol of our appreciation for the support you provided to the Loma Prieta Earthquake,* and thanks for your efforts to succeed during this shocking tragedy... "The perspective we have gained since the earthquake has reinforced the impression of professionalism and dedication that was apparent during the operation. Thank you, *Nohemí* for your exceptional contribution. Sincerely, Tom Mullis, Director of Information and Public Affairs."

In addition, The Office of The Governor, State of California, sent *a letter for Assisting the Governor, Pete Wilson –May 6, 1992. "To: Nohemí." I wanted to write and thank you for all your hard work on behalf of the Tenth Border Governors' Conference earlier this month." We received instructions as the host state that was our own responsibility for planning this important conference and making it success. Although, we worked within serious time constraints, our devotion to duty showed through, and knows from the conversations with fellow Governors and their staffs, that they were very impressed. In the meantime before and after the conference, relied heavily upon the enthusiasm, organizational skills, and creative talent of many people like yours. Without your generous donation of time and energy, the Conference could not have achieved its level of accomplishment. I am enormously proud of the work of everyone associated with this coordinated effort. Gayle joins in extending to you our very best wishes for every continued success in the years ahead. Sincerely, (signed) PETE WILSON, Governor of the State of California. "*

Likewise, was working for the California State government agencies, in charge of translating diversity of the state's documents for the Hispanic community. Also, in charge of the Spanish Media on behalf of the Department of Motors Vehicles, announcing the new laws and regulations for drivers in the State of California.

–From this organization, received all kind of awards as a contribution with their programs, and having close association with Spanish speaking customers.

In addition, help the *Latino Peace Officers Association* announcing the regulations on television to Hispanic people, who could not write or read.

Assisting people in need is a good and essential part of life… It is a kind of destiny. You do not have to wait for rewards… Just help. One of the best feelings in the world is knowing that someone is happy because of you.

Next, the President of the "Mexican Patriotic Committee" in Sacramento, announced, "The contribution is to educate young women; and help them to present their family's heritage and to be able to talk in public, on radio and television, and gatherings". –The outcome was to elect The Queen, and Princess, among the group, being fascinated with the good results! At the end or the training, they were able to talk in public, in crowds, and represent themselves with pride.

The Chicano/Latino Youth Leadership and *The Consulate of Mexico,* granted *Nohemí* the *"Special Commendation Award" for reaching out to Spanish speaking people.*

At The Youth Conference's 10th Anniversary on July 24, 1991, in *company* with Leading Poet and Professor at California State University Sacramento *José Montoya,* delighted youngsters with reading and explaining the heritage and culture embodied with poetry. *– Enjoyed success, since success, is the result of working hard, and being persistent.*

A Governor of California assigned Nohemi, to organize The *Pan-American Day* in Sacramento, California… Since *I was The*

President of Círculo Hispano, with connections to the Spanish people, he delegated me to develop all the details and ceremonies, to succeed in that gigantic project. The results were spectacular! That particular day, thousands of the Hispanic Heritage, and friends from all Latin-American countries, including Mexico, Central-American, South America, and Spain, paraded around the parks and streets of the Center of Sacramento, displaying floats decorated with flags and orchards. At night, we celebrated at the Central Park of Sacramento with Hispanic Dancers, (taught dancers, and rehearsed with members, in the back yard of my own residence).

The culmination of this event had great results, and great pleasure, and we earned a lot of publicity for future events. – Also, organized, several Radio and Television Programs in California to help the community, for which, received awards–.

Also, received accolades from these establishments: The National Library of Poetry, Owing Mills, from Maryland; Sparrowgrass Poetry Forum from, Sistersville, WV; Editorial Poetry Center Orinda, California; Creative Arts & Science Enterprises, Printed Post and Watermark Press, New York, and The Owings Mills, MD.

Also in 1998, as a *Texan resident poet,* obtained rewards from *The International Society of Poets in Washington DC.*

Likewise, received Appreciation certificate from *The Cancer Society* for coverage on television programs related to health issues of concern to the Hispanic Community.

–Received with pride a Certificate as a member in good standing of *International Society of Poets,* and recognized for support of *The Society's Principles of Peace – Education –* Accomplishment Charity and Equality.

"It pays to **KEEP MOVING FORWARD TO HAPPINESS**, and to never give up! *—The past is gone! Let us live in the present!*

This is the outcome! Even if life have inconveniences, we have to continue being assertive to overcome them and obtain happiness.

Just apply cognitive therapy, "The process of squishing sower juice of the grapes, we convert them in wonderful sweet wine".

The famous Marcus Aurelius, said, *"The happiness of your life depends upon the quality of your thoughts: therefore, guard accordingly and take care that you entertain no notions unsuitable to virtue and reasonable nature."*

Sons and daughter are professionals, married and have wonderful kids; some graduated from college, managing their own businesses. Now have two great grand kids, *Ava* and *Autumn*; and between all of them, and with my wonderful husband, *Michael*, completed the dream to be Happy for the rest of life. Have been traveling and indeed very blissful learning and appreciating other cultures.

Having determination, faith and never giving up, are the tools to be happy and successful, no matter the circumstances in life!–Just, remember, me your Great-Grand-Mother is very happy - of course, enjoying life. Now have the reward in life, sharing life with a great-responsible and kind husband on this Hawaiian Island, land of beauty.

IF WE REMOVE OUR FEAR, WE REMOVE THE PROBLEM!

One of these days, we should suggest to the UN, to establish the *International Day of Happiness to remind the whole world that everyone can be happy and earn great rewards.*

All of these are the reasons to KEEP MOVING FORWARD TO HAPPIESS with faith, keeping in mind, to never relinquish. Life is always great for those who have faith, and never give up.

WANT TO THANK LIFE
© *Nohemí*

Want to thank life for its gentle structure
For rolling dawn pleasant scents of apples
For watching the glide of the birdies
Soaring through the sky with peace, bliss and joy

Want to thank life for the virtue of youngsters
For leading their lives through the sway of the wind
For fitting the great gardens, escorted by trees
showing Happiness, Success, and Love.

Want to thank this great, structured soul
That tries to guide life through the years
With standards of masters and gurus
Displaying and screening lessons of honor

Want to thank life, for the placid breeze in Hawaii
Allowing the boats to sail slowly and peacefully
On my fast-paced world that dares
to share existence with dreams and goals.

Continued traveling, since travel expands our capacity for wonder, joy and appreciation; with amazing diversity of happiness, on our lovely planet…   Also, sharing life with the world, enjoying the company of each other, (husband and wife) living near the country in *Honolulu, Hawaii…* with a wonderful environment, we are very happy.

Likewise, enjoying beautiful flowers, kind weather, colorful beaches, and observing Hawaiian natives girls dancing *hula*, and the gorgeous women in colorful *holocaust* and handmade *leis* around their necks, listening to the aloha music played by natives, we enjoy sitting on the grass, full of happiness and good health.

Life is what we make it, whether we conceive one inner force or another… It does not matter. –Relying on that force, it does! "Ask, and you will receive… Knock and it shall be opened to you!"

The possibility of an intelligent and responsive universe, acting and reacting in our interest, is where we see the results! Had learned, "Never to ask whether we can do something" – instead, state, "I am doing it". "Then, fasten the seat belt said, God is efficient… The Universe delivers its treats!

It seems a fitting time, is to reflect on the past, while looking forward about what is ahead. On a personal level, I am relishing the old calendars, having joined the future… Leave the past where it belongs! "I am especially looking forward to meet the happy time. *Hope to see you on board"*.

We all should feel good today and every day! Do not let this confidence waste! Do things with your sweetheart, and turn the dial up on romance!

Your inner light is shining brightly, so know that you can use this, to illuminate the path for others.

Offer a sympathetic ear and comforting shoulder for someone to cry on tonight! Do not let that "someone" cry alone! People will draw to you, like steel to a magnet! Share happiness now, do not waist time!

BEFORE FINISHING THIS BOOK, I want to share with my readers something I do almost every week, that makes me feel very happy…

When I take care, or undusted some wonderful remembrances from life, —like the very tall porcelain Japanese Doll, my Dear Son Herb, sent to me more than forty years ago. I remember this wonderful thought, as yesterday! Son Herb had been at war in Vietnam, for more than a year then, exhausted, for being, day, and night, defending and rescuing wounded people wounded by the enemy…

— Oldest son Herb also needed at that time some time off — and The Marines granted one week. Therefore, he went to Japan… Over there, guess what he bought for his lovely Mom? This wonderful colorful Japanese Doll!" — As you probably agree, I, his mother kept this doll dressed with a long red/gold gown in my heart! (Son could be resting, sleeping in a real bed!) …Instead, he went to the store to buy and mail this doll to his mom, this Royal doll!

This is one of the joyful moments I always keeping in the heart!

Every time I dust the Musical Porcelain Horse Mary Go Round, remember when second Son Joe sent it —for my birthday, many, many, years ago — this gorgeous toy! Always smile listening to the darling music, —Always, I treasure these lovely moments!

When am relaxing even now, at 87 years old, and I open the Poem Book "With love to a wonderful mother "my daughter Pilar gave me thirty-seven years ago. Her note on the first page, dated August 6th, 1980, expressed, "I know very soon you won't be by my side, and God only knows how much time you will be far away from me, (from us)...

"I want to say thanks for everything... for your understanding, for your help, for your love for me and Mal, and especially for understanding, –even you probably don't agree, but among all, for always being there when I needed you the most! I am going to miss you tremendously! Only thinking about it, I start missing you now! –Your daughter, –who loves you so much! Pilar."

At other side of that page, read this very lovely note, –

"With Love, to a Wonderful Mother". I am grateful and feel so fortunate to have shared this past year and a half, with you, not only as a mother, but also as a friend. I will miss you very much! Hope you will have a very safe trip, and that it may offer you great opportunities. Do not worry about your daughter... I will try with all my heart to keep her happy and full of love, – Your son-in-love, Mal."

Want, also to transcribe to the readers, this beautiful poem, sent by daughter, 36 years ago...

"With mother's love you Dear Daughter, is always near, crossing the bridge in perfect safety, translated quietly from war to peace, for the illusion of love will never satisfy, but is reality, which awaits you on the other side, giving you everything." Nohemi

"Dear Mother"

"Dear Mother, when I think of you
Think of all things, good and true."
Of trees and lanes and babbling brooks,
Of mountains, hills and shady nooks

> *Think of flowers of every hue,*
> *Of roses kissed by morning dew,*
> *Of violets blue and daisies bright,*
> *and Stately lilies, pure and white*

I think of cloudless skies of blue,
and Mother dear, because of you,
I think of robins in the spring
and of the joyous songs they sing

> *I think of fields of golden grain,*
> *And, of the soft refreshing rain*
> *I think of honeybees in clover*
> *and of God's sunshine bubbling over.*

I think of children's happy faces,
Of grand old ladies in their laces,
Of all men, noble, brave and true,
because of Mothers, just like you."

> *– by, Pauline Mengedoth"*

Among all the treasures, from my *husband Michael*, -me dropping tears of happiness-, I admire this ("really I am sure it won't be the last") last present for me on his wife' birthday, at 87 years of age, and on our wedding anniversary... A gorgeous piece of art, *a cute woodcarving, showing two dolphins, swimming or dancing together* on a calm lake in Hawaii... – with the thoughtful idea to engrave our names on their delicate skin.

I always look forward for these precious moments, (since I did not have many of these memories at childhood.) Holding husband Michael's hands, we rest together, thanking God for His mercy of making us "parents of our kids, grand-kids, and great-grand-kids in this life. With some difficulties, we accomplished some, even with a great challenge. These are the precious moments; we parents receive at old age, before going to our "last home".

– Time changes things, but we have to change ourselves. I reassure "the only way to move is to move up. And the only way to move up is to move out and to move on".

This particular day in Hawaii, the sky is full of fog and rain...the palms are dancing with the wind... – Observed the drops sliding down at the window, like tears from the absence of all our kids, grandkids, and great-grand kids. Then, the sun appeared suddenly, and the kaleidoscopic rainbow emerged majestic high over the mountains, reminding us the different types of commitments with diverse people. – *It takes every color to make a complete rainbow.*

Decided to continue being HAPPY with all experiences of life forming the mold for it, in my heart. Just remember, –All the dreams come true... –The method that works for one will work for all. - The key to keep the power of love is using what we have, leaving the past in the past!

– Learned the key to make this determination, which is to take the next step! It is much easier when we obtain the clear success of being Happy, abandoning the attachment to the outcome, before obtaining our Goal; then, our life will be incomplete!

It is like Ray Kurzweil, author of The Age of Spiritual machines said, "The primary requirement for the recursive algorithm is a Straight Forward codification of the problem ... In a game of chance, that's easy; but in other situations a clear definition of the problem is not always easy to come by".

Some people read books, visit psychologists, or consult therapists... See the solutions of the problem and say, I am going to change my life, from unhappiness to be happy. Moreover, the results are not showing beneath the surface, it is just about ready to break through, but they just look just at the surface results and say, this stuff does not work. –Do you know why? The universe says, your wish is my command. – Leave the Past in the past! –

Just remember, when we allow a thought of doubt to enter our mind, the law of attraction will soon line up one doubtful thought after another. The moment the thought of doubt comes, release it immediately, and send that thought on its way, replacing it with confidence ..." With determination, and faith, you leave the past in the past, and Move Forward, making your dreams comes true.

Happiness is, to accept one another's differences and work together on the larger issues that affect us all.

The power of decision is our own remedy to regain freedom, instead of being prisoner of this world!

Finally, "Make our year resolutions, a success" **This advice never fails!**

Please, My Dear Readers…read this poem… Keeping your mind on eternal happiness, it will never let you down!

WHAT IS HAPPINESS

© *Nohemi*

Happiness is, when mother delivers a child with pain…
That pain is hope!
Hope is Happiness to observe the child learning how he grows
Growing is Happiness, learning about life
Life is Happiness developing his mind
Mindfulness in Happiness directs his intellect.

Observing the sunrise, is Happiness
Happiness is also observing the sunset
With the sky full of colors, red, blue and gold,
The colors reflect the water, adorning the sky
The sky and the rainbow, in different colors, is Happiness
It delights our eyes…

The rain is also Happiness…
It cools the mountains… The flowers open their petals
The colorful petals give us happiness.
Sorrow is Happiness, when a son goes to war,
Since at his return, mother opens her arms
To welcome him with smiles, for being so brave,
Coming with medals of Honor, full of hope!

Happiness is Pain, observing her daughter
Delivering her first baby,
When she received the dear child,
Her pain, then, is converting into happiness…
Absence is Happiness, when children leave their parents
to unify life with husband or wife.

We, mothers, regain Happiness, after being alone for years
Finding a Caring-darling partner to share our life,
Holding hands, to avoid falling down…
Somebody who look at our silvery hair
With the face full of wrinkles, assuring with his tender smile
And care, saying, "You, Dear, look lovely with silvery hair
Looking mature, who I also respect and admire.

Acknowledgements

Wish to express enormous gratitude to husband *Michael Lewis,* whose guidance and support have been vital to guide my life, and to write this and other books. Ever since we met on a dark night at The Rosicrucian Lodge in Fair Oaks, California in January of 1992; when I was so sad, after the death of Brother *Gustav* one month before; he dried my tears and invited me to meditate inside the lodge. He became my best friend in the truest sense of the word. *Michael* has also been a guardian angel in my literary and personal life, someone I can trust for honest opinions, editorial advice, and moral support. Without him as a publisher, the best books could not exist. – *Michael* is more than simply a knowledgeable Consultant and University Professor, he is an excellent adviser and wonderful husband…– *The love of my life,* with whom I became the happiest person in the world! .

Here and now, want to state appreciation to the General Director of Literary Texts, College Professor, and Director of the Spanish Department at the California State University at Sacramento, California, **Dr. *Jorge Santana,*** *for his believing in me.* He selected the collection of poems of my book *Semblanzas y Recuerdos,* (*Profile and Remembrances*) which has been used in bilingual Literature Classes, throughout the State of California, and all over the world!

In addition, I want to express gratitude, love, and deepest bond, to my *Literature Professor, Poet Laureate Colombian **Poetess Luz Stella**,* who was my first encouragement in literary life, guiding my baby steps toward poetry and writing, who very much appreciated her guidance in growing.

Likewise, wish to express appreciation to son **Herbert**, Psychology Graduate of UCLA in Los Angeles, California, being a College Professor, and teaching with his mom at the same Colleges for many years; nurturing their soul when needed... He still celebrates with grown-up kids The Great Breakfast on Sundays, as his mother did for him and his family, no matter any inconveniences of life!

It is a pleasure to acknowledge the two stars that despite the distance, with some storms, and being busy guiding their grownups adults, tried to light their nights, Son ***Jose,*** and daughter ***Pilar.***

Equally, it is a pleasure to recognize a dear friend of more than half century **Myriam Guevara**, who read my articles in magazines, and all the books, offering insightful remarks and making time from her busy life, to express love, through great cards and phone calls. I feel so blessed when she calls me "Mom".

Wish to express gratefulness to **Anne Murata**, Director of *Marketing at Pacific Aviation Museum of Pearl Harbor, Hawaii*, for her great admiration of all my articles of *Great Heroes around the world.*

Want to convey appreciation and sincere love, to Dear Friend, **Silvia Ichar**, Editor of *Para Todos* Magazine, for always showing gratitude for the positive articles, during so many years. –Since I met you, admired your sincerity and kindness!

Also, wish to express appreciation to my dear friend **Julio Lacayo**, for his faithful friendship for more than thirty years, when we shared producing our television and radio programs for the Spanish community on behalf of the State of California... In addition, for his profound love as "an adopted a son", (even he has a wonderful mother who celebrated recently 100 years of age). On every birthday, Julio calls, saying, *"Hi, Mom, I want to wish you a Happy Birthday, and also calls me on "Mother's Day".* Always hear his voice, singing a beautiful song. –He has been reading all my books, giving me incentive to keep writing. –Thanks, dear Julio-.

Likewise, want to thanks a cherished friend **Okalani Tallet**, *Native Hawaiian, Cultural Practitioner, and Hawaiian Spiritual Leader of Honolulu, Hawaii*, for praising my book **Keep Moving Forward On Your Journey To Happiness.** *Okalani*, also has a dear mother in Hawaii Island, and makes time to call me on *Mother's Day* and to celebrate our birthdays, as mother and son.

In addition, want to show gratitude to friend **Dolores McSweeney**, Graduate from the *University of Northern Iowa*, for being a Literary Critic of the book **Colombina** published in the *English language.*

Furthermore, want to escalate gratefulness to dear **Cynthia Meléndrez**, *Spanish Professor at San Diego State University*, California, for editing my Book **Colombina**, which was also published in the *Spanish language.*

Also, want to show appreciation to **Vickie Andresen Sedillo**, *Faculty, Texas A&M University in Corpus Christy*, as Editor of my book of Poetry **A Journey Through Life with Wisdom to Share.**

Have left the last, but not the least acknowledgement for a deepest bond of the brilliant star that despite the distance lighted the nights... grandson; **Carlos**, for his

Continuous devotion to his Grandma, since the time he was born. In addition, want to reinforce love to Grandson *Erik*, – the **famous excellent Great Designer, and Artist**, thanking him for his devotion as being the *artistic cover creator* for most all my books, with his good taste and professionalism. –Thanks, dear Erik.

Have a dilemma right here! I want, with all my heart, to show love and appreciation to a Sister-in-law, (who I always call *"Dear Sister"* –The bold, brilliant and beautiful, resident of France, *Anne-Marie*, Le Cordon Bleu –who God gave me the opportunity to meet since fifty years ago, in Colombia, as a wife of my now departed brother Gustavo. –She, wonderfully translated *"Colombina Buscando la Felicidad" from Spanish to French, **"Colombina À la Recherche du Bonheur**. In addition, she is the *Literature **Critique "Premiere edition Françoise"**. (She came from Grenoble, France, to Padre Island, Texas, USA to visit, and gave the wonderful surprise of her translation, using my computer at night. – *She is one the most wonderful human beings on earth! –God Bless You, Dear Sister Anne-Marie–.*

Also, appreciate the presence of the **wonderful people from all corners of Earth, who attended my Seminars about HAPPINESS, at *the Queen Mary 2 Worldwide Cruise!*** It is rewarding to receive so many notes of gratitude from my attendees, acknowledging all of you who every morning chooses that you *"Will Choose To be Happy Every Day"*. It is impossible to name hundreds of names from all the corners of the world, in this section, I am only very grateful of your choices! This is a reminder to all writers of the world, who graduated with the shared cumulative accomplishment of life's maximum grade of *Suma Cum Laude.* Who succeed in the rich womblike environment of life, surviving without being millionaires of money, but instead being the billionaires of Happiness, Creativeness, and Insight!

I like to write poetry, incentive books, and stories, passing it down from one generation to another, creating the wonderful legacies of culture… We all share dearly the accomplishments and achievements in life, which results in the recorded story of the development of this wonderful phenomenon of man.

This way we, as writers, collecting documents, and creating the story of the real soul personality, we shared consciousness of mankind. As it progresses in its growth toward higher and highest level of consciousness, and, we develop the world's great cultures, which, continually evolved into a more complete and whole being at one with happiness. –*Nohemí*

LAST A SIMPLE GUIDE TO MAKE THE CHANGE, TO REGAIN CREATIVITY, AND HAPPINESS

Sometimes we have to make changes, honest changes! The process of identifying as self, inevitably involves loss as well as gain...   We discover our new boundaries, and these boundaries, sometimes separate us from our family...   As we eliminate ambiguity, we lose illusion. Well, this is my point... As we clarify our perceptions, we lose our misconceptions. -As we eliminate ambiguity, we lose illusion, as well... We arrive at clarity, and clarity creates "Positive Change".

My Dear Readers, Sons and Daughter...   I finally stopped rescuing sons and family, who needed to grow up, Save Themselves, and Moved Forward!

We have to encounter the truth and meet ourselves to meet our self-expression. Becoming original, is something specific... This is an original, form, which works flows...   As we gain –or regain– our creative identity, we lose the false self we were sustaining.

The loss of this false self, can feel traumatic, is like saying, "I don't recognize me." –The more we feel ourselves to be incognito the more certain, we know that the recovery process is working! (Try to get that recovery, to live in peace!)

The old of you is leaving and grieving, while the new you, celebrates and grows strong! *It is very much like tension and relief.*

Say for instance, you are in a life dilemma, like walking away from a crashed relationship: Your old life has crashed and burned; your new life is not apparent, yet... It may feel you are temporarily without a direction...Don't lie there in pity feeling victimized... just move forward! You will see,- sooner or late-r the light at the end of the channel or tunnel. It is important to know that no matter which form you growth is, it is time... to make another change! Keep moving forward! (It is never too late)

You may have felt be victimized. You were confused! You did not know what you wanted to do... You may have sensed that you would not be able to keep up! You did not see any possibilities...

With time, there will be a change in energy patterns... Sometimes your intuition may guide you, or your dreams may guide you... then, you will become stronger and see clearer and clearer...Life does unfolds itself if you are not locked in a closet...and you are out there (in life)... I promise things will cross your paths for you to choose from...It is your time to be selective!

However, you did not, or have not realized how many small things you could do to improve your own life and the love of your family. Everything will lead you forward, giving you a place to recuperate from your forward motion.

Trusting your perceptions with love is another powerful affirmation to use as you undergo shifts in identity. A stronger and clearer one is emerging.

Choose affirmations according to your needs. As you excavate your buried dreams, like to upgrade the pure constant and pure love of your mother... you will need the assurance that such explorations are permissible.

Then, happily you will say, "I recovered and enjoy my New Identity!

DO YOU WANT TO KNOW, THE SECRET OF HAPPINESS?

IT IS TO

"ACCEPT THE THINGS THAT CAN NOT BE CHANGED

AND CHANGE THE THINGS THAT CAN BE CHANGED"

May **Keep Moving Forward on Your Journey to Happiness** bring you peace, love and delight in your existence (in your heart), that was and is my objective for you and for the world to experience more enjoyment and Happiness in life.

What we allow ourselves to see, to know, and to experiment has a profound impact above all. Life, guards your heart, for it is the wellspring of life; on what we think and what we do, with enjoyment and happiness.

In Hawaii we walk, observing multicolored hues and soft textures… the backdrop is green –deep green, –light green, –even bright green– all in contrast to the clear blue sky, which crisply borders the splash of green on the horizon, and even in the water.

In the background, we observe the Acacia trees, spark their smart red lanterns, carpeting fields accented with tiny buttercups… Everything along the way is Pink, Green, Blue, Purple, and White… Like Happiness, brings all kind of colors, to enjoy our lives. If there is dark at night, this darkness turns into light in the morning…like sadness turns, with determination and faith, into HAPPINESS.

–*Nohemi*

Hope you have enjoyed this book!

NOTES ABOUT THE AUTHOR

Nohemí Molano Lewis grew up in a small town in Colombia, South America; at age of seven, she began to learn English with a retired Catholic Priest and uncle of her mother. As a youngster, attended college, mastered the English language at the American-Colombian College, specialized in Literature; and started writing poetry, under the tutelage of famous writer and Poet Laureate Luz Stella. *She* received her degrees in Colombia, immediately after, was hired as Special Assistant to the President of the State Penal Court, Dr. Caycedo. Later, she was Special Assistant to the President of Sheering Corporation, a North-American, pharmaceutical Company. Performed at the *"Alberto Castilla Conservatory of Music"* in Colombia; USA and with the *Vienna Boys Choir.*

Immigrated to USA in 1963, raised three adolescents without a father, since irresponsible husbands abandoned her and her family. Sons graduated from UCLA, and daughter from California State University, Sacramento. Now the six grandchildren advanced their education, have college degrees and two of them opened their own licensed business; others are finishing their academia studies. Nohemi now has two great grandchildren.

In USA Nohemi was a Professor at different private colleges in California, worked for the government of California as a translator and as a Television director; on her spear time, was a Newspaper Columnist for various bilingual newspapers, magazines, and radio and television stations in Los Angeles, San Francisco, Sacramento California, and San Jose, Costa Rica.

Governors of California and FEMA Federal Emergency Agency; prized her for Assisting victims at Earthquakes and other tragedies in the Northern Area of California. She is an Award Winning Writer of Novels, Political History; Newspaper, Poet, Radio and Television Celebrity, Journalist, Anchor and Talk Show Host in California, and Costa Rica. She has published many articles in newspapers and magazines, as well as 27 Wonderful Books

–Honored by Sacramento State University for her books of poetry in Spanish e.g. *"Semblanzas y Recuerdos"*. Effective columnist in USA at "El Hispano Newspaper", *"Para Todos"* Spanish magazine" and *"Culturs"* English publication; *Pacific Aviation Museum* in Honolulu, Hawaii, interviewed famous people for magazines.

In 2016, Guest Speaker for five Seminars,on CUNARD's "Interest Corner" Queen Mary 2 World Cruise. Nohemi is an internationally acclaimed Celebrity, Author, Journalist, Poet, Translator, Educator, Literary Critic, and renowned Happiness and Wisdom Advisor from Hawaii.com sm. (Some information about the itinerary of the trip around the world is based on flyers distributed to us, the passengers, in a Daily Programs from *Cunard.)*

–THIS IS ONLY PART OF THE SADNESS IN LIFE!–

– When *a police officer in Colombia assassinated Dad*, at the time he was trying to vote in a Presidential Race, leaving his family, in limbo... I was very young, and my mom sent me to live with Aunts and Uncles. Was very happy, with them, then, uncle was murdered when he was riding a horse coming home from town. – I started dealing with a lot of sorrow at young age…

– Later, *Brother Vita, already blind*, due to a car accident where he lost his eyes; burned and died from a Kerosene stove in his kitchen, stroking a match and the gas was on; he actually died at a hospital, where some members of his family witnessed his terrible pain from the severe burning. His wife passed away a few months before, due to cancer, and children were here and there!

–Dear *Sister Helen, –just twenty-five years old*, married against the will of brother Gus, because he considered "a cruel idea to give in matrimony *"beautiful, educated angel"*, to this *"unkind, callous, ruthless and uneducated person."* to that." -He had three little beautiful boys. She took her life in desperation after confirming the infidelity of her husband. – I miss very much!

–Little *Brother Fabian only nine years old* was playing with a dear friend, falls down from the rooftop and crashed his head, dying a few days later.

–As soon as young *Brother Gabby barely thirty-five years old,* finishing the first section of the football game with his two children, he dropped down with a mortal heart attack, living his three children orphaned. –Think of you with love!

–Then, we had to face the death of sixty-five years old' *Mother*, by a heart attack, after suffering from so many tragedies of her family, leaving two young daughters –*Leo* and *Chila*, orphans. Recently they passed away…Love you.

I, her older daughter, took care of the younger sisters *Leonor* and *Martha*; later Leonor got married… After I, Nohemi, moved with my kids to USA, I sent for dear sister *Martha*; so she would get good education, becoming a nurse in California; had a son, a wonderful kid; as an adult, he joined the Air Force of USA. Now he is a father of two beautiful girls, and two beautiful boys. - We all are so proud of him; he learned well with the Dear Mother God provided for him!

At the news of Brother *Charlie*, passing away went to Colombia to attend his funeral… He died after suffering many heart attacks, do the absence of his dear kids, who left with their mother to US many, years back, and never went back. I, his sister witnessed his sadness, drinking to hide his profound pain, due to their absence.

AGAIN, AS WE CREATE AND CLARIFY OUR PERCEPTION, WE LOSE OUR MISCONCEPTION!

As we eliminate ambiguity, we lose illusion, as well…
Today I arrived at clarity, and clarity creates CHANGE!

KEEP MOVING FORWARD ON YOUR JOURNEY TO HAPPINESS!

Dear readers sons and daughter… I finally stopped rescuing sons and daughters who needed to free themselves. I Moved Forward… I kept Moving Forward. It Worked! - People frequently believe the creative life is ground in fantasy… We have to encounter the truth and meet ourselves, to meet our self-expression and become original (Something Specific – *An original form which works and flows.*)

As we gain, or regain our Creative Identity, we lose the False Self we were sustaining… - With the loss of this False Self, we feel traumatized- We do not know who we are! We do not recognize our mind! The more we feel incognito the more uncertain we become. I had infinite patience with all of them, but that way did not produced good results! In addition, I knew that patience calls upon infinite love, but the time was wasted unnecessarily. I had repeatedly said that time was a learning device to be abolished when it was no longer useful, but time is over! I Moved Forward. I kept Moving Forward and It Worked!

I was hoping for them to heal, but knew many healers did not heal themselves. I could not move mountains only with faith; I had to take the determination to heal myself. Why should I listen to the endless insane letters and phone calls criticizing their mother-, since they never appreciated any positive action from the family members; only condemnations? While their father left us with the excuse to find a better job, I, as a single mother, raised the family, and ten years later, he wanted to comeback, to do the same? Drinking, having mistresses, abusing his wife and children? No Way! I Moved Forward. I kept Moving Forward and It Worked! Enough is enough!

My darling grown-up kids, instead of appreciating all the wonderful help from Mom, like giving -free of charge- a gorgeous lot to her younger son-, in the Atlantic Coast of Colombia, and never had the time to go to the Colombian Consulate in US to transfer the proprietorship to him! Then, after the law changed, prohibited to make gifts or real state in Colombia, he insisted to make an unlawful deal. Why? I Moved Forward. I kept Moving Forward and It Worked!

I do not mention all the sacrifices, helping day and night, for months and years, grownups and children, with their wants and needs, and why even at old age do not have the kindness to communicate with me?   I Moved Forward.   I kept Moving Forward and It Works!

I wept at the "sacrifices" I (their Mother, Grand Mother) made to help sons, daughter, grandkids, who to have learned to be reliable and responsible, without their fathers' help…that they who should take the duty to help support and raise them. Nevertheless, I did and had to take care of everything! -Fulfilled all their dreams-…Brought all legally to USA, giving them the great opportunity to be successful, and later to build the future for their kids and grandkids….Many Times I worked 2 and sometimes 3 jobs at a time…I Am Very Proud of All Sacrifices I made to Accomplish This For Them! I Had To Move Forward…   I still Kept Moving Forward, and It Worked! I Never Gave Up!

Sometimes had been reacting with lack of Love, which I perceive as unfair: they became defensive when they frequently disagreed their old mother, who never ceased to help with assets and love, and never gave up! I Had To Move Forward. I Kept Moving Forward On My Journey To Happiness and It Worked, since I Never Gave Up! Life is so beautiful, just loving and care!

Dear Readers, do you remember the sad issues of mother, brothers and sisters, their miserable and cruel life, and death, born in undeveloped countries, where killing innocents, and deceiving wives, were a daily occurrence? -I got tire of that…   I Had to Move Forward! Kept Moving Forward On my Journey To Happiness, and It Worked! Because I Never Gave Up!

I forgave the cruelty of the country, forgave the idiosyncrasy of the people, and forgive myself since being a mother under sad circumstances I did not figure out what I could have done differently…   Therefore, the first step, in undoing unpleasant behavior is to recognize that accidently we had decided some things incorrectly. Moreover, it only occurred to me, because I tried to be a good mother without good example. I know, to make up for their irresponsible father, who never really truly cared about their family, abandoned the children, not having a daddy, throughout the years all sons and daughter, tried to raise their kids with love, responsibility, and kindness, with some rough edges against their mother, for not being perfect! Even though I meditate for them, wishing to have the appropriate qualities to fit the purpose, love, and good health.

Now I understand, in order to be a good mother, we must do the best for our kids, but not everything because if we do, then we are setting them up for failure in life and ruining the future. But, of course, if we don't do everything for them, they think we are completely selfish. I cherish my children, but did not smug about it, I understand, we should not complain about our children, but if we only say good things, we are not being honest and we are fake.

Otherwise, each one should prove to be acting as a responsible one, by being kind with each other, including their mother, and support each other with kindness and love.

Now, I look at things differently.   -since of this insight- I can *Keep Moving Forward On My Journey To Happiness* and, I Will Keep Working Again And Again toward this goal, since Now I Am At Peace, and I Never Will Gave Up!

Now, I am very firm with myself on this concept, and keep being fully aware of the undoing process, which does not come from outside me, but nevertheless from within me, because Life placed it here... And, because I Never Gave Up! I Moved Forward! ***I Kept Moving Forward On My Journey To Happiness and Peace*** … **That's Why It Is Now Working!**

Your part is merely to return your thinking to the point at which the error had been made, and give it over to the atonement process, once and for all! My Dear Readers SAY THIS MANTRA REPEATEDLY AND REGULARLY TO YOURSELF: Now I Keep Moving Forward On My Journey To Happiness and It Keeps Working!

I Meditate Regularly, Follow My Intuition, Keep Moving Forward On My Journey To Happiness, making better decisions and things improved. Keeping Moving Forward on My Journey To Happiness, things work out on a Regular Basis a Whole Lot Better!

Recovering is a process of finding the flow of the river and saying yes. We start ourselves by saying yes, instead of no, to opportunities, as we begin to pry ourselves loose from our old self-concepts; we find our new emerging self, enjoying all sorts of bizarre adventures! For the first time in years, we allow ourselves to laugh feeling happy; why did not I, do this sooner? This newly positive attitude is the beginning of trust... We are starting to look for the "silver lining" instead of continuing looking for adversity."

In the meantime, I just enjoyed reading this beautiful card from son Herb...

"Dear Mother... From time to time, think about the valuable influence you've had on all of us, and the one influencing factor I believe has been our commitment to hard work, and our desire to achieve new goals. When sister was here last week I could not help but noticed how similar to you she has become – the qualities I most admired on her, the most about you, she has!

As the year goes by, I hope that I can instill see in my children the one attribute essential to success in life... discipline... If I can help them achieve that, and helped them how to learn how to have empathy, I believe I will have the ingredients of some pretty well rounded adults. - I wish you many, many more years to see your legacy in the next generation.

(signed) Love, your son Herbert. 7/13/94

Finally, I want to express to you, as sincerely as I can; according to Ancient Wisdom Schools and Hindu Yogi's schools,

*"All your Sincere Efforts create in you, a Magnetic Soul Personality ... What you need will be attracted to you (again via your Magnetic Soul Personality) ... What you need will cross your path!" *

When you notice what is happening, just accept it (seize the gift or opportunity). Never, worry! God, or the Universe, or the Cosmos, - whatever you want to call it, will watch out for you. I totally understand this principle and by experience completely agree! I have been looked out for! I have been greatly blessed! **

Keep Moving Forward On Your Journey To Happiness. I know from my own personal experience that ***Keep Moving Forward On Your Journey to Happiness, really works!***

****Paying it forward primes the pump!***

*****We teach meditation for no fees in Honolulu, HI in order to give back.***

It is an honor to acknowledge the presence of two new members of our *Ananda Meditation Group in Honolulu, Hawaii.*

Vladimir and Son Auriel

Son and Grandson of the Great Artist

ALEK RAPOPORT

Portrait of Vladimir as a Young Man

Alek Rapoport stated, *"I have always been a realist, because I am concerned with what is real in life that is what I depict"*

Michal Dunev' Gallery Owner from San Francisco, California, acknowledged this great man Alek Rapoport, "When I first met the diminutive Russian émigré sometime in 1985, I was struck by the honest intensity of the man, so small in stature yet so great of presence. —Although his work was unknown in San Francisco, and hardly consistent with the aesthetic or philosophical direction of my gallery, the sincerity of his personality and the power of his remarkable paintings impelled me to present his work as a testament to art's ability to survive all hardship and tribulation."

At eighty-seven years old, I still listen to my heart … I hear my thoughts… I attend very carefully…

I had been thinking with devotion, doing what I loved to do, making a special breakfast, decorating the room… As when on Sundays I had time, to adorn the table with linen, some flowers, and bright napkins to feed my darling children on Sundays, happy to observe their smiles full of pleasure, eating something special, cooked by their mom, –even more than sixty years ago.

–Then in the mature days we were rushing, when working sometimes three jobs instead of two, –like on Saturdays, making wigs, while the kids played in the park, besides had to do many other chores. Every day, besides cooking and cleaning, getting my children to take showers and dressed for school, packing lunches, organized their books, and homework. Then, next day, jump into the car to drive them to school, then on my way going to work! –Old Happy Busy Days!

Now on recent days, like Sundays in Honolulu, Hawaii, having time for heightened reasoning and judgment… What a great way to get things done! Pulled out projects, that surfaced recently facing them directly... Made the most of these days' energy, by thinking about ways to do things, more efficiently… –Like writing and publishing books, articles for magazines; teaching meditation, being confident, handling everything without stress!

At this point, we do not go to church every Sunday, or swim every day;   –just three times a week. We do not attend concerts so often, –but occasionally, like when we visit *Ko-Olina, Hawaii*… As long as we do things, we love, –like holding hands, walking a few miles around the park, or near the beach, before the sun is high; observing the birds, especially the *red cardinals*; listening to the breeze moving through the tree's branches, and paying attention to the rhythm in our hearts, with real gladness we are at peace with ourselves, feeling very happy and content!

We harm no one… Nor do we allow anyone to fill up and sink our boat; despite family members who think it would be great for them to do so.

We are responsible for our success… We do not impose on others; we do not blame the world if we are not successful! We choose to *Keep Moving Forward On Our Journey To Happiness* by being proactive and guided by our intellect, intuitive side, and our feelings!

We have our responsibilities to still grow and change in a positive direction! –To improve!– –This we can count on. We believe in ourselves! With doing our part, we know what we need will happen… It always comes our way!

I understand, sometimes we want to rest from the stresses in life that others put upon us… From time to time, we want to let our boat float in the harbor… We do use other ships on our journalistic travels to take us around the world, and in the process, we do enjoy life! We go with the flow, if it seems right for us. –Those who are truthful and honest, kind with us, who love us, who treasure our kind memories, we cherish them. –Others, who do not get these rewards in life, - we try to help!

As the Yogis taught, we have learned to pursue solitude. –They call it living in seclusion… observing the calm ocean, watching the birds flying across the mountains and the colorful trees, reflecting on the rays of the afternoon sun… just doing that, inspiration comes easily to us.

This is what we call, *"Real Contentment, Bliss, and Ecstasy in life… a real large slice of Happiness!"*

I have written this Special Book of my 27 wonderful inspiring manuscripts, to help My Dear Readers, who might be some of the "Walking Wounded" in this world, or might know someone who is in similar circumstances! Or else, just might like to help someone to "get out of the ditch"!

It is never too late to "Choose" a better path to start moving ahead and ***Keep Moving Forward On Your Journey To Happiness".***

I assure you, that after you "Read" this Special Book and put its "Gems" into daily practice, you will get there much faster than you may realize!

My Dear Readers ... Please, look out for my next book.

<u>*Some of the Other Wonderful 27 Books, by Nohemí Molano Lewis*</u>

<u>*(In English, Spanish, and French)*</u>

<u>*English and French Works*</u>

COLOMBINA Searching for Happiness (English)
COLOMBINA À La Recherche du Bonheur (French)
Happiness Does Not Have To Be A Project It Is A Journey (English)
Keep Moving Forward On Your Journey To Happiness (English)

<u>*Poetry in English*</u>

A Journey Through Life with Wisdom to Share
Ashes / Reflections / Sunset

<u>*Works in Spanish*</u>

COLOMBINA Buscando la Felicidad
Ángeles de la oscuridad
Cómo poder aliviar la tensión y tristeza
Pruebas de cariño
Se ha quemado el 'último cartucho

<u>*Poetry in Spanish*</u>

Alborada
Álbum familiar
Cenizas
Gotas de agua
Las rosas de mi huerto, Sutilezas, for Spanish Associates, Sacramento.
Semblanzas y Recuerdos for California State University, Sacramento.

<u>*And Of Course Bilingual Editions for Children in Spanish/English*</u>
Aprenda sus números – Learn Your Numbers
Buenos amigos – Good Friends
Mi hermosa tortuga – My Beautiful Turtle
Mi querida patita – My Darling Little Duck
Nuestro paseo – Our Walk
Conchas del mar –Sea Shells

Your Notes